W9-BPL-055

fifth edition

Classrooms That Work
They Can All Read and Write

Patricia M. Cunningham
Wake Forest University

Richard L. Allington
University of Tennessee, Knoxville

PEARSON

Boston • Columbus • Indianapolis • New York • San Francisco • Upper Saddle River
Amsterdam • Cape Town • Dubai • London • Madrid • Milan • Munich • Paris • Montreal • Toronto
Delhi • Mexico City • Sao Paulo • Sydney • Hong Kong • Seoul • Singapore • Taipei • Tokyo

Editor-in-Chief and Vice President: Aurora Martínez Ramos
Editorial Assistant: Amy Foley
Vice President, Director of Marketing: Chris Flynn
Executive Marketing Manager: Krista Clark
Marketing Manager: Amanda Stedke
Production Editor: Annette Joseph
Editorial Production Service: Lynda Griffiths
Manufacturing Buyer: Megan Cochran
Electronic Composition: Denise Hoffman
Interior Design: Denise Hoffman

For related titles and support materials, visit our online catalog at www.pearsonhighered.com.

Copyright © 2011, 2007, 2003, 1999, 1994 Pearson Education, Inc., publishing as Allyn & Bacon, 501 Boylston Street, Suite 901, Boston, MA 02116.

All rights reserved. No part of the material protected by this copyright notice may be reproduced or utilized in any form or by any means, electronic or mechanical, including photocopying, recording, or by any information storage and retrieval system, without written permission from the copyright owner.

To obtain permission(s) to use material from this work, please submit a written request to Allyn and Bacon, Permissions Department, 501 Boylston Street, Suite 900, Boston, MA 02116; fax your request to 617-671-2290; or e-mail permissionsus@pearson.com.

Between the time website information is gathered and then published, it is not unusual for some sites to have closed. Also, the transcription of URLs can result in typographical errors. The publisher would appreciate notification where these errors occur so that they may be corrected in subsequent editions.

Printed in the United States of America

10 9 8 7 6 5 4 3 2 1   RRD-VA   14 13 12 11 10

www.pearsonhighered.com

ISBN-10: 0-13-704837-8
ISBN-13: 978-0-13-704837-3

brief contents

chapter 1   *Creating Classrooms That Work*   1

chapter 2   *Creating Enthusiastic, Independent Readers*   12

chapter 3   *Building the Literacy Foundation*   28

chapter 4   *Fostering Fluency*   48

chapter 5   *Teaching Phonics and Spelling Patterns*   65

chapter 6   *Building Vivid, Vital, and Valuable Vocabularies*   94

chapter 7   *Developing Thoughtful Comprehenders*   117

chapter 8   *Developing Ready, Willing, and Able Writers*   145

chapter 9   *Reading and Writing across the Curriculum*   180

chapter 10   *Assessment*   204

chapter 11   *Differentiating Instruction for Diverse Learners*   218

chapter 12   *Inside Classrooms That Work*   243

contents

Preface   ix

chapter **1** *Creating Classrooms That Work*   **1**

Observing in the Classrooms of Unusually
Effective Teachers   2

What We Know about Classrooms That Work   8

Creating Your Own Classroom That Works,
Even Better   11

chapter **2** *Creating Enthusiastic,
Independent Readers*   **12**

Assess and Document Your Students' Independent Reading   13

Make Teacher Read-Aloud an Everyday Event   14

Schedule Time Every Day for Independent Reading   18

Accumulate the Widest Possible Variety of
Reading Materials   20

Schedule Conferences So You Can Talk with Your Students
about Their Reading   22

Make Time for Sharing and Responding   24

Summary   27

chapter **3** *Building the Literacy Foundation*   **28**

Concepts That Form the Foundation for Literacy   30

Activities for Building the Foundation   34

Summary   47

chapter **4** *Fostering Fluency*   **48**

Mandate Easy Reading for Everyone   50

Model Fluent, Expressive Reading   53

Provide Engaging Rereading Opportunities   57

Use a Word Wall to Teach High-Frequency Words   59

Summary   63

chapter **5** *Teaching Phonics and Spelling Patterns*   **65**

Guess the Covered Word   68

Using Words You Know   71

Making Words   75

The Nifty-Thrifty-Fifty   87

The Wheel   91

Summary   92

chapter **6** *Building Vivid, Vital, and Valuable Vocabularies*   **94**

How Do We Learn All the Words We Know?   96

Provide as Much Real Experience as Possible   99

Increase Meaning Vocabularies through Reading   104

Teach Morphemes, Context, and the Dictionary to Learn New Words   108

Teach Children to Monitor Their Vocabulary Knowledge   112

Promote Word Wonder   114

Summary   115

chapter 7 *Developing Thoughtful Comprehenders* **117**

Comprehension Strategies   120

Literate Conversations   121

Think-Alouds   126

Informational Text Lessons   132

Story Text Lessons   138

Summary   143

chapter 8 *Developing Ready, Willing, and Able Writers* **145**

Starting the Year with Writer's Workshop   147

Adding Editing to Writer's Workshop   151

Adding Conferencing, Publishing, and Author's Chair to Writer's Workshop   156

Adding Revising to Writer's Workshop   160

Focused Writing   168

Summary   178

chapter 9 *Reading and Writing across the Curriculum* **180**

Use Shared Reading to Teach Your Students How to Read Informational Text   181

Help Your Students Transfer Their Comprehension Strategies When Reading Science and Social Studies   184

Spotlight Vocabulary in Science, Social Studies, and Math   185

Link Vocabulary Development to Comprehension Lessons   186

Writing to Learn   193

Think-Writes   194

Summary   203

chapter **10** *Assessment* **204**

What Is Assessment? 205

Determining Student Reading Level 205

Identifying Good Literacy Behaviors and Documenting
Student Progress 209

Summary 217

chapter **11** *Differentiating Instruction*
for Diverse Learners **218**

Use a Variety of Collaborative Groupings 221

Partner Older Struggling Readers to Tutor Younger
Struggling Readers 232

Find and Train a Tutor for Your Most Needy Child 233

Coordinate with Reading and Other Specialists 237

Use the Latest Technology 238

Increase the Support You Are Providing Your
English Language Learners 240

Summary 241

chapter **12** *Inside Classrooms That Work* **243**

A Day in a Kindergarten Classroom 244

A Day in a Primary Classroom 250

A Day in an Intermediate Classroom 259

References **267**

Index **271**

It is hard to believe we are revising *Classrooms That Work* for the fifth time! Much has changed since we first wrote this book in the early nineties. Systematic phonics programs have replaced whole language as the dominant organizing theme for literacy instruction. Struggling readers are found in the bottom reading group in primary grades and in the low track in intermediate grades. To date, there is no evidence that these changes have made things better for children who struggle with reading and writing.

In the first edition of *Classrooms That Work*, we applauded the authentic reading and writing experiences provided in whole-language classrooms but expressed our fears that children were not being given enough instruction in decoding and spelling. We made the case for balanced, comprehensive literacy instruction that included authentic reading and writing, along with explicit instruction in the skills that would enable children to successfully engage in reading and writing. Of course, the pendulum has once again swung too far. In many classrooms with a lot of at-risk readers, skills instruction and worksheets absorb a huge amount of time and energy, leaving little place for actually engaging in reading and writing.

The most effective classrooms described in Chapter 1 are classrooms that do it all! Authentic reading and writing are combined with explicit skills instruction. Daily instruction includes some whole-class teaching, some one-to-one conferences, and both teacher-led and collaborative groupings. Literacy instruction takes place during the reading/language arts time and throughout the day as the students learn math, science, and social studies. The teachers in these classrooms believe all their students can learn to read and write well and don't believe in an "either-or" approach to their teaching.

The original *Classrooms That Work* argued that all children—particularly children who struggle with reading and writing —need balanced, comprehensive literacy instruction. Our schools today have more children from racial and ethnic minority groups, more children who are learning English, more children from single-parent homes, and more children living in poverty. The need for balanced, comprehensive literacy instruction that pervades the school day and curriculum is greater now than ever. We have revised this book to help you better meet the needs of our increasingly diverse classrooms.

Because fluency is critical to successful reading and writing for beginning readers, we have added a chapter on fostering fluency. Chapter 4 provides you with a variety of ways to increase the amount of reading your students are doing and to make sure that all your students are getting some easy reading in their reading diets, and that they are all learning to quickly and accurately read and spell the most common words.

We have also added a chapter on incorporating literacy activities throughout the day as you teach the content areas of math, science, and social studies. If you incorporate the literacy activities described in Chapter 9, Reading and Writing across the Curriculum, you can dramatically increase the amount of reading and writing your students do each day and provide them with skills that will increase their math, science, and social studies achievement.

Chapter 11, Differentiating Instruction for Diverse Learners, is a new chapter that reflects the reality of the current student population we teach in classrooms across the United States. This chapter suggests a variety of ways successful teachers differentiate their instruction to meet the needs of our increasingly diverse classrooms. To further help you differentiate instruction, we have included "Tech-Savvy Teacher" and "English Language Learners" boxes throughout all the chapters. These boxes contain practical suggestions for using technology and other resources to make your instruction as effective as possible for all the children you teach. In Chapter 8, when we talk about revising, we suggest that you tell your students that revising is how they make their good writing *even better*. We hope the suggestions and activities you find in this book will make your classroom that works well work *even better*—especially for the children whose futures depend on excellent instruction.

Thank you to the following reviewers: Jodi Grubb, Pittsfield Elementary School; Dena Harrison, Mendive Middle School; Madelaine Kingsbury, Overbrook High School; Darlene Stewart, Pittsfield Elementary School; and Paula Witkowski, Webster University.

chapter 1

Creating Classrooms
That Work

How well does your classroom work? If you are like most teachers, you might respond, "Some days better than others" or "Most days, things work pretty well." Or you might respond to the question with a question, "What do you mean by 'work'?"

In 1994, when the first edition of this book was published, it had a bold and optimistic title: *Classrooms That Work: They Can* All *Read and Write*. The claim that *all* children could learn to read and write was, at the time, not widely accepted. Since 1994, the goal of teaching all children has achieved wide acceptance and is most clearly captured in the phrase "No Child Left Behind" (NCLB). Although we have many concerns about the way NCLB was implemented, we were on record long before NCLB existed as believing that the goal of teaching all children to read and write was reasonable and responsible.

In the years since 1994, a great deal of research has focused on schools and classrooms that "beat the odds." All over the country—in rural, suburban, and urban areas—there are classrooms where, year after year, *all* the children succeed in learning to read and write. We know what happens in these overachieving classrooms. We know what kinds of environment, instruction, and activities the teachers provide that result in all children becoming readers and writers. In this chapter, we will invite you into the classrooms of unusually effective teachers by sharing the observations of some very clever and hard-working researchers. We will then summarize some of the characteristics you would see if you could be a "fly on the wall" in one of these "odds-beating" classrooms.

Observing in the Classrooms of Unusually Effective Teachers

One of the first research studies that actually observed what was happening in classrooms to try to determine effective classroom practice was conducted by Michael Knapp in 140 classrooms in moderate- to high-poverty areas of California, Ohio, and Maryland (Knapp, 1995). After two years of observations, Knapp concluded that classrooms with the highest achievement gains were classrooms in which teachers:

- Emphasized higher-order meaning construction more than lower-order skills
- Maximized opportunities to read
- Integrated reading and writing with other subject areas
- Provided opportunities to discuss what was read

A team of researchers headed by Ruth Wharton-McDonald (Wharton-McDonald, Pressley, & Hampston, 1998) carried out the first extensive observational study to determine what actually happens in the classrooms of outstanding first-grade teachers. Administrators in school districts in upstate New York nominated "exemplary" first-grade teachers as well as "more typical—solid but not outstanding" first-grade teachers. In choosing the exemplary teachers, administrators were asked to consider their own observations of the teacher; teacher, parent, and student enthusiasm; the reading and writing achievement of children in that classroom; and the ability of the teacher to teach children with a wide range of abilities.

Five outstanding teachers and five more typical teachers were identified, and the researchers made multiple visits to their classrooms across one school year. In addition to being observed, the teachers were interviewed across the year about their teaching and how they made decisions. Throughout the year, the observers also looked for indicators of how well the children in these 10 classrooms were reading and writing.

At the end of the year, the researchers reclassified the teachers according to the achievement of the children. Three classes had unusually high achievement. Most of the students in these three classrooms were reading books at or above first-grade level. They wrote pieces longer than a page in length, and their writing showed reasonably good coherence, punctuation, capitalization, and spelling. These three classes with the highest reading and writing achievement also had the highest levels of engagement. Most of the students were working productively on reading and writing most of the time.

The researchers then looked at the observation and interview data from these three classrooms with the highest levels of reading, writing, and engagement and compared them with the data from other classrooms. Although there were many similarities across all classrooms, the three outstanding first-grades differed from the others in significant ways:

- All of the teachers provided both skills instruction and reading and writing, but the teachers in the highest-achieving classrooms integrated skills teaching with reading and writing.
- Every minute of time in the highest-achieving classrooms was used well. Teachers in these classrooms turned even mundane routines into instructional events.
- Teachers in the highest-achieving classrooms used lots of scaffolding and coaching—providing support but always trying to get the most out of every child.
- Teachers in the highest-achieving classrooms constantly emphasized self-regulation and self-monitoring.
- In the high-achieving classrooms, there was an abundance of integration of reading and writing. Reading and writing were also integrated with content areas, and teachers made many cross-curricular connections.
- Teachers in the high-achieving classes had high expectations for their children—both for their learning to read and write and for their behavior. Students knew how they were expected to act and behaved accordingly most of the time.
- Teachers in the high-achieving classrooms were excellent classroom managers.

Encouraged by the results of the Wharton-McDonald study and supported by a large grant, faculty at the University of Albany and other researchers planned and carried out an observational study of first-grade classrooms in five states (Pressley, Allington, Wharton-McDonald, Block, & Morrow, 2001). Thirty exemplary or typical teachers were identified in New York, New Jersey, Texas, Wisconsin, and California, and year-long observations and interviews were conducted in their classrooms. At the end of the year, each teacher identified six students—two low achieving, two middle achieving, and two high achieving—and these children were administered a standardized reading test. Based on the results of this test, a most effective and a least effective teacher were identified for each of the five locations. Comparing observations in the classrooms of the most and least effective teachers revealed the following characteristics of the most effective classrooms:

- Skills were explicitly taught and related to reading and writing.
- Books were everywhere and used in a variety of ways—read aloud by the teacher and read and listened to on tape by the children.
- Children did a lot of reading and writing throughout the day and for homework.
- Teachers had high but realistic expectations of children and monitored progress regularly.
- Self-regulation was modeled and expected. Children were taught to check and reflect on their work and to make wise choices.
- Cross-curricular connections were made as children read and wrote while studying science and social studies themes.
- Classrooms were caring, positive, cooperative environments, in which discipline issues were handled quickly and quietly.
- Classroom management was excellent and teachers used a variety of grouping structures, including whole class, one-to-one teaching, and a variety of small groups.
- Classrooms showed high student engagement. Ninety percent of the students were engaged in their reading and writing work 90 percent of the time.

The researchers followed up their first-grade observational study by looking at exemplary teachers in fourth grade (Allington & Johnson, 2002). Thirty fourth-grade teachers from five states were identified. Classroom observations took place for 10 days in each classroom. Teachers and children were interviewed. Samples of student writing, reading logs, and end-of-year achievement tests provided information about the reading and writing abilities of the children. From their observations, interviews, and data, the researchers concluded that the following variables distinguished the most effective classrooms from the less effective classrooms:

- All kinds of real conversations took place regularly in the most effective classrooms. Children had conversations with each other, and teachers had conversations with children.
- Through their conversations and in their instruction, teachers constantly modeled thinking strategies. More emphasis was put on How could we find out? than on right and wrong answers.
- All kinds of materials were used for reading and writing. Teachers "dipped" into reading, science, and social studies textbooks but rarely followed the lesson plans for these materials. Students read historical novels, biographies, and informational books. Magazines and the Internet were used to gather information.

- Word study focused on building interest in words and on looking for patterns in words.

- Learner interest and engagement were important variables in the teachers' planning. Teachers taught the standard curriculum but tailored it to their students' interests, needs, strengths, and weaknesses.

- *Managed choice* was a common feature in these classrooms. Students were often presented with a topic or problem and allowed to choose which part of it they would pursue and what resources they would use.

- Instruction took place in a variety of formats. Whole-class, various types of small groups, and side-by-side teaching were seen throughout the day.

- Students were expected to work collaboratively and take responsibility for their learning. Working together was valued. When problems occurred, teachers helped students figure out how to solve these problems so the group could successfully complete its task.

- Reading and writing were integrated with science and social studies. Many of the books chosen for the class to read tied into science and social studies topics.

- Teachers evaluated student work with consideration for improvement, progress, and effort. Self-evaluation was also encouraged and modeled.

In the late 1990s, Barbara Taylor, David Pearson, and other researchers at the Center for the Improvement of Early Reading Achievement (CIERA) began investigating school and classroom practices in schools with unexpectedly high achievement and compared them to what was happening in similar schools in which the children were not "beating the odds" (Taylor, Pearson, Clark, & Walpole, 2000). They identified 70 first-, second-, and third-grade teachers from 14 schools in Virginia, Minnesota, Colorado, and California. Teachers were observed monthly and kept weekly logs of instructional activities. They also completed a questionnaire on their reading/language arts instructional practices. Some of the teachers and principals also participated in interviews. In each classroom, data were gathered for two low and two average readers in the fall and in the spring. When comparing the classroom practices of the most effective teachers with those of the less effective teachers, researchers concluded that the most effective teachers shared these qualities:

- Had higher pupil engagement
- Provided more small-group instruction
- Provided more coaching to help children improve in word recognition
- Asked more higher-level comprehension questions
- Communicated more with parents
- Had children engage in more independent reading

For a peek into preschool and kindergarten classrooms that work, we invite you into classrooms observed by Connie Juel and associates (Juel, Biancarosa, Coker, & Deffes, 2003), who followed 200 low-income urban children from preschool to first grade. Juel and her associates tracked the development of these young children in two important areas—decoding and oral vocabulary. While it is generally accepted that young children need to develop phonemic awareness and phonics skills to become successful readers, meaning vocabulary—that is, the number of words students have meanings for in their speaking and listening vocabularies—is often ignored. Meaning vocabulary, however, is essential to comprehension, and deficits in the oral vocabularies of young children are apt to show up as comprehension deficits in future years.

When the 200 children were evaluated on their decoding and meaning vocabulary skills as they entered preschool, most showed deficits in both areas. The children improved in their decoding skills each year. By the middle of first grade, their average decoding scores were slightly above national norms. Although the children did make gains in oral vocabulary between preschool and first grade, they never caught up to national norms. In their vocabulary development, these low-income children were as far behind (nearly one standard deviation) in first grade as they had been in preschool.

Juel and her associates then looked at their classroom observations and coded all the instruction observed into five categories: letter-sound, oral language, anchored word, reading, and writing. The only category of activities that had a positive effect on oral vocabulary was anchored word instruction. Anchored word instruction was defined using an example from Pat Hutchins's *Rosie's Walk*:

> The teacher had printed the words *pond, mill* and *haystack* on large cards which she places on the floor in front of her students. As she rereads the story, she points to the word cards and asks the students to walk around them the way Rosie walks around each of the locations in the book. The class discusses the meaning of the words *pond, mill* and *haystack.* (p. 13)

The article goes on to explain that the teacher then helps children with the sounds in the words *pond, mill,* and *haystack* but only after having the children actively involved in adding these words to their oral vocabularies. Choosing important words from reading, printing them on cards, and focusing specifically on their meanings is what Juel defines as *anchored word instruction*.

First-graders who had experienced more anchored word instruction had higher oral vocabulary scores. This increase occurred for children who entered preschool with low, average, and high levels of oral vocabulary. Conversely, the oral vocabulary scores of children in classrooms that spent the largest amount of time in letter-sound instruction decreased. This decrease in scores occurred for children who entered preschool with low, average, and high levels of oral vocabulary. Juel concluded her research with one of the best arguments for the need for balanced instruction at all grade levels:

> Ultimately, effective early reading instruction must help students learn to identify words and know their meanings. With so much research emphasizing the importance of early development in both word reading and language skills, we must consider how to provide instruction that fosters students' vocabulary development without losing the promising results of effective instruction in decoding. It does little good, after all, to be able to sound out the words *pond, mill* and *haystack* if you have no idea what they mean. (p. 18)

In 2005, Pat Cunningham conducted a study of effective schools (Cunningham, 2006; 2007). She identified six schools with high levels of poverty and large numbers of children who passed their states' literacy tests. The six schools were located in five different states. All but one school were located in medium-sized cities in the midwest, northeast, and southeast. The non-urban school was on an army base. The percentage of children in these schools who qualified for free/reduced-price lunch ranged from 68 to 98 percent. Students in two of the schools were predominately Hispanic and most of these students were English language learners. One school was almost exclusively African American. Two of the schools had mixed populations of children, with approximately half Caucasian and half African American students. In the army base school, 70 percent of the students were Caucasian. The tests taken by the students varied according to the states in which they were located. Scores on the 2005 state literacy tests indicated that between 68 and 87 percent of students met or exceeded the state's standards for proficiency. All six schools scored better on their literacy tests than other schools in their districts that had lower levels of poverty.

The third factor all three schools shared was that they used the Four Blocks framework to organize their literacy instruction. Four Blocks, a framework for balanced literacy in the primary grades, began in the 1989 school year in one first-grade classroom (Cunningham, Hall & Defee, 1991). Since then, it has expanded to include a Building Blocks framework in kindergarten and a Big Blocks framework in upper grades. At all grade levels, instructional time and emphasis is divided between a Words Block, which includes sight words, fluency, phonics, and spelling; a Guided Reading Block, which focuses on comprehension strategies for story and informational text and building prior knowledge and vocabulary; a Writing Block, which includes both process writing and focused writing; and a Self-Selected Reading Block, which includes teacher read-alouds and independent reading.

The six schools had three things in common: They had large numbers of poor children, they had done better than expected on their states' literacy tests, and they all used the Four Blocks framework. What did they do that allowed them to achieve their success? To attempt to answer this question, 12 factors were identified that research suggests are important to high literacy achievement: assessment, community involvement, comprehensive curriculum, engagement, instruction, leadership, materials, parent participation, perseverance, professional development, specialist support, and time spent reading and writing. Through interviews and school visits, it was determined that all 12 factors were valued by the schools and played important roles in school decision making. To determine which of the 12 factors was most important to the schools' success, teachers and administrators completed a survey in which they ranked these 12 factors according to their perceived importance.

None of these factors is unimportant, but when the teachers and administrators in these schools were forced to decide what contributed most to their success ranked instruction, *time spent reading and writing*, the *engagement* of their students in the literacy activities, and their *perseverance* in sticking with the Four Blocks framework as the most important factors.

What We Know about Classrooms That Work

Based on the research studies of effective classrooms, we can draw some firm conclusions about what it takes to create classrooms in which all the children learn to read and write.

The Most Effective Classrooms Provide Huge Amounts of Balanced, Comprehensive Instruction

Balance is an overused word these days, but it is still an important concept in classroom instruction. Balance can be thought of as a multiple vitamin. We know that many vitamins are required for good health, and we try to eat a balanced diet. Many of us take a multiple vitamin each day as extra insurance that we are getting all the most important nutrients. The most effective teachers provide all the important ingredients that go into creating thoughtful, avid readers and writers. Exceptional teachers teach skills and strategies and also provide lots of time each day for children to read and write. The Juel study, in particular, points out the importance of balance (Juel et al., 2003). When teachers spend too much time on one component—teaching decoding—the development of another important component—oral vocabulary—suffers.

Children in the Most Effective Classrooms Do a Lot of Reading and Writing

We have long known that the amount of reading and writing children do is directly related to how well they read and write. Classrooms in which all the students learned to read and write are classrooms in which the teachers gave more than "lip service" to the importance of actually engaging in reading and writing. They planned their time so that children did a lot of reading and writing throughout the day—not just in the 100 minutes set aside for reading and language arts.

Science and Social Studies Are Taught and Integrated with Reading and Writing

In a misguided effort to raise test scores, some schools have eliminated science and social studies in the primary grades and asked teachers just to focus on "the basics." Unfortunately, children who have not had regular science and social studies instruction usually enter the intermediate grades with huge vocabulary deficits. Science and social studies are the "knowledge" part of the curriculum. Young children need to be increasing the size and depth of their meaning vocabularies so that they can comprehend the more sophisticated and less familiar text they will be reading as they get older. Exemplary teachers don't choose reading and writing over science and social studies. Rather, they integrate reading and writing with the content areas. As children engage in science and social studies units, they have daily opportunities to increase the size of their meaning and knowledge stores and real reasons for reading and writing.

Meaning Is Central and Teachers Emphasize Higher-Level Thinking Skills

In today's society, where almost every job requires a high level of literacy, employers demand that the people they hire be able to communicate well and thoughtfully as they read and write. Low levels of literal comprehension and basic writing are no longer acceptable in the workplace. The most effective teachers emphasize higher-level thinking skills from the beginning. They ask questions that do not have just one answer. They engage students in conversations and encourage them to have conversations with one another. They teach students to problem solve, self-regulate, and monitor their own comprehension. Classrooms in which all the children learn to read and write are classrooms in which meaning is central to all instruction and activities.

Skills Are Explicitly Taught, and Children Are Coached to Use Them while Reading and Writing

Excellent teachers know what skills children need to be taught, and they teach these skills explicitly—often through modeling and demonstration. More importantly, these excellent teachers never lose sight of the goals of skills instruction. When working with children in a small group or in a one-on-one reading or writing setting, these teachers remind children to use what they have been taught. Because the children are doing a lot of reading and writing, they have numerous opportunities to apply whatever skills they are learning.

Teachers Use a Variety of Formats to Provide Instruction

The argument about whether instruction is best presented in a whole-class, small-group, or individual setting is settled when you observe excellent teachers. Teachers who get the best results from their children use a variety of formats, depending on what they want to accomplish. In addition to providing whole-class, small-group, and individual instruction themselves, excellent teachers use a variety of collaborative grouping arrangements to allow children to learn from one another. Excellent teachers group children in a variety of ways and change these groupings from day to day, depending on what format they determine will best achieve their goals.

A Wide Variety of Materials Are Used

In some schools today, there is a constant search for the "magic bullet" to increase reading achievement. "What program should we buy?" is the question these schools ask. Not a single one of the exemplary teachers found in the various observational studies was using only one program or set of materials. All the teachers gathered and used the widest range of materials available to them. Administrators who restrict teachers to any one set of materials will find no support for this decision in the research on outstanding teachers.

Classrooms Are Well Managed and Have High Levels of Engagement

In order to learn, children must be in a safe and orderly environment. If there are many disruptions and behavior management issues in a classroom, they will take the teacher's time away from teaching and the children's focus away from learning. All the teachers in the most effective classrooms had excellent classroom management. They expected children to behave in a kind and courteous manner and made these expectations known. These classrooms all had high levels of engagement. Almost all the children were doing what they were supposed to be doing almost all the time. If this seems a bit unreal to you, think about all the factors underlying these well-managed, highly engaging classrooms. Instead of doing a lot of worksheets and repetitive drills, the children were engaged in a lot of reading and writing. Because the teachers took into account the interests and needs of the children, the students were interested in what they were reading and writing. The fourth-grade classrooms, in particular, featured a great amount of managed choice and collaborative learning. Children spent time investigating topics they cared about with friends with whom they were encouraged to have conversations. Teachers focused their evaluations on improvement and progress, and they guided the children in becoming self-reliant and responsible for their own learning. Classrooms in which the activities seem real and important to the children are classrooms in which children are more engaged with learning and less apt to find reasons to be disruptive.

Creating Your Own Classroom That Works, Even Better

From the first edition to the current edition, we have been writing this book for you—the classroom teacher. It has been clear to everyone for decades that the teacher is the most important variable in how well children learn to read and write. The critical role of the teacher in determining reading achievement was confirmed by Nye, Konstantopoulos, and Hedges (2004) in a large study that showed that teacher effects were more powerful than any other variable, including class size and socioeconomic status. Although there are many restrictions on what elementary classroom teachers can do, most teachers are still given a great deal of freedom in deciding exactly how their classrooms will be run, how the various materials will be used, what the daily schedule will be like, what kinds of instructional formats they will use, how they will monitor and assess the progress of their students, and how they will create a well-managed, engaging environment. By learning from the most exemplary teachers—teachers who "beat the odds" in helping all their children achieve thoughtful literacy—you can create classrooms that work *even better* than they have in the past. We hope the practical information contained in the rest of this book will help you make your teaching even more exemplary and more effective.

chapter 2

Creating Enthusiastic, Independent Readers

In Chapter 1, we described the characteristics of classrooms that work, classrooms in which all the children become the very best readers and writers they can be. These classrooms share many important features. Teachers in these classrooms provide a comprehensive curriculum and devote time and energy to all the important components of literacy. They model, demonstrate, and encourage. They emphasize meaning and integrate reading and writing with the content areas. They use a variety of groupings and side-by-side teaching. They use a wide assortment of materials and are not tied to any one published program. They have excellent classroom management, based primarily on engaging their students in meaningful and worthwhile endeavors. Children spend a lot of their time actually engaged in reading and writing.

In this chapter, we will focus on the essential component that must be in place in any classroom where all the children learn to read and write. In order to become literate, children must become readers. Readers are not just children who *can* read—they are children who *do* read. The amount of reading children do is highly correlated with how well they read. The number of words in your meaning vocabulary store is directly related to how much you read, and your reading comprehension is heavily dependent on having meanings for the words you read. *Fluency*—the ability to read quickly and with expression—is also related to how much you read.

Reading is complex, and teaching children to read is equally complex. The fact that children must do a lot of reading to become good readers, however, is simple and straightforward. Because creating enthusiastic and independent readers is the essential foundation on which all good instruction can be built, we begin this book by describing how to create classrooms in which all children become readers. We hope that as you think about how to make your classroom one in which all children become readers, you will begin by considering how much and how willingly they read and what steps you can take to increase both those levels.

Assess and Document Your Students' Independent Reading

One of the characteristics of the most effective teachers is that they regularly assess how children are progressing toward meeting important goals and then adjust their instruction based on these assessments. Suppose that having all your children read more enthusiastically is one of your most important goals. You will be more apt to achieve this goal if you have some way of knowing where your children are early in the year and how they are progressing toward that goal.

Many teachers do a status assessment early in the year to determine how the children feel about themselves as readers. They file these assessments away and then have the children respond to the same questions halfway through the year and at the end of the year. After the children assess themselves halfway through the year, the teachers give them the reports they completed early in the year and have them compare how they are "growing up" as readers. Both the early-in-the-year reports and the midyear reports are then filed away. At the end of the year, the teachers have children self-report their reading habits one last time. After the students complete the final report, the teachers give them the first and second reports and have them write paragraphs summarizing their change and growth as readers. Many children are amazed (and proud!) to see how much more they like to read. The "Reading and Me" form is one example of the type of report you might use to help you and your students assess their growth as readers.

• Reading and Me •

My name is _____.

Here is how I feel about reading as of _____ (today's date).

The best book I ever read was _____.

I like it because_____.

The best book I read in the last 4 months was _____.

I like it because_____.

My favorite author is _____.

My favorite kind of book is _____.

When I am home, I read: (Circle one)

    Almost Never   Sometimes   Almost Every Day   Every Day

This is how I feel about reading right now: (Circle one)

    I love reading.   I like reading.   I don't like reading.   I hate reading.

Make Teacher Read-Aloud an Everyday Event

Do you read aloud to your students at least once every day? Teacher read-alouds have been shown to be one of the major motivators for children's desire to read. In 1975, Sterl Artley asked successful college students what they remembered their teachers doing that motivated them to read. The majority of students responded that teachers reading aloud to the class was what got them interested in reading. More recently, elementary students were asked what motivated them to read particular books. The most frequent response was "My teacher read it to the class" (Palmer, Codling, & Gambrell, 1994). Ivey and Broaddus (2001) surveyed 1,765 sixth-graders to determine what motivates them to read. The responses of this large group of diverse preteens indicated that their major motivation for reading came from having time for independent reading of books of their own choosing and teachers reading aloud to them.

Reading aloud to children is a simple and research-proven way to motivate children of all ages to become readers. When thinking about your struggling readers, however, you also need to consider *what* you are reading aloud. Did you know that most of the fictional books sold in bookstores are sold to women and most of the informational books are sold to men? Now, this doesn't mean that women never read informational texts or that men never read fiction; it just means that males seem to have a preference for information and females for fiction.

Including Both Fact and Fiction

Reading aloud matters to motivation, and what you read aloud may really matter to your struggling readers. In *True Stories from Four Blocks Classrooms* (Cunningham & Hall, 2001), Deb Smith describes her daily teacher read-aloud session. Each day, Deb reads one chapter from a fiction book, a part of an information book, and an "everyone" book. She chooses the everyone book by looking for a short, simple book that "everyone in her class will enjoy and can read." (She *never* calls these books "easy" books!) By reading from these three types of books daily, Deb demonstrates to her students that all kinds of books are cherished and acceptable in her classroom. Deb follows her teacher read-aloud with independent reading time. The informational books and "everyone" books are popular choices, especially with her boys who struggle with reading.

Reading aloud to students is more common in primary grades than in upper grades, even though it might be even more important for teachers of older children to read aloud. Most children develop the reading habit between the ages of 8 and 11. Reading aloud to older children provides the motivation for them to read at the critical point when they have the literacy skills to take advantage of that motivation. Intermediate teachers need to make a special effort to read books from

My Epiphany

I (Pat) first heard this report on female/male preferences for fiction versus informational texts on *All Things Considered* while driving home from a workshop I had just done on motivation to read. I was instantly transported back to a fourth-grade class I taught many years ago. I had five "resistant" readers—all boys who I tried all kinds of things with to motivate them to read. I can clearly hear their voices telling me that they didn't want to read because "Reading is dumb and silly." At the time, I thought this was just their way of rationalizing the fact that they weren't good readers.

I read to my fourth-graders every day, but I am embarrassed to admit I can't think of a single nonfiction title I read aloud. I read *Charlotte's Web* but never a book about real spiders. What if their "reading is dumb and silly" attitude was engendered by the fanciful text I so enjoyed reading to them?

Reading to children motivates many of them to want to read—and particularly to want to read the book the teacher read aloud. I wonder if my struggling boys' attitude toward reading was an unintended consequence of years of being read to by female teachers who were reading their favorite books—which just happened to be mostly fiction! If I could go back in time, I would resolve to read equal amounts of fiction and informational text. Yes, I would still read *Charlotte's Web,* but I would also read Gail Gibbon's wonderful book *Spiders.*

Male Reading Models

Most elementary teachers are women, and most struggling readers are boys. A lot of boys believe that "Real men don't read books!" Many schools have reported an increase in students' motivation to read after some "real men" came in to read books to their classes.

Finding these real men and getting them to come to school regularly is not easy, but if you are on the lookout for them, they can often be found. Service organizations such as the Jaycees and the Big Brothers are a place to begin your search. City workers, including policemen and firemen, may also be willing to help. Would the person who delivers something to your school each week be flattered to be asked to come and read to your class? If some construction is being done in your neighborhood, the construction company may feel that it is good public relations to allow its workers to volunteer to come into your classroom for a half hour each week and read to your class.

Cindy Visser (1991), a reading specialist in Washington, reported how her school formed a partnership with the local high school football team. Football players came once a month and read to elementary classes. Appropriate read-aloud books were chosen by the elementary teachers and sent to the high school ahead of time. Interested athletes chose books and took them home to "polish their delivery." On the last Friday of the month, the athletes donned their football jerseys and rode the team bus to the elementary school. The arrival of the bus was greeted by cheering elementary students, who escorted the players to their classes. There, they read to the children and answered questions about reading, life, and, of course, football. This partnership, which was initiated by an elementary school in search of male reading models, turned out to be as profitable for the athletes as it was for the elementary students. The coach reported a waiting list of athletes who wanted to participate and a boost in the self-esteem of the ones who did.

all the different sections of the bookstore. Most of us who are readers established our reading preferences in these preteen years. If you read *Cam Jensen* mysteries then, you probably still enjoy reading mysteries today. If you read *Star Wars* and *Star Trek* books then, you probably still enjoy science fiction today. If you packed biographies of famous people and informational books about sports to take to camp, the books you pack in your vacation travel bags today are probably still more information than fiction.

One way you can motivate more of your students to become readers is to read some books in a series and some books by authors who have written many other books. Remember that your students often want to read the book you read aloud. Read aloud one of David Adler's *Cam Jensen* mysteries, and then show students several more of these mysteries that you wish you had time to read aloud to them. Read aloud one of Gail Gibbon's informational books on animals—perhaps *Sharks* or *Whales* or *Dogs*—and then show students the other 40 Gibbon animal books you wish you had time to read to them. Your students who like mysteries may have "choice anxiety" trying to decide which *Cam Jensen* mystery they want to read first, and your animal lover informational readers will not know where to begin with all of Gail Gibbon's wonderful animal books. Unlike most anxiety, this kind of choice anxiety is a good thing!

You may want to make a list of different genres, titles, and authors, on which you can record the books you have read aloud. By keeping a Teacher Record Sheet, you can be sure you are opening the doors to all the different kinds of wonderful books there are.

• Teacher Record Sheet: •
Books and Magazines Read Aloud This Year

Type	Title	Author
Mystery	_____	_____
Science Fiction	_____	_____
Fantasy	_____	_____
Contemporary Fiction	_____	_____
Historical Fiction	_____	_____
Multicultural Fiction	_____	_____
Sports Fiction	_____	_____
Other Fiction	_____	_____
Sports Informational	_____	_____
Animals Informational	_____	_____
Multicultural Informational	_____	_____
Science Informational	_____	_____
Other Informational	_____	_____
Biography	_____	_____
Easy Chapter-Series	_____	_____
Authors with Other Books	_____	_____
Magazines	_____	_____

the tech-savvy
TEACHER

Rich Resources for Multicultural Literature

A treasure trove of good multicultural children's literature is available and there are many sources of multicultural books on the web. Here are a few of our favorites:

> ncrel.org/sdrs/areas/issues/educatrs/
> presrvce/pe3lk28

> nea.org/readacross/resources/
> 50multibooks

> multiculturalchildrenslit.com

If you teach older children, you can show your students the whole range of items that adults read by bringing real-world reading materials, such as newspapers and magazines, into the classroom and reading tidbits from these with an "I was reading this last night and just couldn't wait to get here and share it with you" attitude. You may also want to keep a book of poetry handy and read one or two poems whenever appropriate. No intermediate-aged student can resist the appeal of Jack Prelutsky's or Judith Viorst's poems. In addition to poetry, your students will look forward to your reading to them if you often read snippets from *The Guinness Book of World Records* and from your favorite joke and riddle books. Be sure to include some of the wonderful new multicultural books in your read-aloud, so that all your students will feel affirmed by what you read aloud to them.

Schedule Time Every Day for Independent Reading

The goal of every elementary teacher should be to have all children read for at least 20 minutes each day from materials they have chosen to read. Use an analogy to help your students understand that becoming good at reading is just like becoming good at anything else. Compare learning to read with learning to play the piano or tennis or baseball. Explain that in order to become good at anything, you need three things: (1) instruction, (2) practice on the skills, and (3) practice on the whole thing. To become a good tennis player, you need to (1) take tennis lessons, (2) practice the skills (backhand, serve, etc.), and (3) play tennis. To become a good reader, you also need instruction, practice on the important skills, and practice reading! Point out that sometimes we get so busy that we forget to take the important time each day to read. Therefore, we must schedule it, just like anything else we do.

At least 20 minutes daily for independent reading is the goal, but you may want to start with a shorter period of time and increase it gradually as your children establish the reading habit and learn to look forward to this daily "read what you want to" time. Consider using a timer to signal the beginning and end of the independent reading time. When engaging in activities regularly, some natural time rhythms are established. Using a timer to monitor independent reading will help children establish these rhythms. When the timer sounds at the end of the session, say something like "Take another minute if you need to get to a stopping point."

When the time for independent reading has begun, do not allow your students to move around the room, looking for books. You may want to suggest to the children that they choose several pieces of reading material before the time begins. Alternately, place a crate of books on each table, and let children choose from that crate. Every few days rotate the crates from table to table so that all the children have access to many different books "within arm's reach." Depending on the arrangement of your classroom, you might want some of your students to read in various spots around the room. Make sure that they all get to their spots before the reading time begins and they stay in that spot until the time is up. Help your students understand that reading requires quiet and concentration and that people wandering around are distracting to everyone.

Establishing and enforcing the "No wandering" rule is particularly important for struggling readers. If your students have not been successful with reading in the past and they are allowed to move around the room to look for books during the independent reading time, then they will be apt to spend more time wandering than reading. Remember that one of your major reasons for committing yourself to this daily independent reading time is that you know how much children read plays a critical role in how well they read. If your good readers read for almost all the allotted time and your struggling readers read for only half the time, the gap between your good and poor readers will further widen as

RICH resources

Independent Reading

For inspiration and lots of practical ideas for independent reading, we have found no better resource than *The Book Whisperer* by Donalyn Miller. You will feel like you are talking with Donalyn as she describes her own sixth-grade classroom in which all students are expected to read at least 40 books each year. She will convince you that it is time to stop assigning book reports, vocabulary lists, and worksheets—all activities that consume student time and foster negative attitudes toward books and reading. She will persuade you that when students choose what they want to read and have sustained time to do that reading, reading becomes its own reward. No external, extrinsic reward is required to motivate students to read. We strongly believe in letting readers (including teachers) choose what they want to read, but if we ruled the world, we would mandate *The Book Whisperer* as required reading for all elementary teachers.

Big Buddy Readers

Having easy-to-read books available for older struggling readers will not get you anywhere if those readers refuse to be seen reading "baby books"! One way to get older children to read easy books is to give them a real-life reason to do so. In some schools, older children (big buddies) go to the kindergarten and read aloud to their little buddies books that they have practiced ahead of time. Arranging such partnerships allows older poor readers to become reading models. The buddy system also serves another critical function in that it legitimizes the reading and rereading of very easy books.

Once you have a buddy system set up, you can have the kindergarten teacher send up a basket of books from which each of your big buddies can choose. Tell them that professional readers always practice reading a book aloud several times before reading it to an audience. Then, let them practice reading the book—first to themselves, then to a partner in the classroom, and finally to a tape recorder.

the year goes on. Having a large variety of materials within arm's reach is crucial if your struggling readers are going to profit from this precious time you are setting aside each day for independent reading.

If you begin with just five or six minutes, kindergartners and early first-graders can engage in independent reading even before they can read. Think about your own children or other young children you have known. Those who have been regularly read to often look at their books and pretend they are reading. Encourage your kindergartners and early first-graders to get in the habit of reading even before they can do it. Many teachers of young children encourage them to "Pretend that you are the teacher and you are reading the book." Kindergarten children are also very motivated to read when they are allowed to pick a stuffed animal or a doll to read to!

Accumulate the Widest Possible Variety of Reading Materials

To have successful independent reading, it is crucial that students choose their own reading materials and have plenty of materials to choose from. Collecting a lot of appealing books requires determination, cleverness, and an eye for bargains. In addition to obvious sources—such as getting free books from book clubs when your students order books, asking parents to donate, begging for books from your friends and relatives whose children have outgrown them, and haunting yard sales and thrift shops—there are some less obvious sources. Libraries often sell or donate used books and magazines on a regular basis. Some bookstores will give you a good deal on closeouts and may even set up a "donation basket," where they will collect used books for you. (Take some pictures of your eager readers and have them write letters that tell what kind of books they like to read for the store to display above the donation basket.)

Many classrooms subscribe to some of the popular children's magazines. You will have far fewer resistant readers if the latest issue and back copies of *Your Big Backyard, Children's Digest, Cricket, Soccer Junior, Ranger Rick, 3-2-1 Contact, Sports Illustrated for Kids, National Geographic for Kids,* and *Zoobooks* are available for your students to read during independent reading.

Another inexpensive source of motivating reading materials is the variety of news magazines for children, including *Scholastic News, Weekly Reader,* and *Time for Kids.* They generally cost about $4.00 per year, and you get a "desk copy" with an order of

The Rotating Book Crates Solution

The goal of every teacher of struggling readers should be to have a variety of appealing reading materials constantly and readily available to the children.

In one school, four intermediate teachers became convinced of the futility of trying to teach resistant children to read with almost no appealing materials in the classroom. The teachers appealed to the administration and the parent group for money and were told that it would be put in the budget "for next year." Not willing to "write off" the children they were teaching this year, each teacher cleaned out her or his closets (school and home), rummaged through the bookroom, and used other means to round up all the easy and appealing books they could find. Then they put these materials into four big crates, making sure that each crate had as much variety as possible. Mysteries, sports, biographies, science fiction, informational books, cartoon books, and the like were divided up equally.

Since the teachers did this over the Christmas holiday, they decided that each classroom would keep a crate for five weeks. At the end of each five-week period, a couple of students carried the crate of books that had been in their room to another room. In this way, the four teachers provided many more appealing books than they could have if each had kept the books in his or her own classroom.

The four-crate solution was one of those "necessity is the mother of invention" solutions that the teachers came up with to get through the year without many books; fortunately, it had serendipitous results. When the first crate left each classroom at the end of the

initial five-week period, several children complained that they had not been able to read certain books or that they wanted to read some again. The teacher sympathized but explained that there were not enough great books to go around and that their crate had to go to the next room. The teacher then made a "countdown" calendar and attached it to the second crate. Each day, someone tore off a number so the children would realize that they had only 10, 9, 8, 7, and so on days to read or reread anything they wanted to from this second crate. Reading enthusiasm picked up when the students knew that they had limited time with these books.

When the third crate arrived, students dug in immediately. A racelike atmosphere developed as children tried to read as many books as possible before the crate moved on. When the fourth (and final) crate arrived, children already knew about some of the books that were in it. Comments such as "My friend read a great mystery in that crate, and I am going to read it, too" let the teachers know that the children were talking to their friends in other classes about the books in the crates!

While the enthusiasm generated by the moving crates of books had not been anticipated by the teachers, they realized in retrospect that it could have been. We all like something new and different, and "limited time only" offers are a common selling device. The following year, even with many more books available, the teachers divided their books up into seven crates and moved them every five weeks so that the children would always have new, fresh material.

Accumulate the Widest Possible Variety of Reading Materials

10 to 12. Teachers across a grade level often share the magazines, with each classroom receiving two or three copies. These news magazines deal with topics of real interest to kids, and reading interest is always heightened on the day that a new issue arrives.

Schedule Conferences So You Can Talk with Your Students about Their Reading

Early in the year, when you are getting your students in the habit of reading every day and gradually increasing the time for independent reading, circulate around and have whispered conversations with individual children about their books. Once the self-selected reading time has been well established, set up a schedule so that you can conference with one-fifth of your students each day. Use this time to monitor your children's reading, to encourage them in their individual reading interests, and to help them with book selection if they need that help.

If your reading conferences are going to be something your students look forward to (instead of dreading!), you need to think of them as conversations rather than interrogations. Here are some "conference starters" you can use to set a positive and encouraging tone for your conferences:

> "Let's see. What have you got for me today?"
>
> "Oh good, another book about ocean animals. I had no idea there were so many books about ocean animals!"
>
> "I see you have bookmarked two pages to share with me. Read these pages to me, and tell me why you chose them."
>
> "I never knew there was so much to learn about animals in the ocean. I am so glad you bring such interesting books to share with me each week. You are turning me into an ocean animals expert!"
>
> "I can't wait to see what you bring to share with me next week!"

One way to make sure your conferences are kid-centered conversations, rather than interrogations, is to put the job of preparing for the conference on your students. Before you begin conferences, use modeling and role-playing to help children learn what their job is in the conference. Your children are to choose the book (or magazine) they want to share and bookmark the part they want to discuss with you. Make sure your students know they must prepare and be ready for the conference, since you will only have three or four minutes with each student. After role-playing and modeling, many teachers post a chart to remind children what they are to do on the day of their conference.

• Getting Ready for Your Reading Conference •

1. Choose the book or magazine you want to share.

2. Pick a part to read to me and practice this part.

3. Write the title and page number on a bookmark and put the bookmark in the right place.

4. Think about what you want to talk to me about. Some possibilities are:

   • What you like about this book

   • Why you chose this part to read to me

   • Other good parts of the book

   • What you think will happen (if you haven't finished the book)

   • What you are thinking about sharing with me next week

   • Who you think would also like this book

Rather than arbitrarily assigning one-fifth of the class to the different conference days, consider dividing your struggling and avid readers across the days. Spend an extra minute or two with the struggling reader scheduled for the day. Many of these readers need help selecting books they can read. After your struggling reader shares the book chosen for that day, take a minute to help that student select some books or magazines to read across the next week. Advanced readers also often need an extra minute for help with book selection. These excellent readers are sometimes reading books that are very easy for them. Although reading easy books is good for all of us, it is nice to take a minute to nudge them forward in their book selection. Clever teachers do this in a "seductive" rather than a heavy-handed way.

> "Carla, I know you love mysteries. The other day when I was in the library, I found two mysteries that made me think of you. Listen to this." (Teacher reads "blurb" on the back of each mystery to Carla.) "Now, I have to warn you: These mysteries are a little longer and harder than the ones you usually read. But you are such a good reader, I know you could handle them if you wanted to read them."

Carla will probably be delighted that you thought of her and believed she could read harder mysteries. She will very likely "take the bait" and go off with some mysteries closer to her advanced reading level.

English Language Learners

Spread your English language learners out across the days and take a few extra minutes to develop language and confidence as you talk with them about the book they have chosen.

Reading books you want to read motivates you to read more. Sharing those books once a week with someone who "oohs and aahs" about your reading choices is also a sure-fire motivator.

Make Time for Sharing and Responding

Children who read also enjoy talking to their classmates about what they have read. In fact, Manning and Manning (1984) found that providing time for children to interact with one another about reading material enhanced the effects of sustained silent reading on both reading achievement and attitudes.

One device sure to spark conversation about books is to create a classroom bookboard. Cover a bulletin board with white paper, and use yarn to divide it into 40 or 50 spaces. Select 40 to 50 titles from the classroom library, and write each title in one of the spaces. Next, make some small construction paper rectangles in three colors or use three colors of small sticky notes. Designate a color to stand for various reactions to the books.

- Red stands for "Super—one of the all-time best books I've ever read."
- Blue indicates that a book was "OK—not the best I've ever read but still enjoyable."
- Yellow stands for "Yucky, boring—a waste of time!"

Encourage your students to read as many of the bookboard books as possible and to put their "autographs" on red, blue, and yellow rectangles and attach them to the appropriate titles. Every week or two, lead your class in a lively discussion of the reasons for their book evaluations. If some books are universally declared "reds," "blues," or "yellows," ask your students to explain why the books were so wonderful or so lame. The most interesting discussions, however, can be centered on those books that are evaluated differently by your students. When most of your students have read some of the books on your bookboard, begin a new bookboard. This time, you may want to let each student select a book and label/decorate the spot for that book.

Another way to have your students share books with each other is to end the independent reading time with a *Reader's Chair,* in which one or two children do a book talk each day. Each child shows a favorite book and reads or tells a little about it and then tries to "sell" this book to the rest of the class. The students' selling techniques are quite effective, since these books are usually quickly seen in the hands of many of their classmates.

Another popular sharing option is to hold "reading parties" one afternoon every two or three weeks. Your students' names are pulled from a jar and they form groups of three or four, in which everyone gets to share his or her favorite book. Reading parties, like other parties, often include refreshments such as popcorn or cookies. Your students will develop all kinds of tasty associations with books and sharing books!

English Language Learners

Sharing books in small groups motivates all your students to read but it is especially important for your students who are learning English. Often, these children are not comfortable speaking in front of the whole class. The small group is much less threatening. Sharing a book, including the pictures, gives them something concrete to use their burgeoning language skills to talk about.

Finding time for children to talk about books is not easy in today's crowded curriculum. There is, however, a part of each day that is not well used in most elementary classrooms—the last 15 minutes of the day. Many teachers have found that they can successfully schedule weekly reading sharing time if they utilize those last 15 minutes one day each week. Here is how this sharing time works in one classroom.

Every Thursday afternoon, the teacher gets the children completely ready to be dismissed 15 minutes before the final bell rings. Notes to go home are distributed. Bookbags are packed. Chairs are placed on top of the desks. The teacher has previously written down each child's name on an index card. The index cards are now shuffled and the first five names—which will form the first group—are called. These children go to a corner of the room that will always be the meeting place for the first group. The next five names that are called will form the second group and will go to whichever place has been designated for the second group. The process continues until all five or six groups have been formed and all the children are in their places. Now, each child has two minutes to read, tell, show, act out, or otherwise share something from what he or she has been reading this week. The children share in the order that their names were called. The first person called for each group is the leader. Each person has exactly two minutes and is timed by a timer. When the timer sounds, the next person gets two minutes. If a few minutes remain after all the children have had their allotted two minutes, the leader of each group selects something to share with the whole class. If you establish a regular sharing time, you will find that your students are more enthusiastic about reading. Comments such as "I'm going to stump them with these riddles when I get my two minutes" and "Wait 'til I read the scary part to everyone" are proof that your students are looking forward to sharing and that this anticipation is increasing their motivation to read. The popularity next week of books shared this week is further proof of the motivation power of book sharing.

Do Incentive Programs and Book Reports Demotivate Reading?

Many schools set up reading incentive programs in an attempt to get children to read real books. These programs can take many different forms. In some, children are given T-shirts that proclaim "I have read 100 books!" and in others, whole classes are rewarded with pizza parties if they have read "the most" books.

These reward systems are set up with the best intentions and may even motivate some children to begin reading. Unfortunately, another message can get communicated to children who are exposed to such incentive programs. The message goes something like "Reading is one of those things I must do in order to get something that I want." Reading thus becomes a means to an end, rather than an end in itself. Many teachers (and parents) report that children only read "short, dumb books" so that they can achieve the "longest list."

Doing book reports is another device used to motivate reading that can often have the opposite effect of what it was intended to have. When adults are asked what they remember about elementary school that made them like reading, they mention having their teachers read books aloud to the class, being allowed to select their own books, and having time to read them. When asked what things teachers did that made them dislike reading, doing book reports is most commonly mentioned. Likewise, few children enjoy doing book reports, and their dislike is often transferred to the act of reading. Some children report on the same books year after year, and others even admit lying about reading books.

Children who are going to become readers must begin to view reading as its own reward. This intrinsic motivation can only be nurtured as children find books that they "just can't put down" and subsequently seek out other books. Incentive programs and book reports must be evaluated on the basis of how well they develop this intrinsic motivation.

Summary

The more you read, the better you read! Nagy and Anderson (1984) showed that good readers often read 10 times as many words as poor readers during the school day. Guthrie and Humenick (2004) analyzed 22 studies of reading achievement and found that access to interesting books and choice about what to read were strongly correlated with reading achievement scores. Stanovich (1986) labeled the tendency of poor readers to remain poor readers as "the Matthew effect" and attributed the increasing gap between good readers and poor readers in part to the difference in time spent reading.

Wide reading is highly correlated with meaning vocabulary, which, in turn, is highly correlated with reading comprehension. Students who read more encounter the same words more frequently, and repeated exposure to the same words has been shown to lead to improvements in fluency (Topping & Paul, 1999). A. E. Cunningham and Stanovich (1998) found that struggling readers with limited reading and comprehension skills increased vocabulary and comprehension skills when time spent reading was increased.

Wide reading is also associated with the development of automatic word recognition (Stanovich & West, 1989). Share (1999) reviewed the research and concluded that self-teaching of word recognition occurs while readers are decoding words during independent reading. Good decoders teach themselves to recognize many words as they read for enjoyment.

This chapter has described classroom-tested ways to create a classroom in which your students read enthusiastically and independently. Reading aloud to your students from all the different types of books and magazines is your best tool for motivating independent reading. Scheduling time every day for independent reading demonstrates to your students the importance of reading and ensures that all your students spend some time every day developing the reading habit. Having a wide variety of books and magazines available is critical to the success of independent reading—particularly with your struggling readers, who may yet have discovered the perfect books for them. Sharing what they are reading in a weekly conference with you and periodically with their peers further motivates students to read and is consistent with a sociocultural view of literacy.

Building the
Literacy Foundation

Ask most adults when they learned to read, and most will tell you about their experiences in kindergarten or first grade. In reality, learning to read begins much earlier for many children. Think back to your own preschool years. You probably couldn't read in the way we usually think of it. You probably couldn't pick up a brand-new book and read it by yourself. But you probably did have some literacy skills in place before you were ever given any reading instruction in school.

Did you have a favorite book that someone read to you over and over? Did you ever sit down with a younger child or a stuffed animal and pretend you could read that book? Perhaps it was a predictable book, such as *Are You My Mother?* or *Pat the Bunny* or *Brown Bear, Brown Bear, What Do You See?* You probably didn't know all the individual words in the book, but you could sound like you were reading by telling in book language what was happening on the different pages.

Pretend reading is a stage that many 3- and 4-year-olds go through and is probably crucial to the ease with which they learn to read once they start school. Children who pretend to read a book know what reading is—that it has to "sound right" and "make sense." They also know that reading is enjoyable and something all the "big people" can do and thus something they are very eager to be able to do, too. Pretend reading is a way of experiencing what reading feels like even before you can do it and is an indicator of future success in reading.

Did you write before you came to school? Could you write your name and the names of your siblings, cousins, pets, or favorite restaurants?

Did you ever write a note like this?

Did you ever make a sign for your room that looked like this?

Many 4-year-olds love to write. Sometimes they write in scribbles.

Young children want to do everything that grown-ups can do. For the things they can't do yet, they just pretend they can! They pretend to drive, to take care of babies, to cook—and if they grow up in homes where the grown-ups read and write, they pretend they can read and write. As they engage in these early literacy behaviors, they learn important concepts.

Concepts That Form the Foundation for Literacy

Why We Read and Write

Ask 5-year-olds from strong literacy backgrounds why people read and write, and they reel off a string of answers:

> "Well, you have to able to read. You read books and signs and cereal boxes and birthday cards that come in the mail and recipes and . . . You write notes and stories and signs and lists and you write on the computer and you send postcards when you are on a trip and you write to your aunt and . . . "

You can tell from these answers that children who come to school with clear ideas about the functions of reading and writing have had many real-world experiences with reading and writing. Reading and writing are things all the bigger people they know do, and they intend to do them, too!

Background Knowledge and Vocabulary

A lot of what we know about the world, we have learned from reading. This is also true of young children. When parents or other people read to young children, they don't just read; they also talk with the children about what they are reading:

> "Do you know what that animal is called?"
>
> "Yes, it's a bear. The bears in this story are not real bears. We can tell because we know that real bears don't wear clothes or live in houses. Where could we go to see a real bear?"
>
> "Maybe we can find a book about real bears the next time we go to the library."

Comprehension is very highly correlated with prior knowledge and vocabulary. The more you know about any topic, the greater will be your understanding of what you read related to that topic. Your store of background knowledge and vocabulary directly affects how well you read. Young children who have had many books read to them simply know more than children who haven't.

Print Concepts

Print is what you read and write. Print includes all the funny little marks—letters, punctuation, spaces between words and paragraphs—that translate into familiar spoken language. In English, we read across the page in a left-to-right fashion. Because our eyes can see only a few words during each stop (called a *fixation*), we must actually move our eyes several times to read one line of print. When we finish that line, we make a return sweep and start all over again, left to right. If there are sentences at the top of a page, a picture in the middle, and more sentences at the bottom, we read the top first and then the bottom. We start at the front of a book and go toward the back. These arbitrary rules about how we proceed through print are called *conventions.*

Jargon refers to all the words we use to talk about reading and writing. Jargon includes such terms as *word, letter, sentence,* and *sound.* We use this jargon constantly as we try to teach children how to read:

> "Look at the **first word** in the **second sentence**."
> "How does that **word begin**?"
> "What **letter** has that **sound**?"

Children who have been read to and whose early attempts at writing have been encouraged often walk in the door of kindergarten with these critical print conventions and jargon. From being read to in the "lap position," they have noticed how the eyes "jump" across the lines of print as someone is reading. They have watched people write grocery lists and thank-you letters to Grandma, and they have observed the top-to-bottom, left-to-right movement. Often, they have typed on the computer and observed these print conventions. Because they have had people to talk with them about reading and writing, they have learned much of the jargon. While writing down a dictated thank-you note to Grandma, Dad may say,

> "Say your **sentence** one **word** at a time if you want me to write it.
> I can't write as fast as you can talk."

When the child asks how to spell *birthday,* he may be told,

> "It **starts with** the **letter *b***, just like your dog, Buddy's, name. *Birthday* and *Buddy* **start with the same sound and the same letter.**"

Knowing these print concepts is an essential part of the foundation for becoming literate. Young children who have had lots of informal early experiences with reading and writing have already begun to develop understandings about print conventions and jargon.

Phonemic Awareness

The ability to recognize that words are made up of a discrete set of sounds and to manipulate those sounds is called *phonemic awareness,* and children's level of phonemic awareness is very highly correlated with their success in beginning reading. Phonemic awareness develops through a series of stages, during which children first become aware that language is made up of individual words, that words are made up of syllables, and that syllables are made up of phonemes. It is important to note here that it is not the jargon children learn. Five-year-olds cannot tell you there are three syllables in *dinosaur* and one syllable in *Rex.* What they can do is clap out the three beats in *dinosaur* and the one beat in *Rex.* Likewise, they cannot tell you that the first phoneme in *mice* is *m,* but they can tell you what you would have if you took the "mmm" off *mice—ice.* Children develop this phonemic awareness as a result of the oral and written language they are exposed to. Nursery rhymes, chants, and Dr. Seuss books usually play a large role in this development.

Phonemic awareness is an oral ability. You hear the words that rhyme. You hear that *baby* and *book* begin the same. You hear the three sounds in *bat* and can say these sounds separately. Only when children realize that words can be changed and how changing a sound changes the word are they able to profit from instruction in letter-sound relationships.

Children also develop a sense of sounds and words as they try to write. In the beginning, many children let a single letter stand for an entire word. Later, they put in more letters and often say the word they want to write, dragging out its sounds to hear what letters they might use. Children who are allowed and encouraged to "invent-spell" develop an early and strong sense of phonemic awareness.

Some Concrete Words

Another area that demonstrates that early and easy readers know things about how words work is the use of *concrete words.* If you were to sit down with children in their first week of school and try to determine if they can read by giving them a simple book to read or testing them on some common words, such as *the, and, of,* and *with,* you would probably conclude that most of them can't read yet. But many young children do know some words. The words they know are usually "important-to-them" concrete words—*David, tiger, Pizza Hut, Cheerios.* Knowing a few words is important, not because you can read much with a few words but because in learning these first words, you have accomplished a critical task. You have learned how to learn words, and the few words you can read gives you confidence that you can learn words.

Some Letter Names and Sounds

Many children know some letter names and sounds when they come to school. They can't always recognize all 26 letters in both upper- and lowercase, and they often don't know the sound of *w* or *c,* but they have learned the names and sounds for the most common letters. Usually, the letter names and sounds children know have come from those concrete words they can read and write. Many children have also learned some letter names and sounds through repeated readings of alphabet books and through making words with magnetic letters on the refrigerator. In addition, children have learned some letter names and sounds as adults have spelled out words they were trying to write. This immersion in print has allowed children to make connections among the letters they have seen in many places.

Desire to Learn to Read and Write

Children who have had lots of early literacy encounters can't wait to learn to read! All the big people can do it, and they want to, too! We all know of children who have come home disappointed after the first day of school because "We were there all day and didn't learn to read!" This "can't wait" attitude motivates and sustains them through the work and effort required to learn to read.

The Foundation

From early reading and writing experiences, children learn these critical concepts:

- Why we read and write
- Background knowledge and vocabulary
- Print concepts
- Phonemic awareness
- Some concrete words
- Some letter names and sounds
- Desire to learn to read

These concepts are not, however, all or nothing. Some children come to school with all of the concepts quite well developed. Some children come with some developed but not all. Some children come with few of these concepts. Successful classrooms for young children are filled with lots of activities to help all children move along in their development of these crucial concepts.

Activities for Building the Foundation

Reading to Children and Independent Reading Time

The previous chapter outlined the importance of doing activities to promote enthusiastic and independent readers. If you have committed yourself to reading aloud to children and including a time for independent reading each day, you are well on your way to helping children build a firm foundation for learning to read. Many children are read to at home and are encouraged as they "pretend read" favorite books and attempt to read signs, labels, and other environmental print. For these children, your teacher read-alouds and independent reading encouragement will just move them further along in their literacy development. For children who have not had these experiences before coming to school, daily teacher read-alouds and independent reading time will give them a successful start in building the foundation for literacy.

Reading to children and providing time for them to read independently will also help children build their oral vocabularies. You may want to capitalize on an anchored vocabulary activity found to be effective in helping low-income young children build their oral vocabularies by picking important words from the books you read aloud to them and focusing their attention on those words. Find or copy a picture to go with each word. Put these words together in a book, with each page having one picture and the word that goes with it. Label the book according to the category the word belongs in. Make these books available for self-selected reading, and you will have lots of simple books that even your most struggling readers can find success with and enjoy.

Supporting and Encouraging Writing

Some people believe that if children are allowed to write before they can spell and make the letters correctly, they will get into bad habits that will be hard to break later. There is a certain logic in this argument, but the logic does not hold up to scrutiny when you actually look at what children do before they come to school. Just as many children "read" before they can read by pretend reading a memorized book, they "write" before they can write. Their writing is not initially decipherable by anyone besides themselves, and sometimes they read the same scribbling different ways! They write with pens, markers, crayons, paint, chalk, and normal-sized pencils with erasers on the ends. They write on chalk-boards, magic slates, paper, and, alas, walls! You can encourage and support fledgling attempts at writing in numerous ways.

Model Writing for the Children   As children watch you write, they observe that you always start in a certain place, go in certain directions, and leave spaces between words. In addition to these print conventions, they observe that writing is "talk written down." There are numerous opportunities in every classroom for the teacher to write as the children watch—and sometimes help with what to write.

In many classrooms, the teacher begins the day by writing a morning message on the board. The teacher writes this short message as the children watch. The teacher then reads the message, pointing to each word and inviting the children to join in on any words they know. Sometimes, the teacher takes a few minutes to point out some things students might notice from the morning message:

"How many sentences did I write today?"
"How can we tell how many there are?"
"What do we call this mark I put at the end of this sentence?"
"Which words begin with the same letters?"
"Which is the shortest word?"

These and similar questions help children learn conventions and jargon of print and focus their attention on words and letters.

Provide a Variety of Things to Write With and On   Young children view writing as a creation and are often motivated to write by various media. Many teachers grab free post-cards, scratch pads, counter checks, pens, and pencils and haunt yard sales—always on the lookout for an extra chalkboard or an old but still working typewriter. A letter home to parents at the beginning of the year, asking them to clean out desks and drawers and donate writing utensils and various kinds of paper, often brings unexpected treasures. In addition to the usual writing media, young children like to write with sticks in sand, with paintbrushes or sponges on chalkboards, and with chocolate pudding and shaving cream on tables.

Help Children Find Writing Purposes through Center Activities   Children need to develop the basic understanding that writing is a message across time and space. Once they have that understanding, they are able to identify a purpose for a piece of writing. For most young children, the purpose of writing is to get something told or done. Children will find some real purposes for writing if you incorporate writing in all your classroom centers. Encourage children to make grocery lists while they are playing in the housekeeping center. Menus, ordering pads, and receipts are a natural part of a restaurant center. An office center would include various writing implements, a typewriter or computer, along with index cards, phone books, and appointment books.

Children can make birthday cards for friends or relatives or write notes to you or their classmates and then mail them in the post office center. They can make signs (Keep Out! Girls Only!) and post them as part of their dramatic play. When children put a lot of time into building a particularly wonderful creation from the blocks, they often do not want to have it taken apart so that something else can be built. Many teachers keep a large pad of tablet paper in the construction center. Children can draw and label records of their constructions before disassembling them.

Once you start looking for them, there are numerous opportunities for children to write for real purposes as they carry out their creative and dramatic play in various centers.

Provide a Print-Rich Classroom   Classrooms in which children are encouraged to write have lots of print in them. In addition to books, there are magazines and newspapers. There are also charts of recipes made and directions for building things. Children's names are on their desks and on many different objects. There are class books, bulletin boards with labeled pictures of animals under study, and labels on almost everything. Children's drawings and all kinds of writing are displayed. In these classrooms, children see that all kinds of writing are valued. Equally important, children who want to write "the grown-up way" can find lots of words to make their own.

Accept the Writing They Do   Accepting a variety of writing—from scribbling to one-letter representations to invented spellings to copied words—is the key to having young children "write" before they can write. Talk to your students on the very first day of school about the forms they can use for writing. Show them examples of other children's scribbles, pictures, single letters, vowel-less words, and other kinds of writing. Tell them they all started out at the scribble stage, and they will all get to conventional writing. For now, they should use the stage of writing that is most comfortable to share the message they have, and you will help them move along to the next stage.

Teach Concrete Words

All children need to be successful in their first attempts at word learning. If the words you focus on with your beginners are the most common words—*the, have, with, to*—then those children who have not had many literacy experiences are going to have a hard time learning and remembering these words. The problem with the most common words is that they do not mean anything. *The, have, with,* and *to* are abstract connecting words. Children do need to learn these words (lots more about that in the next chapter), but doing so will be much easier if they have already learned some concrete important-to-them words. Most kindergarten and first-grade teachers begin their year with some get-acquainted activities. As part of these activities, they often have a "special child" each day. In addition to learning about each child, you can focus attention on the special child's name and use that name to develop some important understandings about words and letters.

To prepare for this activity, write all the children's first names (with initials for last names, if two first names are the same) in permanent marker on sentence strips. Cut the strips so that long names have long strips and short names have short strips. Each day, reach into the box and draw out a name. This child becomes the "King or Queen for a Day," and his or her name becomes the focus of many activities. Reserve a bulletin board and add each child's name to the board. (Some teachers like to have children bring in snapshots of themselves or take pictures of the children to add to the board as the names are added.) The following sections describe some day-by-day examples of what you might do with the names.

Day 1   Close your eyes. Reach into the box, shuffle the names around, and draw one out. Crown that child "King (or Queen) for a Day!" Lead the other children in interviewing this child to find out what he or she likes to eat, play, or do after school. Does she or he have brothers? Sisters? Cats? Dogs? Mice? Many teachers record this information on a chart or compile a class book, with one page of information about each child.

Now focus the children's attention on the child's name—*David.* Point to the word *David* on the sentence strip and develop children's understanding of jargon by pointing out that this *word* is David's name. Tell them that it takes many *letters* to write the word *David,* and let them help you count the letters. Say the letters in *David*—D-a-v-i-d—and have the children chant them with you. Point out that the word *David* begins and ends with the same letter. Explain that the first and the last *d* look different because one is a capital *D* and the other is a small *d* (or uppercase/lowercase—whatever jargon you use).

Take another sentence strip and have the children watch as you write *David.* Have them chant the spelling of the letters with you. Cut the letters apart and mix them up. Let several children come up and arrange the letters in just the right order so that they spell *David,* using the original sentence strip on which *David* is written as a model. Have the other children chant to check that the order is correct.

Give each child a large sheet of drawing paper, and have all of them write *David* in large letters on one side of their papers using crayons. Model at the board how to write each letter as the children write it. Do not worry if what they write is not perfect (or even if it does not bear much resemblance to the letter you wrote). Also resist the temptation to correct what they write. Remember that children who write at home before coming to school often reverse letters or write them in funny ways. The important understanding is that names are words, that words can be written, and that it takes lots of letters to write them.

Finally, have everyone draw a picture of David on the other side of the drawing paper. Let David take all the pictures home!

Day 2 Draw another name—*Caroline.* Crown "Queen Caroline" and do the same interviewing and chart making that you did for David. (Decide carefully what you will do for the first child because every child will expect equal treatment!) Focus the children's attention on Caroline's name. Say the letters in *Caroline,* and have the children chant them with you. Help the children count the letters and decide which letter is first, last, and so on. Write *Caroline* on another sentence strip and cut it into letters. Have children arrange the letters to spell *Caroline,* using the first sentence strip name as their model. Put *Caroline* on the bulletin board under *David,* and compare the two. Which has the most letters? How many more letters are in the word *Caroline* than in the word *David?* Does *Caroline* have any of the same letters as *David?* Finish the lesson by having everyone write *Caroline.* Have everyone draw Caroline pictures, and let Caroline take all of them home.

Day 3 Draw the third name—*Dorinda.* Do the crowning, interviewing, and chart making. Chant the letters in Dorinda's name. Write it, cut it up, and do the letter arranging. Be sure to note the two *d*'s and to talk about first and last letters. As you put *Dorinda* on the bulletin board, compare it to both *David* and *Caroline.* This is a perfect time to notice that both *David* and *Dorinda* begin with the same letter and the same sound. Finish the lesson by having the children write *Dorinda* and draw pictures for Dorinda to take home.

Day 4 *Mike* is the next name. Do all the usual activities. When you put *Mike* on the bulletin board, help the children realize that *David* has lost the dubious distinction of having the shortest name. (Bo may now look down at the name card on his desk and call out that his name is even shorter. You will point out that he is right but that Mike's name is the shortest one on the bulletin board right now. What is really fascinating about this activity is how the children compare their own names to the ones on the board, even before their names get there. That is exactly the kind of word/letter awareness you are trying to develop!)

When you have a one-syllable name with which there are many rhymes (*Pat, Jack, Bo, Sue,* etc.), seize the opportunity to help the children listen for words that rhyme with that name. Say pairs of words, some of which rhyme with Mike—*Mike/ball, Mike/bike, Mike/hike, Mike/cook, Mike/like.* If the pairs rhyme, everyone should point at Mike and shout "Mike." If not, they should shake their heads and frown.

Day 5   Next, the name *Cynthia* is drawn from the box. Do the various activities, and then take advantage of the fact that the names *Caroline* and *Cynthia* both begin with the letter *c* but with different sounds. Have Caroline and Cynthia stand on opposite sides of you. Write their names above them on the chalkboard. Have the children say *Caroline* and *Cynthia* several times, drawing out the first sound. Help them understand that some letters can have more than one sound and that the names *Caroline* and *Cynthia* demonstrate this fact. Tell the class that you are going to say some words, all of which begin with the letter *c*. Some of these words will sound like *Caroline* at the beginning, and some of them will sound like *Cynthia.* Say some words and have the children say them with you—*cat, celery, candy, cookies, city, cereal, cut.* For each word, have the children point to Caroline or Cynthia to show which sound they hear. Once they have decided, write each word under *Caroline* or *Cynthia.*

Day 6/Last Day   Continue to have a special child each day. For each child, do the standard interviewing, charting, chanting, letter arranging, writing, and drawing activities. Then take advantage of the names you have to help children develop an understanding about how letters and sounds work. Here are some extra activities many teachers do with the names:

- Write the letters of the alphabet across the board. Count to see how many names contain each letter. Make tally marks or a bar graph, and then decide which letters are included in the most names and which letters are included in the fewest names. Are there any letters that no one in the whole class has in his or her name?
- Pass out laminated letter cards—one letter to a card, lowercase on one side, uppercase on the other. Call out a name from the bulletin board, and lead the children to chant the letters in the name. Then let the children who have those letters come up and display the letters and lead the class in a chant, cheerleader style: "David—D-a-v-i-d—David—Yay, David!"

Learning Other Concrete Words   The activities just described for names can be used to teach many concrete words. Many teachers bring in cereal boxes as part of a nutrition unit. In addition to talking about the cereals, children learn the names of the cereals by chanting, writing, and comparing. Places to shop is another engaging topic. Ads for local stores—Wal-Mart, Kmart, Sears—are brought in. Children talk about the stores and, of course, learn the names by chanting, writing, and comparing. Food is a topic of universal interest. Menus from popular restaurants—Burger King, McDonald's, Pizza Hut—spark lots of lively discussion from children, and, of course, children love learning to read and spell these very important words. You can teach the color words through chanting, writing, and drawing. When studying animals, add an animal name to an animal board each day. Children love chanting, writing, and drawing the animals.

the tech-savvy TEACHER

Concrete Words for English Language Learners

Beginning with names and other concrete words is especially important for your children who are learning English. Learning to read and write their names and the names of their classmates gives them an initial successful experience and boosts their confidence. If you have a Jack and a Juan or a Julio, treat their names just as the example described for Carolina and Cynthia and have all your students listen for the two sounds of *j*. A wonderful resource for helping your English language learners develop a bank of concrete words can be found at **enchantedlearning.com**. There, you will find a *Little Explorers Picture Dictionary* with hundreds of printable pictures and the words for these pictures in both English and many other languages, including German, French, Spanish, Portuguese, Swedish, and Japanese.

These activities with the children's names and other concrete words can be done even when many children in the class do not know their letter names yet. Young children enjoy chanting, writing, and comparing words. They learn letter names by associating them with the important-to-them words they are learning.

Develop Phonemic Awareness

Phonemic awareness is the ability to take words apart, put them back together again, and change them. Phonemic awareness activities are done orally, calling attention to the sounds—not the letters or which letters make which sounds. Here are some activities to include in your classroom to ensure that all your children continue to develop in their ability to hear and manipulate sounds in words.

Use Names to Build Phonemic Awareness   Capitalize on your children's interest in names by using their names to develop a variety of phonemic awareness skills. The first way that children learn to pull apart words is into syllables. Say each child's name, and have all the children clap the beats in that name as they say it with you. Help children to discover that *Dick* and *Pat* are one-beat names, that *Manuel* and *Patrick* are two beats, and so on. Once children begin to understand, clap the beats and have all the children whose names have that number of beats stand up and say their names as they clap the beats with you.

Another phonemic awareness skill is the ability to hear when sounds are the same or different. Say a sound, not a letter name, and have all the children whose names begin with that sound come forward. Stretch out the sound as you make it: "s-s-s." For the "s-s-s" sound, Samantha, Susie, Steve, and Cynthia should all come forward. Have everyone stretch out the "s-s-s" as they say each name. If anyone points out that *Cynthia* starts with a *c* or that *Sharon* starts with an *s,* explain that they are correct about the letters but that now you are listening for sounds.

You can use the names of some of your children to help them understand the concept of *rhyme.* Choose the children whose names have lots of rhyming words to come forward—*Bill, Jack, Brent, Kate, Clark.* Say a word that rhymes with one of the names (*hill, pack, spent, late, park*), and have the children say the word along with the name of the rhyming child. Not all your children's names will have rhymes, but the children who do will feel special and appreciated because they are helping everyone learn about rhyming words.

All your children will feel special if you call them to line up by stretching out their names, emphasizing each letter of each name. As each child lines up, have the class stretch out his or her name with you. The ability to segment words into sounds and blend them back together is an important phonemic awareness ability.

Encourage Phonics Spelling Think about what you have to do to "put down the letters you hear" while writing. You have to stretch out the sounds in the word. Children who stretch out words develop the phonemic awareness skill of *segmenting.* When children are just beginning, it doesn't really matter if they represent all the sounds with the right letters. What matters is the stretching out they are doing to try to hear the sounds. As phonics instruction continues, their phonics spelling will more closely match the actual spelling of the word.

Count Words This activity lets you build math skills as you develop the basic phonological awareness concept of separating words. For this activity, each child should have 10 counters in a paper cup. (Anything that is manipulative is fine. Some teachers use edibles, such as raisins, grapes, or small crackers, and let the children eat their counters at the end of the lesson. This makes clean-up quick and easy!) Begin by counting some familiar objects in the room, such as windows, doors, trash cans, and the like, having each child place one of the counters on the desk for each object.

Tell the children that you can also count words by putting down a counter for each word you say. Explain that you will say a sentence in the normal way and then repeat the sentence, pausing after each word. The children should put down counters as you say the words in the sentence slowly and then count the counters and decide how many words you said. As usual, children's attention is better if you make sentences about them:

> Carol has a big smile.
> Paul is back at school today.
> I saw Jawan at the grocery store.

Once the children catch on to the activity, let them say some sentences—first in the normal way, then one word at a time. Listen carefully as they say their sentences, because they usually need help saying them one word at a time. Not only do children enjoy this activity and learn to separate words in speech but they are also practicing critical counting skills!

Clap Syllables   In addition to using your students' names to develop syllable awareness, you can use any of the environmental print words that you are helping children learn. *Cheerios* is a three-beat word. *Kix* takes only one clap and has one beat. When children can clap syllables and decide how many beats a given word has, help them see that one-beat words are usually shorter than three-beat words—that is, they take fewer letters to write. To do this, use your sentence strips and write some words that children cannot read. Cut the strips into words so that short words have short strips and long words have long strips. Have some of the words begin with the same letters but be of different lengths. This will require the children to think about word length in order to decide which word is which.

For the category of animals, you might write *horse* and *hippopotamus, dog* and *donkey, kid* and *kangaroo,* and *rat, rabbit,* and *rhinoceros.* Tell the children that you are going to say the names of animals and that they should clap to show how many beats each word has. (Do not show them the words yet!) Say the first pair of words, one at a time—*horse hippopotamus*. Help children to decide that *horse* is a one-beat word and that *hippopotamus* takes a lot more claps and is a five-beat word. Now, show children the two words and say, "One of these words is *horse,* and the other is *hippopotamus.* Who thinks they can figure out which one is which?" Explain that because *hippopotamus* takes so many beats to say, it probably takes more letters to write.

Play Blending and Segmenting Games   In addition to using the names of your children to help them learn to blend and segment, you can use a variety of other words that help build their meaning vocabularies while simultaneously practicing blending and segmenting. Use pictures related to your unit or from simple concept and alphabet books. Let each child take a turn saying the name of the picture (one sound at a time), and call on another child to identify the picture. In the beginning, limit the pictures to five or six items whose names are very different and short—*truck, frog, cat, pony, tiger,* for example. After children understand what they are trying to do, they love playing a variation of "I Spy," in which they see something in the room, stretch out its name, and then call on someone to figure out what was seen and to give the next clue.

Read Rhyming Books and Nursery Rhymes   One of the best indicators of how well children will learn to read is their ability to recite nursery rhymes when they walk into kindergarten. Since this is such a reliable indicator and since rhymes are so naturally appealing to children at this age, kindergarten and first-grade classrooms should be filled with rhymes. Children should learn to recite these rhymes, sing the rhymes, clap to the rhymes, act out the rhymes, and pantomime the rhymes. In some primary classrooms, they develop "raps" for the rhymes.

As part of your read-aloud, include lots of rhyming books, including such old favorites as *Hop on Pop; One Fish, Two Fish, Red Fish, Blue Fish;* and *There's a Wocket in My Pocket.* As you read the book for the second time—once is never near enough for a favorite book of young children—pause just before you get to the rhyme and let the children chime in with the rhyming word.

Read and Invent Tongue Twisters Children love tongue twisters, which are wonderful reminders of the sounds of beginning letters. Use children's names and let them help you create the tongue twisters. Have students say them as fast as they can and as slowly as they can. When students have said them enough times to have them memorized, write them on posters or in a class book.

Teach Letter Names and Sounds

Through all the activities just described, children will begin to learn some letter names and sounds. You can accelerate this learning with some of the following activities.

RICH resources

Two Wonderful Tongue-Twister Books

Alphabet Annie Announces an All-American Album, by Susan Purviance and Marcia O'Shell (1988).

The Biggest Tongue Twister Book in the World, by Gyles Brandreth (1978).

Use Children's Names to Teach Letter Names and Sounds When you focus on a special child each day, chanting and writing that child's name and then comparing the names of all the children, many children will begin to learn some letter names and sounds. Once all the names are displayed, however, and most of the children can read most of the names, you can use these names to solidify knowledge of letter names and sounds.

Imagine that these children's names are displayed on the word wall or name board:

David	Rasheed	Robert	Catherine	Cindy
Mike	Sheila	Larry	Joseph	Julio
Amber T.	Matt	Erin	Shawonda	Bianca
Erica	Kevin	Adam	Delano	Brittany
Bill	Tara	Amber M.	Octavius	Kelsie

Begin with a letter that many children have in their names and that usually has its expected sound. With this class, you might begin with the letter *r*. Have all children whose names have an *r* in them come to the front of the class, holding cards with their names on them. First count all the *r*'s. There are 12 *r*'s in all. Next, have the children whose names contain an *r* divide themselves into those whose names begin with an *r*—*Robert* and *Rasheed;* those whose names end with an *r*—*Amber T.* and *Amber M.*; and those with an *r* that is not the first or the last letter—*Brittany, Erica, Tara, Erin, Catherine,* and *Larry.* Finally, say each name slowly, stretching out the letters, and decide if you can hear the usual sound of that letter. For *r,* you can hear them all.

Now choose another letter, and let all those children come down and display their name cards. Count the number of times that letter occurs, and then have the children divide themselves into groups according to whether the letter is first, last, or in between. Finally, say the names, stretching them out, and decide if you can hear the usual sound that letter makes. The letter *D* would be a good second choice. You would have *David* and *Delano* beginning with *d; David* and *Rasheed* ending with *d; Cindy, Shawonda,* and *Adam* having a *d* that is not first or last. Again, you can hear the usual sound of *d* in all these names.

Continue picking letters and having children come up with their name cards until you have sorted for some of the letters represented by your names. When doing the letters *s, c, t,* and *j,* be sure to point out that they can have two sounds and that the *th* in *Catherine* and the *sh* in *Sheila, Shawonda,* and *Rasheed* have their own special sounds. You probably should not sort out the names with an *h* because although *Shawanda, Sheila, Rasheed, Catherine,* and *Joseph* all have *h's,* the *h* sound is not represented by any of these. The same would go for *p,* which only occurs in *Joseph.* When you have the children come down for the vowels—*a, e, i, o,* and *u*—count and then sort the children according to first, last, and in between but do not try to listen for the sounds. Explain that vowels have many different sounds and that the children will learn more about the vowels and their sounds all year.

Use Favorite Words with Pure Initial Sounds as Key Words   Capitalize on the concrete words you have been teaching your children by choosing one or two of these words to represent each of the important sounds. Use your children's names when they have the appropriate sounds and then use other concrete words you have been learning.

When teaching the first letter-sound relationships, begin with two letters that are very different in look and sound and that are made in different places of the mouth—*b* and *l,* for example. Also choose two letters for which your children's names can be the examples. Show the children the two words, *Bill* and *Larry,* which will serve as key words for these letters. Have the children pronounce the two key words and notice the positions of their tongues and teeth as they do. Have Bill stand in the front of the room and hold the word *Bill.* Also have Larry hold a card with his name on it. Say several concrete words that begin like *Bill* or *Larry*—*bike, lemon, box, book, ladder, lady, boy*—and have the children say them after you. Have them notice where their tongues and teeth are as they say the words. Let the children point to the child holding the sign *Bill* or *Larry* to indicate how each word begins.

The Alphabet Song and Alphabet Books   "The Alphabet Song" has been sung by generations of children. Not only do children enjoy it, but it seems to give them a sense of all the letters and a framework in which to put new letters as they learn them. Many children come to school already able to sing "The Alphabet Song." Let them sing it and teach it to everyone else. Once the children can sing the song, you may want to point to alphabet cards (usually found above the chalkboard) as they sing. Children also enjoy "being the alphabet" as they line up to go somewhere. Simply pass out your laminated alphabet cards— one to each child, leftovers to the teacher—and let the children sing the song slowly as they line up. Be sure to hand out the cards randomly, so that no one always gets to be the *A* and lead the line or has to be the *Z* and bring up the rear every day!

Wonderful alphabet books are also available. You can read these books aloud over and over. Your children can select these books to "read" during their independent reading. Teacher aides, as well as parent and grandparent volunteers, can "lap read" these in the reading corner and so on. Your class can create its own alphabet book modeled after the children's favorite alphabet books. Be sure to focus on the meanings of the words in all alphabet books you use, so that children will add words to their oral vocabularies.

Letter Actions   Young children love movement! Teach children actions for the letters, and they will remember those letters. Write a letter on one side of a large index card and an action on the other. The first time you teach each letter, make a big deal of it. Get out the rhythm sticks and the marching music when you *march* for *M*. Go out on the playground and do *jumping jacks* for *J*. Play *hopscotch* and *hop* like bunnies for *H*.

When the children have learned actions for several letters, you can do many activities in the classroom without any props. Have all the children stand by their desks and wait until you show them a letter. Then, they should do that action until you hide the letter behind your back. When they have all stopped and you have their attention again, show them another letter and have them do that action. Continue this with as many letters as you have time to fill. Be sure to make comments such as "Yes, I see everyone marching because *M* is our marching letter."

In another activity, pass out the letters for which children have learned the actions to individual children. Each child then gets up and does the action required and calls on someone to guess which letter he or she was given. In "Follow the Letter Leader," the leader picks a letter card and does that action. Everyone else follows the leader, doing the same action. The leader then chooses another card and the game continues.

Teachers have different favorites for letter actions, and you will have your own favorites. Try to select actions with which everyone is familiar and that are only called by single names. Following is a list of actions we like:

bounce	hop	nod	vacuum
catch	jump	paint	walk
dance	kick	run	yawn
fall	laugh	sit	zip
gallop	march	talk	

The action for *s* is our particular favorite. You can use it to end the game. Children say, "It is not an action at all," but remember that "*s* is the sitting letter." You may want to take pictures of various members of your class doing the different actions and make a book of actions they can all read and enjoy.

English Language Learners

Using concrete words, alphabet picture books, and actions will help all your students learn letter names and sounds. Your English language learners will reap the extra benefit of adding these words to their oral vocabularies.

Summary

Emergent literacy research began with the work of Charles Read (1975) and his mentor, Carol Chomsky (1971). Read's work described for many of us at the time what we were seeing in the writing of young children. Read taught us that young children's spellings are developmental and could be predicted by analyzing the consonant and vowel substitutions students consistently made. Chomsky's article, "Write First, Read Later," was seminal in helping to shift instruction toward the field that came to be known as *emergent literacy*.

Much of the emergent literacy research has been done in the homes of young children, tracing their literacy development from birth until the time they read and write in conventional ways (Sulzby & Teale, 1991). From this observational research, it became apparent that children in literate home environments engage in reading and writing long before they begin formal reading instruction. These children use reading and writing in a variety of ways and pass through a series of predictable stages on their voyage from pretending and scribbling to conventional reading and writing. When parents read to children, interact with them about the print they see in the world (signs, cereal boxes, advertisements), and encourage and support their early writing efforts, children establish a firm foundation for learning to read.

This chapter has summarized the crucial understandings essential to building the foundation for success. Through early reading and writing experiences, children learn why we read and write. They develop background knowledge and vocabulary, print concepts, and phonemic awareness. They learn some concrete important-to-them words and some letter names and sounds. Most important, they develop the desire to learn to read and gain self-confidence in their own ability to become literate. Classrooms in which all children develop a firm foundation of emergent literacy provide a variety of reading, writing, and word activities to help all children get off to a successful start in literacy.

Fostering
Fluency

Sometimes to understand what something is, you have to understand what it is not. To experience what it feels like to read without fluency, read this paragraph **aloud** WITHOUT first reading it to yourself. When you have finished reading it, cover it and summarize what you read.

FLUENCYISTHEABILITYTOREADMOSTWORDSINCONTEXTQUICKLYAND
ACCURATELYANDWITHAPPROPRIATEEXPRESSIONFLUENCYISCRITICAL
TOREADINGCOMPREHENSIONBECAUSEOFTHEATTENTIONFACTOR
OURBRAINSCANATTENDTOALIMITEDNUMBEROFTHINGSATATIMEIF
MOSTOFOURATTENTIONISFOCUSEDONDECODINGTHEWORDSTHERE
ISLITTLEATTENTIONLEFTFORTHECOMPREHENSIONPARTOFREADING
PUTTINGTHEWORDSTOGETHERANDTHINKINGABOUTWHATTHEYMEAN

If you paused to figure out some of the words and if your phrasing and expression was not very smooth, you have experienced what it feels like when you cannot read something fluently. If your summary lacked some important information, you have experienced the detrimental effects of the lack of comprehension. If you are developing a headache, you have experienced what a painful task reading can be to readers who lack fluency.

Fluency is the ability to read most words in context quickly and accurately and with appropriate expression. It is critical to reading comprehension because of the attention factor. Our brains can attend to a limited number of things at a time. If most of our attention is focused on decoding the words, there is little attention left for the comprehension part of reading—putting the words together and thinking about what they mean.

The paragraph you just read is exactly the same as the one written in caps with no punctuation and no spaces between words. If, this time, you read it quickly and effortlessly and with good comprehension, you read it the way you normally read everything— fluently.

In order to become avid and enthusiastic readers who get pleasure and information from reading, children must develop fluency. Children who have to labor over everything they read, as you did with the opening paragraph, will only read when forced to read and will never understand how anyone can actually enjoy reading!

Fluency is not something you have or don't have. In fact, how fluent a reader you are is directly related to the complexity of the text you are reading. If you are reading a text on a familiar topic with lots of words you have read accurately many times before, you probably recognize those familiar words immediately and automatically. All your attention is then available to think about the meaning of what you are reading. If you are reading a text on an unfamiliar topic with lots of new words, you will have to stop and decode these words in some way—using the letter-sound and morphemic patterns you know to turn the printed letters into sounds and words. In order to comprehend what you have read, you may have to reread the text once or even twice so that your attention is freed from decoding and available for comprehending.

The National Reading Panel (2000) explains this relationship between reading comprehension and fluency:

> If text is read in a laborious and inefficient manner, it will be difficult for the child to remember what has been read and to relate the ideas expressed in the text to his or her background knowledge. (p. 11)

Fluency is fast, expressive reading. Close your eyes and try to imagine the voices of your good and struggling readers as they read aloud. The good readers probably sound "normal." They identify almost all the words quickly and accurately and their voices rise and fall and pause at appropriate points.

Some of your struggling readers however read one word at a time hes—si—ta—ting and and and re—peat—ing words. Every teacher has had the experience of working with students who can read many words but for whom reading is a tortured, labored, word-by-word, sometimes syllable-by-syllable, process. Dysfluent reading is slow, labored, and lacking in expression and phrasing. Fluency is the ability to quickly and automatically identify the words. Fluent reading is not saying one word at a time. Fluent reading puts words together in phrases and has the expression you would use if you were speaking the words. All your students can become fluent readers. This chapter will describe activities you can use to make it happen.

Mandate Easy Reading for Everyone

Most of the reading you do is not at your reading level. In fact, most of what you read is much too easy for you! If your reading in the past month has included the latest best-selling novel, a travel guide in preparation for your summer break, a journal article on effective teaching strategies, and your favorite section of your local newspaper, all this reading was most likely at your independent level. Because these are all things you chose to read and were interested in, you had huge amounts of background knowledge for these topics and you instantly recognized 98 to 99 percent of the words.

The best readers in your classroom—the ones whose instructional reading levels are above the grade level they are placed in—also spend most of their time reading text that is very easy for them. The science and social studies textbooks in their desks are written at the average reading level for your grade but they are easy for your best readers who read above grade level—so are the books you assign them for guided reading and take-home readers. The books and magazine articles they choose to read for independent reading time at home and school are also probably very easy for them. Your best readers became fluent readers by reading and rereading lots of easy books. Many of these children have favorite books at home in their own personal libraries and have read these books over and over. Many good readers get "hooked" on a series of books—the Arthur books or the Babysitter Club books, for example—and they devour these books.

Now think about the materials your struggling readers are reading. They probably have the same grade-level science and social studies books in their desks and these books are much too hard for them to read. Hopefully, the books you assign them for guided reading and as take-home readers are at their level—but that doesn't mean they are easy. The reading level of most children is determined to be the level at which they can read 90 to 95 percent of the words and can comprehend 75 percent of the ideas. Even in material that is determined to be at their instructional reading level, they will encounter a word they don't recognize every two or three sentences. When they encounter these unfamiliar words, they have to stop and use whatever decoding strategies they have to figure out these words, and this stopping to decode interrupts their fluency and interferes with comprehension.

Our best readers are fluent readers who spend a huge proportion of their reading time reading things that are easy for them. Our struggling readers spend a huge proportion of their reading time struggling through text that is much too hard and a little bit of time working to read material that is at their level. When reading both the too hard text and the on-their-level text, they have to work hard to read and their reading is not fluent. The first commitment you have to make to help all your students become fluent readers is to make sure all your students are spending some of their time reading easy text—text in which they are interested and thus have background knowledge and text in which they can recognize 98 to 99 percent of the words.

At this point, you may be thinking, "Easier said than done! I struggle to find appropriate materials at the instructional levels of my struggling readers. Where will I find easy books? And if I find easy books, won't my students be insulted if I offer them these 'baby' books?"

Finding easy materials for your struggling readers and getting them to read them is actually easier than you think, and we have already shared some ideas clever teachers use to accomplish this. Look back to Chapter 2 and think again about Deb Smith including an "everyone book" as part of her teacher read-aloud. An everyone book is a book that

RICH resources

Easy Informational Books

Once you start looking, you will be amazed at how many you can find. These are a few of our favorite sets. Many more may be available by the time this book is printed.

- National Geographic publishes hundreds of small informational books as part of its *Windows on Literacy* series. Some of the titles in their social studies sets include *The Park, What's on the Ships, What Did They Drive?*, and *The Earth*. Science titles include *When a Storm Comes, Spiders Spin Silk,* and *Fossils*. All books have small amounts of text that comes to life through the incredibly engaging photos.

- Scholastic publishes a Rookie Read-About Science series that also has small amounts of text and engaging photos. Titles include *What Is Friction?, All about Light,* and *What Magnets Can Do*.

- HarperCollins has a Let's Read and Find Out About Science series. Captivating illustrations bring the text to life in titles including *Energy Makes Things Happen; Switch On, Switch Off;* and *What's It Like to Be a Fish?*

everyone can read and that would be easy for even your struggling readers. Fortunately, many publishers have recently published sets of small informational books. These books have very little text on the page and the text is accompanied by engaging pictures—often photos. Because these books are informational and on high-interest topics—trucks, turtles, magnets, football, and much more—your students won't perceive them as "baby" books. Because you include them in your read-aloud (they only take two minutes to read!), and you marvel at all the interesting facts in the book, your students won't be embarrassed to be seen reading and enjoying the books you obviously enjoy.

Chapter 2 contains another clever way you can lure your struggling readers into reading easy books. Set up a buddy reading program with a kindergarten class. Gather some classic kindergarten favorites—such as *Hop on Pop, Go Dog Go,* and *Mr. Brown Can Moo*—and have your struggling readers choose one and practice reading it in preparation for reading to their little buddy. (If you don't have these books, consider asking your students' parents if they have any books their kids have outgrown and would like to donate, borrow some from a kindergarten or first-grade teacher, or check the local thrift shops.) Many of your struggling readers are familiar with these books but were not able to read them when they were younger. They will be delighted to be able to read them now, and the repetition of sight words and rhyming words in these books will go a long way toward increasing the fluency of your struggling readers.

the tech-savvy
TEACHER

Donors Choose

Are you excited about providing all your students with easy reading materials but short on funds? Go to **www.donorschoose.org** and enter your request there. Donors Choose is a clever but simple idea. Many people are concerned about schools that lack the resources to provide their students with the extras often provided by PTOs in wealthier communities. Teachers can write short grants that explain what they need and why and how much the items will cost. Donors can log on and use their credit cards to fund worthy projects. Donors Choose is not available in all 50 states and as of today, 74,784 projects have been funded.

Depending on the age of your children, a magazine subscription to *Zoobooks, Your Big Backyard,* or another magazine easy enough for your struggling readers to read may provide the needed easy reading resources. With magazines, it is not essential that the children be able to read every word or every article. Just as adults do, children tend to pick and choose from magazine articles and read the ones they are most interested in. Those high-interest articles will be easier to read because they are usually on a topic on which your struggling reader has a lot of background knowledge and vocabulary.

Independent reading is a critical daily component of a balanced reading program in any classroom. Some significant amount of time every day in every classroom should be devoted to children choosing for themselves something to read and then settling down to read it. Independent reading is often promoted in terms of the motivation and interest children develop as they have time to pursue their own personal interests through books. In addition, reading easy materials during independent reading promotes fluency. In Chapter 2, it was suggested that you conference with one-fifth of your students each day during their independent reading time and that you spread your struggling readers out across the days. Use the opportunity of this weekly conference to monitor what your struggling readers are reading and entice them into reading some easier books if they are consistently choosing books that are too hard for them to read fluently.

For your struggling readers who don't yet read fluently, you need to think about increasing the amount of easy reading they do beyond the independent reading time. Consider getting some volunteers to come to your classroom who "drop in when they drop off." Parents who drive or walk their children to schools are often willing to come to a classroom for 20 minutes when they know a child is counting on them to read them a book and then listen to them read from a book they have been reading during independent reading time. Consider letting your students choose books they want to take home to read to a younger brother, sister, or cousin. Make sure they have practiced the book they are taking home and that they can read the book fluently.

If you have lots of struggling readers, consider forming an "After Lunch Bunch" reading club in your classroom. Each day, invite five or six of your children to read with you some "just plain fun" books. Include all your students at least once each week but include the struggling readers on several days. Choose "old favorites" and read the books chorally with your students. Remember that all good readers spend a significant amount of time reading easy materials. Provide your struggling readers with a lot of easy reading opportunities and watch them become fluent readers.

Fluency and Rate Increase across the Grade Levels

Reading rate is one indicator of fluency. By the end of first grade, the average first-grader who is reading at grade level reads about 60 to 90 words per minute. Average reading rates increase across grade levels and are estimated by Harris and Sipay (1990) to be :

Grade 1 = 60–90 wpm

Grade 2 = 85–120 wpm

Grade 3 = 115–140 wpm

Grade 4 = 140–170 wpm

Adult = 250–300 wpm

Model Fluent, Expressive Reading

In addition to making sure everyone in your classroom has some easy reading in their reading diets, you can promote fluency by modeling fluent reading. Be sure that you are reading as expressively as possible whenever you read aloud to students. Give your students the opportunity to practice expressive reading by doing echo reading and choral reading with plays and poems.

Echo Reading

One teacher had been doing echo reading for months when a child suddenly asked, "What's an echo?" The teacher invited class members to explain what an echo is and discovered that many children hadn't heard an echo. After some "field research," the teacher located a spot in the auditorium where sound would echo and the class all got to hear their voices echoing back to them. Echo reading made a lot more sense to them after that and they tried to "be the echo." It is easy to forget that our students don't know everything we know. If your children haven't heard an echo, you might try to find a place to take them where they can have firsthand experience with echoes.

Echo reading is the perfect venue for modeling expressive oral reading because in echo reading, your voice is the first voice and your students are trying to make their voice sound just like your voice. Echo reading is usually done one sentence at a time and is fun to do when the text has different voices. If you teach young children, consider using some of their favorite big books for echo reading. Children enjoy doing the different voices in *Brown Bear, Brown Bear; I Went Walking;* and *Hattie and the Fox.* Echo reading also works well for stories such as *There's an Alligator Under My Bed* in which one boy is telling the story. Stories told in the first person format are called *"I" stories.* When you echo read "I" stories, try to sound the way the different voices would sound. Some favorite "I" stories include *One of Three* by Angela Johnson, *Enzo the Wonderfish* by Cathy Wilcox, and *My Friend* by Taro Gomi.

Elementary children of all ages enjoy plays, and echo reading is the perfect format for reading plays. There are many books of reproducible plays available and several sets of leveled readers include plays.

RICH resources

Multilevel Plays

Rigby publishes a set of *Tales and Plays,* which are particularly useful because in the same book, the story is told in the traditional tale format and then as a play. These tales and plays are written on many different reading levels and include favorites such as *Town Mouse and Country Mouse* and *Robin Hood and the Silver Trophy.* Another set of plays perfect for echo reading are the *Speak Out! Readers' Theater* series published by Pacific Learning. In the Speak Out plays, different parts of the plays are written on different reading levels. Benchmark Education also publishes plays with multileveled scripts. Their plays include fables, legends, myths, and a wide variety of science and social studies topics. Using these scripts, you can group together children who read on a variety of reading levels and assign children parts that match their levels.

In addition to plays you find, you can easily turn some of your children's favorite stories into plays using a Readers' Theatre format. The trick to turning a story into a play is to choose a story with a lot of dialogue and to include a narrator who describes what you can't describe with dialogue. Imagine that your students have read *The Little Red Hen*—or you have read it aloud to them. Here is the beginning of the Readers' Theatre you could easily create:

> **Narrator:** The Little Red Hen was walking in the barnyard. Her friends—the cat, the pig, and the duck—were playing. The Little Red Hen found a grain of wheat.
>
> **Hen:** "Who will help me plant this wheat?"
>
> **Cat:** " Not I!"
>
> **Dog:** " Not I!"
>
> **Pig:** " Not I!"
>
> **Narrator:** So, the Little Red Hen planted the wheat herself. The wheat grew and grew.
>
> **Hen:** "Who will help me cut this wheat?"
>
> **Cat:** " Not I!"
>
> **Dog:** " Not I!"
>
> **Pig:** " Not I!"

As you can see, you don't need any particular talents to turn a favorite story with a lot of dialogue into a Readers' Theatre play. If you teach older students, you can have them take a story and turn it into a play. Let different groups create different plays. Make copies for everyone and use the echo reading format to model fluent, expressive reading of all the plays. Have students take the plays home and corral their family members into reading the plays at home. This is one take-home reading assignment the whole family will willingly participate in.

Choral Reading

Another format you can use to model expressive oral reading is choral reading. When you do choral reading of plays, assign groups of students to the different roles. If you are doing a choral reading of *The Little Red Hen*, for example, divide your students into five groups and let different groups chorally read the parts of the narrator, hen, cat, duck, and pig. Reassign the parts and read it several times so that all your students

the **tech-savvy** TEACHER

Readers' Theatre Scripts

Google Readers' Theatre Scripts and you will find oodles of sites to get Readers' Theatre scripts for your students. Some cost money, but some sites allow you to print them for free. A few of our favorite free sites are:

www.aaronshep.com/rt/RTE12.html

www.timelessteacherstuff.com/

www.proteacher.com/070173.shtml

Model Fluent, Expressive Reading

get to read all the parts. Make sure that you assign your struggling readers to the easier parts first. For much of *The Little Red Hen*, the cat, duck, and pig roles only require the students to read, "Not I!" After a couple of readings, your struggling readers may be able to fluently read the hen's part. If your struggling readers are very dysfluent readers, you may not want to assign them the narrator's part, which always requires the most sophisticated reading skills.

In addition to choral reading of plays and Readers' Theatres, consider leading your students in reading some poetry you have arranged in a choral reading format. Nursery rhymes and other rhymes and finger-plays are naturals for choral reading. Begin by reading the rhyme to your children using the echo reading format. After the echo reading, assign different groups of voices to read different parts. Keep the choreography simple by having the children count off to read different parts or assigning girls and boys to read different parts. Here is an example for the beginning of *Five Little Monkeys:*

> **All:** Five little monkeys jumping on the bed.
>
> **Voice 1:** One fell off and bumped his head.
>
> **All:** Momma called the doctor and the doctor said,
>
> **Voice 2:** "No more monkeys jumping on the bed!"

After reading it the first time, reassign the students so that those who were voice 1 now read the part of voice 2.

Many of these poems lend themselves to pantomiming. Divide your class into actors and readers. For actors, you will need five monkeys, the doctor, and the momma. Have all the readers read the first line chorally—*Five little monkeys jumping on the bed*. Then stop the readers so the five monkeys can pantomime jumping on the bed. Continue leading your readers to read and stopping them so the actors can act. Read the poem several times so that all your students get to be actors as well as readers.

English Language Learners

Modeling fluent reading through echo and choral reading are excellent opportunities for your students learning English to practice their reading skills in a comfortable, supportive environment. Using poems and plays with repeated patterns will help them develop their understanding of English syntax and add some common phrases to their speaking vocabularies.

Sometimes, fluency is talked about as if it is only rate of reading. Some tests (The Diebels, for example) claim to measure fluency but really only measure how quickly and accurately students read. Reading with expression (called *prosody*) is a critical part of fluency. When we read fluently, our voices go up and down in pitch at the right times, we pause and we group words together in phrases. If you want your students to read with expression, you have to model how that expressive reading sounds. When you regularly engage your students in echo and choral reading of plays and poetry, you are modeling for them and giving them opportunities to practice fluent, expressive reading.

Provide Engaging Rereading Opportunities

One of the major ways that we become fluent readers is to read something over several times. The first time, a lot of our attention is on identifying the words. The second time, we are able to read in phrases as our brain puts the phrases together into meaningful units. The third time, we read more rapidly, with good expression and in a seemingly "effortless" way. Good readers often reread favorite books. Do you remember the stage in your life when you were hooked on a favorite series of books such as Nancy Drew, American Girl, Junie B. Jones, or Harry Potter? Did you ever go back and reread some of the first ones you read? If you were lucky enough to have a magazine subscription when you were a child, did you save these magazines and return to *Zoobooks* or *Highlights* or *Ranger Rick* and reread some of your favorite articles?

Rereading is important for fluency and if you reread the previous sections of this chapter, you will find that getting your students to reread text plays a role in many of the activities. In the section on easy reading, we suggested that you pair your struggling readers with a "drop-off, drop-in" volunteer and that after the volunteer had read to the student, that student read something he had already read to the volunteer. That section also suggests that students will do more easy reading if you let your struggling readers choose something they enjoyed to take home and read to family members, especially younger siblings and cousins. When you model expressive reading through echo and choral reading, you lead the students through several readings of the plays and poems. Having your students take copies of the plays and poems home and engage their families in echo and choral reading provides more opportunities for rereading.

Easy reading, echo reading, and choral reading all provide opportunities for rereading. You can provide more opportunities for rereading if you include some recorded reading and fluency development lessons in the fluency instruction portion of the balanced reading diet you are providing your students.

Recorded Reading

Children—and many adults—enjoy listening to recorded books. Many of these books are recorded by authors or professional readers and they are marvelous models of fluent expressive reading. For your readers who need to work on fluency, have them select a book on their reading level and then let them listen to that book as many times as they need to until they can read the book fluently. When your students are able to read the selection fluently without the aid of the recording, let them show off their fluency skills by reading the book to whomever you can commandeer to listen. Send them to a class of younger-aged students and let them read the book to a small group in that class. Let them take the book home and challenge them to see how many signatures they can collect on an "I can read this book" card. Young children like to read to their pets and stuffed animals. Grandparents would love to hear their precious grandchild reading the book over the phone.

Consider recording some of the books and magazine articles as you are reading them aloud to your students. Have your students participate by clapping as a turn-page signal. Likewise, you may want to record some of the echo and choral reading you do with your students. If you record just a few pieces you are reading to your students, you will soon have a large recorded library customized to the interests of your students. Children often want to read the book the teacher has read to them. Recording some of what you read to your students makes this possible for more of your students.

Fluency Development Lessons

In 1998, Tim Rasinski and Nancy Padak published a study that drew everyone's attention to how widespread fluency problems are for readers who are in remedial or special education classes. They had looked at a large number of remedial readers and evaluated their abilities in comprehension, decoding, and fluency. Almost all the children were well below grade level in all three areas, but fluency was by far the biggest area of concern. The children read the test passages in such a slow and laborious manner that the investigators were surprised that they had any comprehension at all. In response to their findings, Rasinski and Padak developed a lesson for teaching fluency they call a Fluency Development Lesson, or FDL (Rasinski & Padak, 2008). Here is how the Fluency Development Lesson strategy works. This is adapted from a more detailed and rich explanation in Tim Rasinski's (2003) wonderfully practical book, *The Fluent Reader*.

The teacher chooses a short passage—often a poem—that is apt to be appealing to the students and reads the passage aloud several times, modeling fluent reading. Meaning for the poem or passage and for any difficult vocabulary words is built through discussion.

Using individual copies of the poem or the poem written on a chart, the teacher and the class do a choral reading of the poem. The poem is read chorally several times, often with different children reading different parts or verses.

The children are paired and take turns reading the passage to each other. Each person reads the passage three times. The children help each other and respond to each other's reading with praise, support, and encouragement.

When the class gathers together again, children can volunteer to read the passage aloud for everyone. If possible, children read the passage to other classes or to other school personnel.

The children choose two or three words from the passage to add to their personal word banks. They study these words and often use them in a variety of word sorts and games.

Children put one copy of the text in their poetry folder and are given a second copy to take home. They are encouraged to read the passage to whoever will listen. Children and parents alike report that this is one "homework" assignment they all look forward to.

The following day, the previous day's passage is read again and then the whole cycle begins with a new passage. Rasinski recommends a fast pace for this activity and suggests that once the class learns the routines, the whole FDL can be completed in 15 to 20 minutes.

Fluency Development Lessons are easy to do and enjoyed by both teachers and students. Rasinski reports that children engaged in these lessons made greater gains in reading than a similar group of children who read the same passages but did not use the FDL procedure. Fluency Development Lessons would be a welcome addition to any classroom routine but would be especially helpful in remedial and special education classes.

Use a Word Wall to Teach High-Frequency Words

Did you know that approximately 100 words make up half of all the words we read and write our whole lives? To read and write fluently, your students must quickly and automatically recognize and spell these most common words. Unfortunately, the most common words are often the hardest words for beginning readers to learn. Most of these words—*of, and, the, is*—are meaningless, abstract, connecting words. Young children use these words in their speech, but they are not aware of them as separate entities. Read these sentences in a natural speech pattern, and notice how you pronounce the italicized words:

> What *do* you see?
> I want that piece *of* cake.
> What are *they*?

In natural speech, the *what* and the *do* are slurred together and sound like "wadoo." The *of* is pronounced like "uh." The *they* is tacked on to the end of *are* and sounds like "ah-thay."

All children use high-frequency words such as *what, of,* and *they* in their speech, but they are not as aware of these words as they are of the more concrete, tangible words, such as *run* and *pizza.* To make learning to read and write even more difficult, many of these high-frequency words are not spelled in regular, predictable ways. *What* should rhyme with *at, bat,* and *cat. Of* should be spelled *u-v. They,* which clearly rhymes with *day, may,* and *way,* should be spelled the way many children do spell it—*t-h-a-y.*

When you consider that most high-frequency words are meaningless, abstract words that children use but do not realize are separate words and that many of these words are irregular in spelling/pronunciation, it is a wonder that any children learn to recognize and spell them! In order to read and write fluently, however, children must learn to instantly recognize and automatically spell these words.

Because these words occur so often, children who read and write will encounter them in their reading and need to spell them as they write. Many teachers have found it effective to display high-frequency words in a highly visible spot in their classrooms and provide daily practice with these words. Teachers often refer to the place where the words are displayed as their *word wall* (Cunningham, 2009a).

Doing a Word Wall

Doing a word wall is not the same thing as *having* a word wall. Having a word wall might mean putting all these words up somewhere in the room and telling your students to use them. In our experience, struggling readers cannot use these words because they do not know them or know which is which! To *do* a word wall, you have to:

- Be selective and "stingy" about which words to include, limiting the words to the most common words.
- Add words gradually—no more than five or six a week.
- Make the words very accessible by putting them where everyone can see them, writing them in big black letters, and using a variety of paper colors so that the constantly confused words (*went, want, what, with, will, that, them, they, this,* etc.) are on different colors.
- Practice the words by chanting and writing them, because struggling readers are not usually good visual learners and can't just look at and remember words.
- Do a variety of review activities to provide enough practice so that children can read and spell the words instantly and automatically.

Teachers who *do* word walls (rather than just *have* word walls) report that *all* their students learn these critical words.

Selecting Words for the Wall

How do you decide which words merit a place on your word wall? The selection of words varies from classroom to classroom, but the selection principle is the same: Include words your students need often in their reading and writing and that are often confused with other words. If you teach first grade and are using a commercial reading series, you may want to select the most common words taught in your reading program. Alternatively, you can select words from a high-frequency word list.

Beyond first grade, look for words commonly misspelled in your students' writing and add them to the wall. These common misspelled words often include homophones, and these should be added with a picture or phrase clue attached to all but one of the words. For example, add a card with the number 2 next to *two* and attach the word *also* and the phrase *too late* next to *too*. Your students can use this clue to correctly spell the homophone by thinking about whether they are writing the number *two*, the "too late *too*," or "the other one."

Displaying the Words

Write the words with a thick, black, permanent marker on pieces of different-colored paper. Place the words on the wall above or below the letters they begin with. When confusable words are added, make sure they are on a different color of paper from the other words they are usually confused with. Highlight helpful rhyming patterns. Add five or six new words each week and do at least one daily activity in which your children find, chant, and write the spellings of the words.

[handwritten margin note: word wall scavanger hunt — T gives clues to diff word wall words. e.g. "Starts with" "rhymes with"]

Chanting and Writing the Words

Lead your students each day in a quick activity to practice the words on the wall by having them chant and write the words. Get your students out of their seats and lead them to chant (cheerleader style) the spelling of the words you are focusing on.

"What. w h a t what."
"They. t h e y they."

[handwritten note: spell w̄ actions e.g. punch on consonants clap on vowels]

This chanting of the words provides your students with an auditory/rhythmic route to learning and remembering the words.

Next, have your students write each word after you model the correct writing. Many teachers tie this daily writing of five or six words into handwriting instruction and model for their students how to make each letter as the children write the words. When the words have been written, lead your students to check/fix their own papers.

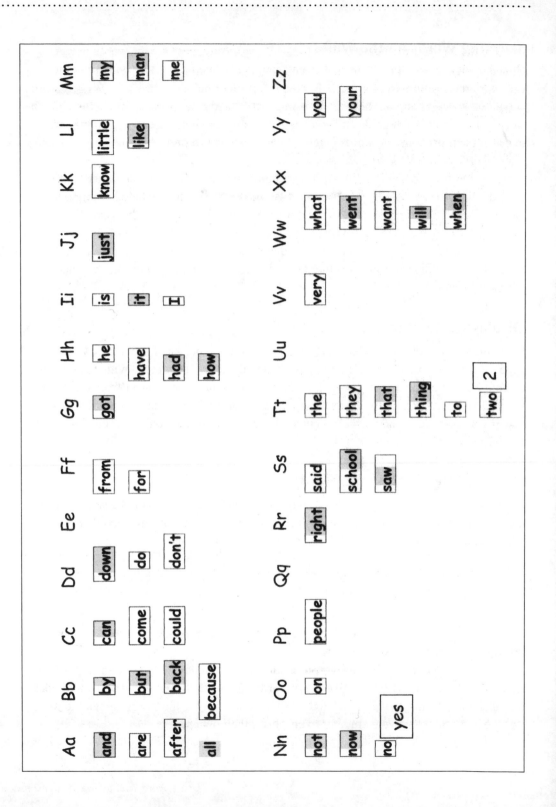

Aa Bb Cc Dd Ee Ff Gg Hh Ii Jj Kk Ll Mm

and by can down from got he is just know little my

are but come do for have it like man

after back could don't had I me

all because how

Nn Oo Pp Qq Rr Ss Tt Uu Vv Ww Xx Yy Zz

not on people right said the very what went want will when you your

now no yes school they that

no saw to thing

two 2

On the day you add new words to the wall, make sure these are the words that get changed and written. Review these same new words on the following day. During the rest of the week, however, choose five or six words, including old and new words, to chant and write.

Reading, Writing, and Word Walls

Once you have a word wall growing in your room, there will be no doubt that your students are using it as they are reading and writing. You will see their eyes quickly glance to the exact spot where a word that they want to write is displayed. Even when children are reading, they will sometimes glance over to the word wall to help them remember a particularly troublesome word.

Word walls provide children with an immediately accessible dictionary for the most troublesome words. Because the words are added gradually, stay in the same spots forever, are alphabetical by their first letters, are visually distinctive by different colors of paper, and are practiced daily though chanting and writing, all your students can learn to read and spell almost all of the word wall words. Because the words you selected are words the students need constantly in their reading and writing, their recognition of these words will become automatic and their attention can be devoted to less frequently occurring words and to constructing meaning as they read and write. When combined with easy reading, your modeling of expressive reading, repeated readings, and recognition of the most common words will result in more fluent reading for your students.

Summary

Fluency includes three components: accuracy, speed, and prosody (commonly called expression) (Rasinski, 2003). Developing fluency needs to be one of the major goals of reading instruction. When children are first starting to read, their reading is not apt to be fluent. They must stop at almost all the words and take a second or two to recognize the word or figure it out. As their word-identification skills develop and their reading vocabularies increase, their reading becomes more fluent.

Allington (2009) suggests three reasons some students struggle to become fluent readers. First, much of what struggling readers are given to read is too difficult. Second, struggling readers read much less than more capable readers. Finally, teachers often ask struggling readers to read aloud and then immediately interrupt that reading to correct reading errors. These struggling readers come to rely on the teacher to correct their errors and don't develop self-monitoring strategies.

Fluency develops when children do a lot of reading and writing—including a great deal of easy text. In addition to making sure that all students are reading some text that is easy for them, teachers can model fluent, expressive reading using echo and choral reading lesson formats.

Repeated reading helps children develop fluency because with each reading, their word identification becomes quicker and more automatic, freeing attention for expression, phrasing, and comprehension. Letting children choose books they want to read and practice reading those books along with a recording help build both fluency and confidence. Fluency Development Lessons have been demonstrated to help students become fluent readers. These lessons are especially important for struggling readers whose reading is well below grade level.

In English, words such as *of, said, the, have, they,* and many others occur in almost every text we read. These words are called "high-frequency words" because they occur so often in everything we read and write. In order to read and write fluently, children must be able to instantly and accurately identify these high-frequency words. Teachers can display these high-frequency words on a word wall and provide opportunities for students to practice these difficult words by chanting and writing them.

Teaching Phonics and Spelling Patterns

When you are reading or writing, your brain is busy constructing meaning and simultaneously identifying or spelling words. Most of the time, you don't even know that you are identifying or spelling words because you have read or written these words so many times that their identification and spelling has become automatic. In the previous chapter, you learned that your students must develop fluency and be able to quickly and effortlessly identify most words.

Even when you can instantly recognize most words, you will occasionally come to a word you have never before seen. Imagine that while reading, you encounter the word *triremes.* When your eyes see the letters of a word you have never seen before, your brain cannot immediately identify that word. You must stop and figure it out. This figuring out may include determining the pronunciation for the word and the meaning for the word. In this case, you can probably pronounce *triremes,* but since no meaning is triggered by your pronunciation, this word can't join the others in your working memory and help them construct some meaning to shift to long-term memory. Your reading is stalled by the intrusion of this unknown word. You have to either figure out what it is and what it means or continue reading, hoping the other words—the *context*—will allow you to continue to construct meaning, in spite of the unfamiliar word *triremes.* Curious about the meaning of *triremes*? (It is true that "inquiring minds want to know.") Triremes were Greek war ships. The name derives from the sets of three oars on each side of the ship.

All proficient readers have the ability to look at regular words they have never seen before and assign probable pronunciations. Witness your ability to pronounce these made-up words:

cate   frow   perdap   midulition

Now, of course, you were not reading because having only pronounced these words, you would not construct any meaning. But if you were in the position of most young readers, who have many more words in their listening/meaning vocabularies than in their sight-reading vocabularies, you would often meet words familiar in speech but unfamiliar in print. Your ability to rapidly figure out the pronunciations of "unfamiliar-in-print" words enables you to make use of your huge store of "familiar-in-speech" words and thus create meaning.

Before we go on, how did you pronounce the made-up word *frow?* Did it rhyme with *cow* or with *snow?* Because English is not a one-sound, one-letter language, there are different ways to pronounce certain letter patterns. Even so, the number of different ways is limited, and with real words, unlike made-up words, your speaking vocabulary lets you know which pronunciation to assign.

Not only do readers use their phonics knowledge to read words they have not seen before, but this same knowledge also enables them to write. If the four made-up words had been dictated to you and you had to write them, you would have spelled them reasonably close to the way we spelled them.

All good readers and writers develop this ability to come up with pronunciations and spellings for words they have never read or written before. Many struggling readers do not. When good readers see a word they have never before seen in print, they stop briefly and study the word, looking at every letter in a left-to-right sequence. As they look at all the letters, they are not thinking of a sound for each letter, because good readers know that sounds are determined not by individual letters but by letter patterns. Good readers look for patterns of letters they have seen together before and then search their mental word banks, looking for words with similar letter patterns. If the new word is a big word, they "chunk" it—that is, they put letters together to make familiar chunks.

Based on their careful inspection of the letters and their search through their mental bank for words with the same letter patterns, good readers try out a pronunciation. If the first try does not result in a word they have heard, they will usually try another pronunciation. Finally, they produce a pronunciation that they recognize as sounding like a real word that they know. They then go back and reread the sentence that contained the unfamiliar-in-print word and see if their pronunciation makes sense, given the meaning they are getting from the context of surrounding words. If the pronunciation they came up with makes sense, they continue reading. If not, they look again at all the letters of the unfamiliar word and see what else would "look like this and make sense."

Imagine a young boy reading this sentence:

The dancer came out and took a bow.

Imagine that he pauses at the last word and then pronounces *bow* so that it rhymes with *show*. Since that is a real word that he remembers hearing, his eyes then glance back and he quickly rereads the sentence. He then realizes, "That doesn't make sense." He studies all the letters of *bow* again and searches for similar letter patterns in his mental word bank. Perhaps he now accesses words such as *how* and *now*. This gives him another possible pronunciation for this letter pattern, one that is also recognized as a previously heard word. He tries this pronunciation, quickly rereads, realizes his sentence now "sounds right," and continues reading.

From this scenario, we can infer the strategies this good reader used to successfully decode an unfamiliar-in-print word:

1. Recognize that this is an unfamiliar word, and look at all the letters in order.

2. Search your mental word bank for similar letter patterns and the sounds associated with them.

3. Produce a pronunciation that matches that of a real word that you know.

4. Reread the sentence to cross-check your possible pronunciation with meaning. If meaning confirms pronunciation, continue reading. If not, try again!

Had the unfamiliar word been a big word, the reader would have had to use a fifth strategy:

5. Look for familiar morphemes, and chunk the word by putting letters together that usually go together in the words you know.

To be a good reader, you must be able to automatically recognize most words and you must be able to quickly decode the words you do not immediately recognize. To be a good writer, you must be able to automatically spell most of the words and come up with reasonable spellings for the words you cannot automatically spell. While children are learning to read and spell high-frequency words and doing lots of easy and repeated reading to develop fluency, they also need to be learning to decode unfamiliar words. Once children know the common sounds for most letters, they need to start paying attention to the patterns in words so that they can use these patterns to decode and spell words. A variety of lesson formats you can use to help your students learn and pay attention to patterns in words will be described in the remainder of this chapter.

Guess the Covered Word

Many words can be figured out by thinking about what would make sense in a sentence and seeing if the consonants in the word match what you are thinking of. You must do two things simultaneously—think about what would make sense and think about letters and sounds. Struggling readers often prefer to do one or the other but not both. Thus, they may guess something that is sensible but ignore the letter sounds they know, or they may guess something that is close to the sounds but makes no sense in the sentence! Doing a weekly Guess the Covered Word activity will help your students combine these strategies effectively.

Before class begins, write four or five sentences on the board that start with your students' names, follow a similar word pattern, and end with words that vary in their initial sounds and word length.

> Rasheed likes to play *soccer.*
>
> Kate likes to play *softball.*
>
> Rob likes to play *basketball.*
>
> Juan likes to play *hockey.*

Cover the last word in each sentence with a sticky note, tearing or adjusting it to the length of the word.

> Rasheed likes to play
>
> Kate likes to play
>
> Rob likes to play
>
> Juan likes to play

Begin the activity by reading the first sentence and asking students to guess the covered word. Write four guesses on the board, next to the sentence.

Rasheed likes to play ▮▮▮▮

ball   video games   monopoly   football

Next, uncover all the letters up to the vowel. Erase the guesses that do not begin with that group of letters. Have students continue offering guesses that make sense and begin with the correct letter. Write their responses on the board. Keep the students focused both on meaning and on beginning letters.

Rasheed likes to play *s*▮▮▮▮

soccer   softball

When the first letter is revealed, some students will guess anything that begins with that letter. For example, if the first letter is an *s,* they may guess *sand.* Respond with something like "*Sand* does begin with an *s,* but I can't write *sand* because people don't play *sand.*" Finally, uncover the whole word and see if any guesses were correct. Repeat the procedure on the remaining sentences.

Rasheed likes to play *soccer.*

Once students understand how Guess the Covered Word works, include some sentences in which the covered word begins with the digraphs *sh, ch, th,* and *wh.* Explain that the rules of this game require you to show your children all the letters up to the first vowel. Then show them some sentences that contain the digraphs *sh, ch, th,* and *wh* as well as single consonants. Include examples for both sounds of *c.* Vary your sentence pattern and where in the sentence the covered word is.

Caroline likes to eat *ch*▮▮▮▮

W▮▮▮▮▮ is Chad's favorite fruit.

Jessica likes strawberries on her *c*▮▮▮

Bo likes strawberry *sh*▮▮▮▮

Melinda bakes pumpkin pies for *Th*▮▮▮▮▮

I don't know *wh*▮▮ pie I like best.

(If you guessed *cherries, watermelon, cereal, shortcake, Thanksgiving* and *which,* you are a true word wizard!)

Guess the Covered Word works for teaching and reviewing *blends,* groups of letters in which you can hear the sounds blended together, such as *br, pl,* and *str.* As with digraphs, vary the sentence pattern and where in the sentence the covered word is.

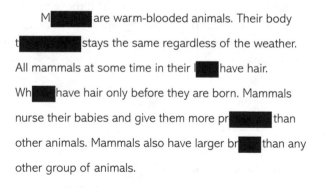

Justin likes to sw██ in the s███████

Curtis plays baseball in the spr███

Sk███ is Jennifer's favorite sport in the winter.

Andrew likes to sk███ all year round.

Val likes to play all kinds of sp████

Be sure that when you uncover the beginning letters, you uncover everything up to the vowel. If you have uncovered an *s* and one of your students guesses the word *snow,* tell him or her that that was good thinking for the *s.* Then, have everyone say *snow* slowly and hear the *n.* Say something like "My rule is I have to show you everything up to the vowel, so if the word were *snow,* I would have to show you not just the *s* but the *n,* too."

Sometimes, struggling readers get the idea that the only time you use reading strategies is during reading! It is important to show them how cross-checking can help them figure out words when they are reading all kinds of things. You might write a paragraph, such as the following, that is related to the science or social studies topic you are studying. Cover the words in the usual way, and have the whole sentence read before going back to guess without any letters and then with all the letters up to the vowel.

M██████ are warm-blooded animals. Their body

t██████████ stays the same regardless of the weather.

All mammals at some time in their l███ have hair.

Wh████ have hair only before they are born. Mammals

nurse their babies and give them more pr██████ than

other animals. Mammals also have larger br███ than any

other group of animals.

(Did you use the context, all the letters up to the vowel and word length to figure out the words, *mammals, temperature, lives, whales, protection,* and *brains*?)

One more way to vary Guess the Covered Word is to cover some words in a "big book." Use the same procedure of guessing without any letters and then with all the letters up to the vowel. Help your students verbalize the strategy they are using to decode the covered word. "When you come to a word you can't figure out, read the whole sentence and then think what would make sense, be about the right length, and have *all* the correct letters up to the vowel."

English Language Learners

If your English language learners come from Spanish-speaking homes, you will need to be alert to some confusion these children may have, given the different sounds some letters represent in Spanish versus English. Spanish-speaking children often experience great difficulty with vowels because the vowel system in Spanish is much simpler than that in English. Spanish does not have the vowel sounds represented by the *a* in *man*, the *e* in *pen*, the *i* in *is*, the *u* in *up*, the *er* in *her*, the *ou* in *could*, the *a* in *along*, or the *au* in *caught*.

Furthermore, some sounds that both English and Spanish share are spelled differently in Spanish. The *a* sound in *cake*, for example, is spelled with an *e* in Spanish. The *e* sound in *bee* is spelled with an *i*. The *i* sound in *like* is spelled with an *ai*. The *o* sound in *on* is spelled with an *a*. When teaching phonics to children whose first language is Spanish, it is probably best to start with the letters that have the same sounds. The consonant letters *p, b, t, k, m, n, f, s, w,* and *y* have almost the same sounds in both languages and provide a good place to begin. As children develop some confidence in their decoding ability, the sounds that do not exist in Spanish and the letters that have different sounds in Spanish and English can be introduced.

Using Words You Know

Using Words You Know is an activity designed to help students learn to use the words they already know to decode and spell lots of other words. Here are the steps of a Using Words You Know lesson:

1. Show students three to five words they know, and have these words pronounced and spelled. For our sample lesson, we will tell students that some of the ways they travel—including bikes, cars, vans, and trains—can help them spell other words.

2 Divide the board, a chart, or a transparency into four columns, and head each column with one of these words: *bike, car, train,* or *van.* Have students set up the same columns on their own papers and write these four words.

bike	car	train	van

3 Tell students that words that rhyme usually have the same spelling pattern. The spelling pattern in a short word begins with the vowel and goes to the end of the word. Underline the spelling patterns *i-k-e, a-r, a-i-n,* and *a-n,* and have students underline them on their papers.

4 Tell students that you are going to show them some new words and that they should write each one under the word with the same spelling pattern. Show them words that you have written on index cards. Let a different student go to the board, chart, or transparency and write each new word there as the other students write the word on their papers. Do not let the students pronounce a word aloud until it has been written on the board. Then help the students pronounce the words by making them rhyme. Use less common words that your students will have in their listening vocabularies but don't immediately recognize. When you have 10 to 12 words written, have the students read the rhyming words and identify the spelling pattern

bike	car	train	van
hike	jar	pain	span
pike		chain	scan
spike		drain	
		Spain	
		sprain	

⑤ Explain to your students that thinking of rhyming words can help them spell. This time, do not show them the words but rather say the words. Have students decide which words they rhyme with and use the spelling pattern to spell them. Have these words added to the chart.

b<u>ike</u>	c<u>ar</u>	tr<u>ain</u>	v<u>an</u>
h<u>ike</u>	j<u>ar</u>	p<u>ain</u>	sp<u>an</u>
p<u>ike</u>	sc<u>ar</u>	ch<u>ain</u>	sc<u>an</u>
sp<u>ike</u>	m<u>ar</u>	dr<u>ain</u>	pl<u>an</u>
str<u>ike</u>	sp<u>ar</u>	Sp<u>ain</u>	br<u>an</u>
		spr<u>ain</u>	cl<u>an</u>
		st<u>ain</u>	
		str<u>ain</u>	
		br<u>ain</u>	
		gr<u>ain</u>	

⑥ End this first part of the lesson by helping students verbalize that in English, words that rhyme often have the same spelling pattern and that good readers and spellers do not sound out every letter but rather try to think of a rhyming word and read or spell the word using the pattern in the rhyming word.

For the second part of the lesson (probably on the next day), use the same procedures and four key words again:

① Head four columns on the board, chart, or transparency and have students head four columns on their papers with these words and underline the spelling patterns. Explain to the students that using the rhyme to help read and spell words works with longer words, too.

② Show students some words written on index cards, and have them write each word under the appropriate word. Once the word has been written on the board or chart, have students pronounce the word, making the last syllable rhyme:

guitar	caravan	Japan	maintain
cigar	unlike	entertain	hitchhike

Using Words You Know

3 Now say these words and have students decide which word the last syllable rhymes with and use that spelling pattern to spell it. Give help with the spelling of the first part, if needed:

lifelike	restrain	streetcar	boxcar
dislike	caveman	trashcan	contain

4 Again, end the lesson by helping students notice how helpful it is to think of a rhyming word you are sure how to spell when trying to read or spell a strange word.

bike	car	train	van
hike	jar	pain	span
pike	scar	chain	scan
spike	mar	drain	plan
strike	spar	Spain	bran
hitchhike	cigar	sprain	clan
unlike	guitar	stain	caravan
lifelike	boxcar	strain	Japan
dislike	streetcar	brain	caveman
		grain	trashcan
		maintain	
		entertain	
		restrain	
		complain	

In Using Words You Know lessons, you should always choose the words students will read and spell. Do not ask students for rhyming words, because, especially for the long vowels, there is often another pattern. *Crane, Jane,* and *rein* also rhyme with *train,* but you should only use words that rhyme and have the same pattern. You can do Using Words You Know lessons with any words your students can already read and spell. To plan a lesson, select known words that have lots of rhyming words with the same spelling pattern. A rhyming dictionary, such as *The Scholastic Rhyming Dictionary* (Young, 1994), is a great help in finding suitable rhyming words.

Most Common Spelling Patterns

Knowing 37 spelling patterns will allow children to read and spell over 500 words commonly used by young children (Wylie & Durrell, 1970). Many teachers display each pattern with a word and picture to help children learn the pattern that will help them spell many other words.

Here are the 37 high-frequency spelling patterns (with possible key words):

ack (black)	ail (pail)	ain (train)	ake (cake)	ale (whale)	ame (game)
an (pan)	ank (bank)	ap (cap)	ash (trash)	at (cat)	ate (skate)
aw (claw)	ay (tray)	eat (meat)	ell (shell)	est (nest)	ice (rice)
ide (bride)	ick (brick)	ight (night)	ill (hill)	in (pin)	ine (nine)
ing (king)	ink (pink)	ip (ship)	it (hit)	ock (sock)	oke (Coke)
op (mop)	ore (store)	ot (hot)	uck (truck)	ug (bug)	ump (jump)
unk (trunk)					

Making Words

Making Words is a popular activity with both teachers and children. Children love manipulating letters to make words and figuring out the secret word that can be made with all the letters. While your students are having fun making words, they are also learning important information about phonics and spelling. As they manipulate letters to make words, they learn how making small changes, such as changing just one letter or moving two letters around, results in completely new words. They also learn to stretch out words and listen for the sounds they hear and the order of those sounds. When you change the first letter, you also change the sound you hear at the beginning of the word. Likewise, when you change the last letter, you change the sound you hear at the end of the word. These ideas seem commonplace and obvious to those of us who have been reading and writing for almost as long as we can remember. But they are a revelation to many beginners—one that gives them tremendous independence in and power over the challenge of decoding and spelling words.

The Making Words activity is an example of a type of instruction called *guided discovery.* In order to truly learn and retain strategies, children must discover them. But some children do not make discoveries about words very easily on their own. In a Making Words lesson, you can guide your students to make these discoveries by carefully sequencing the words they are to make and giving them explicit guidance about how much change is needed.

Making Words lessons have three steps. In the first step, you make words. Begin with short, easy words and move to longer, more complex words. The last word is always the secret word—a word that can be made with all the letters. As the children make each word, a child who has made it successfully goes up to the pocket chart or chalk ledge and makes the word with big letters. Children who have not made the word correctly quickly fix their word to be ready for the next word. The small changes made between most words encourages even those children who have not made a word perfectly to fix it, because they soon realize that spelling the current word correctly increases their chances of spelling the next word correctly. In each lesson, have students make 10 to 15 words, including the secret word that can be made with all the letters.

In the second step of a Making Words lesson, sort the words into patterns. Many children discover patterns just through making the words in the carefully sequenced order, but some children need more explicit guidance. This guidance happens when all the words have been made and you guide the children to sort them into patterns. Depending on the sophistication of the children and the words available in the lesson, words might be sorted according to their beginning letters—all the letters up to the vowel. Alternatively, to focus on just one sound-letter combination, you may ask children to sort out all the words that begin with *sp* or *sn*. Once the words with these letters have been sorted, you and the children should pronounce the words and discover that most words that have the same letters also have the same sound.

Another pattern that children need to discover is that many words have the same root word. If they can pronounce and spell the root word and if they can recognize the root word with a prefix or suffix added, they can decode and spell many additional words. To some children, every new word they meet is a new experience! They fail to recognize how new words are related to already known words and thus are in the difficult, if not impossible, position of starting from "scratch" and trying to learn and remember every new word. To be fluent, fast, automatic decoders and spellers, children must learn that *play, playing, played, plays, player,* and *replay* all have *play* as their root and use their knowledge of how to decode and spell *play* to quickly transfer to these related words.

In every lesson, sort the rhyming words. Each lesson should contain several sets of rhyming words. Children need to recognize that words that have the same spelling pattern from the vowel to the end of the word usually rhyme. When you sort the words into rhyming words and point out that the words that rhyme have the same spelling pattern, children learn rhyming patterns and how to use words they know to decode and spell lots of other words.

The final step of a Making Words lesson is the transfer step. All the working and playing with words you do while making words will be worth nothing if children do not use what they know when they need to use it. Many children know letter sounds and patterns and do not apply this knowledge to decode unknown words they encounter during reading or to spell words they need while writing. All teachers know that it is much easier to teach children phonics than it is to actually get them to use it. This is the reason that you need to end every Making Words lesson with a transfer step. Once you have the words sorted according to rhyme, have your students use the sorted rhyming words to spell some new words with the same rhyming pattern.

the **tech-savvy** TEACHER

Our Secret

Would you like to know our secret to planning a good Making Words lesson? Go to **wordplays.com** and click on Words in a Word. Enter the word you have chosen for the secret word and, like magic, all the words that can be made from the letters of the secret word appear. Choose the words that will give you lots of sorting possibilities. Don't tell your students about this site. It's our secret!

Steps in Planning a Making Words Lesson

1. Choose your secret word, a word that can be made with all the letters. In choosing this word, consider child interest, the curriculum tie-ins you can make, and the letter-sound patterns to which you can draw children's attention through the sorting at the end.

2. Make a list of other words that can be made from these letters

3. From all the words you could make, pick 12 to 15 words using these criteria:
   • Words that you can sort for the pattern you want to emphasize
   • Little words and big words to create a multilevel lesson (Making little words helps your struggling students; making big words challenges your highest achieving students.)
   • Words that can be made with the same letters in different places (*barn/bran*) so children are reminded that ordering letters is crucial when spelling words
   • A proper name or two to remind the children that we use capital letters
   • Words that most students have in their listening vocabularies

4. Write all the words on index cards and order them from shortest to longest.

5. Once you have the two-letter words together, the three-letter words together, and so on, order them so you can emphasize letter patterns and how changing the position of the letters or changing/adding just one letter results in a different word.

6. Choose some letters or patterns to sort for.

7. Choose some transfer words—uncommon words you can read or spell based on the rhyming words.

8. Store the cards in an envelope. Write the words in order on the envelope, the patterns you will sort for, and the transfer words.

Here is an example of how you might conduct a Making Words lesson and cue the children to the changes and words you want them to make. This lesson is taken from *Making Words 2nd Grade* (Cunningham & Hall, 2009a).

Beginning the Lesson

The children all have the letters: **a   e   u   c   c   k   p   s**

These same letters—big enough for all to see—are displayed in a pocket chart. The letter cards have lowercase letters on one side and capital letters on the other side. The vowels are in a different color.

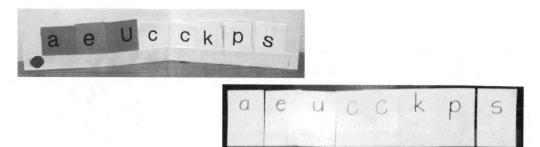

The words the children are going to make are written on index cards. These words will be placed in the pocket chart as the words are made and will be used for the Sort and Transfer steps of the lesson.

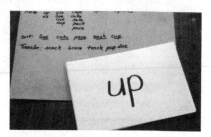

The teacher begins the lesson by having the children hold up and name each letter as the teacher holds up the big letters in the pocket chart.

> "Hold up and name each letter as I hold up the big letter. Let's start with your vowels. Show me your **a**, your **u**, and your **e**. Now show me your two **c**'s, **k**, **p**, and **s**. Today you have 8 letters. In a few minutes, we will see if anyone can figure out the secret word that uses all 8 letters."

Part One: Making Words

> "Use 2 letters to spell the word **up**. I got **up** at 6:30."

(Find someone with **up** spelled correctly and send that child to spell **up** with the big letters.)

> "Change 1 letter to spell **us**. The fifth-graders put on a play for **us**."
> "Add a letter you don't hear to spell **use**. We **use** our letters to make words."
> "Move the same letters to spell the name **Sue**. Do you know anyone named **Sue**?"

(Find someone with **Sue** spelled with a capital **S** to spell **Sue** with the big letters.)

"Change 1 letter to spell **cue**. When you are an actor, you listen for your **cue**."

(Quickly send someone with the correct spelling to make the word with the big letters. Keep the pace brisk. Do not wait until everyone has **cue** spelled with their little letters. It is fine if some children are making **cue** as **cue** is being spelled with the big letters. Choose your struggling readers to go to the pocket chart when easy words are being spelled and your advanced readers when harder words are being made.)

"Change 1 letter in **cue** to spell **cup**. The baby drinks from a sippy **cup**."

"Change the vowel to spell **cap**. Do you ever wear a **cap**?"

"Add a silent letter to change **cap** into **cape**. Batman wore a **cape**."

"Change 1 letter to spell **cake**. Do you like chocolate **cake**?"

"Change 1 letter to spell **sake**. I hope for your **sake** that it doesn't rain during the game."

"Change the last 2 letters to spell **sack**. A **sack** is another name for a bag."

"Change 1 letter to spell **pack**. **Pack** your clothes for the sleepover."

"Change the last letter to spell another 4 letter word, **pace**. The racers ran at a very fast **pace**."

"Add 1 letter to spell **space**. When we write, we leave a **space** between words."

"I have just one word left. It is the secret word you can make with all your letters. See if you can figure it out."

(Give the children one minute to figure out the secret word. Then give clues if needed.) Let someone who figures it out go to the big letters and spell the secret word: **cupcakes**.

Part Two: Sorting the Words into Patterns   Using the index cards with words you made, place them in the pocket chart as the children pronounce and chorally spell each. Give them a quick reminder of how they made these words:

"First we spelled a 2 letter word, **up, u-p**."
"We changed the last letter to spell **us, u-s**."
"We added the silent e to spell **use, u-s-e**."
"We used the same letters with a capital S to spell **Sue, S-u-e**."
"We changed the first letter to spell **cue, c-u-e**."
"We changed the last letter to spell **cup, c-u-p**."
"We changed the vowel to spell **cap, c-a-p**."
"We added the silent e to spell **cape, c-a-p-e**."
"We changed 1 letter to spell **cake, c-a-k-e**."
"We changed 1 letter to spell **sake, s-a-k-e**."
"We changed 2 letters to spell **sack, s-a-c-k**."
"We changed 1 letter to spell **pack, p-a-c-k**."
"We changed the last letter to spell **pace, p-a-c-e**."
"We added a letter to spell **space, s-p-a-c-e**."
"Finally, we spelled the secret word using all our letters, **cupcakes, c-u-p-c-a-k-e-s**."

Next have the children sort the rhyming words. Take one of each set of rhyming words and place them in the pocket chart.

Sue	cake	pace	sack	cup

Ask three children to find the other words that rhyme and place them under the ones you pulled out.

Sue	cake	pace	sack	cup
cue	sake	space	pack	up

Have the children chorally pronounce the sets of rhyming words.

Part Three: Transfer   Tell the children to pretend it is writing time and they need to spell some words that rhyme with some of the words they made today. Have the children use whiteboards or half-sheets of paper to write the words. Say sentences that children might want to write that include a rhyming word. Work together to decide which words the target word rhymes with and to decide how to spell it.

> "Boys and girls, let's pretend it is writing time. Terry is writing about what he likes to eat for a **snack** and he is trying to spell the word **snack**. Let's all **say** snack and stretch out the beginning letters. What 2 letters do you hear at the beginning of **snack**?"

Have the children stretch out **snack** and listen for the beginning letters. When they tell you that **snack** begins with **sn**, write **sn** on an index card and have the children write **sn** on their papers or whiteboards.

Take the index card with **sn** on it to the pocket chart and hold it under each column of words as you lead the children to chorally pronounce the words and decide if **snack** rhymes with them:

> "Sue, cue, snack." Children should show you "thumbs down."
> "Cake, sake, snack." Children should again show you "thumbs down."
> "Pace, space, snack." Children should again show you "thumbs down."
> "Sack, pack, snack." Children should show you "thumbs up."

Finish writing **snack** on your index card by adding **ack** to **sn** and place **snack** in the pocket chart under **sack** and **pack**.

Make up sentences and use the same procedure to demonstrate how you use **pace** and **space** to spell **brace** and **sack** and **pack** to spell **track**.

Sue	cake	pace	sack	cup
cue	sake	space	pack	up
due			brace	snack	pup
				track

Kathleen C.
snack
brace
track
pup
due

We hope this sample lesson has helped you see how a Making Words lesson works and how Making Words lessons help children develop phonemic awareness, phonics, and spelling skills. Most important, we hope you see that in every lesson children will practice applying the patterns they are learning to reading and spelling new words.

One-Vowel Lessons

Vowels are the tricky part of English spelling, so the first lessons we do with students have only one vowel. Here are some one-vowel lessons taken from *Making Words 1st Grade* (Cunningham & Hall, 2008b).

Letters:	a d h n s	

Words to Make: as an and has had sad sand hand hands

Sort:	and	had	as
	sand	sad	has
	hand		

Transfer: Use rhyming words to spell *bad*, *band*, *land*, and *mad*

Letters: e d n p s

Words to Make: Ed Ned end den pen pens dens send spend

Sort:	Ed	end	pen	dens
	Ned	send	den	pens
		spend		

Transfer: Use rhyming words to spell *bed*, *lend*, *ten*, and *hens*

Letters: i p r s t

Words to Make: is it sit pit tip sip rip trip strip trips

Sort:	it	rip
	sit	sip
	pit	tip
		trip
		strip

Letters:	o m p s t
Words to Make:	Tom pot top mop mops tops pots spot stop stomp

Sort:	pot	top	mops
	spot	mop	tops
		stop	

Transfer:	Use rhyming words to spell *hot*, *hop*, *trot*, and *drops*

Letters:	u g n s t
Words to Make:	us Gus sun gun tug nut nuts snug sung stung

Sort:	us	sun	tug	sung
	Gus	gun	snug	stung

Transfer:	Use rhyming words to spell *hug*, *bus*, *bug*, and *plug*

Making Big Words

For older students, we choose a secret word that has some related words. We print the letters on a strip and copy them. The students tear the strips into letters and use them to make words. (These lessons are taken from *Making Words 3rd Grade* and *Making Words 4th Grade* [Cunningham & Hall, 2009b, 2009c].)

a	e	e	b	c	c	l	l	r	y

Make:	all call ball bell cell real able cable cycle clear really caller/recall clearly recycle recyclable

Sort Related Words:	call, caller, recall; real, really; clear, clearly; cycle, recycle, recyclable (Use related words in sentences that show relationship.)

Sort Rhymes (with same spelling pattern):

all	bell	able
ball	cell	cable
call		

Transfer:	Have students use rhyming words to spell *table*, *stable*, *swell*, and *shell*.

a	e	i	d	h	h	r	s	s	w

Make:	ear hear dish wish wash wise rise herd heard arise dishes wishes washes radishes dishwasher
Sort homophones:	herd, heard (Put in a sentence to make meaning clear.)
Sort Related Words:	hear, heard; rise, arise; wish, wishes; dish, dishes, dishwasher, wash, washes (Use related words in sentences that show relationship.)

Sort Rhymes (with same spelling pattern):

ear	dish	wise	dishes
hear	wish	rise	wishes
		arise	

Transfer:	Have students use rhyming words to spell *year*, *spear*, *revise*, and *franchise*.

e	e	i	g	h	l	s	s	t	w

Make:	hit with wish heel tile while wheel sheet sleet sweet light sight wishes weight hitless whistle weightless
Sort Related Words:	wish, wishes; hit, hitless; weight, weightless (Use related words in sentences that show relationship.)

Sort Rhymes (with same spelling pattern):

heel	tile	sheet	light
wheel	while	sleet	sight
		sweet	

Transfer:	Have students use rhyming words to spell *mile*, *smile*, *slight*, and *parakeet*.

Modeling How to Decode Big Words

Big words present special decoding problems. Most of the words we read are one- and two-syllable words, but polysyllabic words often carry most of the content. Decoding and spelling polysyllabic words is based on patterns, but these patterns are more sophisticated and require students to understand how words change in their spelling, pronunciation, and meaning as suffixes and prefixes are added. The *g* in *sign* seems quite illogical until you realize that *sign* is related to *signal, signature,* and other words. Finding the *compose/composition* and *compete/competition* relationship helps students understand why the

Steps in Teaching a Making Words Lesson

1. Place the large letter cards needed in a pocket chart or along the chalk tray.

2. Have children pass out letters or pick up the letters needed.

3. Hold up and name the letters on the large letter cards, and have the children hold up their matching small letter cards.

4. Write the numeral 2 (or 3 if no two-letter words are in this lesson) on the board. Tell them to take two letters and make the first word. Have them say the word after you stretch out the word to hear all the sounds.

5. Have a child who makes the first word correctly make the same word with the large letter cards on the chalk tray or pocket chart. Do not wait for everyone to make the word before sending a child to make it with the big letters. Encourage anyone who did not make the word correctly at first to fix the word when he or she sees it made correctly.

6. Continue to make words, giving students clues, such as "Change the first letter only" or "Move the same letters around and you can make a different word" or "Take all your letters out and make another word." Send a child who has made the word correctly to make the word with the large letter cards. Cue students when they are to use more letters by erasing and changing the number on the board to indicate the number of letters needed.

7. Before telling students the last word, say, "Has anyone figured out the secret word—the word we can make with all our letters?" If someone has, offer congratulations and let him or her make it. If not, give students clues until someone figures out the secret word.

8. Once all the words have been made, take the index cards on which you wrote the words and place them one at a time (in the same order that children made them) along the chalk ledge or in the pocket chart. Have children say and spell the words with you as you do this. Ask children to sort these words for patterns—including beginning letters, rhymes, and related words.

9. To encourage transfer to reading and writing, show students how rhyming words can help them decode and spell other words. Say some words that rhyme and have students spell these new words by deciding which words they rhyme with.

second syllable of *composition* and *competition* sound alike but are spelled differently. To decode and spell big words, your students must (1) have a mental store of big words that contain the spelling patterns common to big words; (2) chunk big words into pronounceable segments by comparing the parts of new big words to the big words they already know; and (3) recognize and use common prefixes and suffixes.

Modeling is the most direct way to demonstrate to your students what to do when they encounter a long, unfamiliar word. When you model, you show someone how to do something. In real life, we use modeling constantly to teach skills. We would not think of explaining how to ride a bike. Rather, we would demonstrate and talk about what we were doing as the learner watched and listened to our explanation. Vocabulary introduction is a good place to model how you figure out the pronunciation of a word for students. Here is an example of how you might model for students one way to decode the word *international*. Write a sentence on the board or overhead:

> The thinning of the ozone layer is an international problem.

"Today, we are going to look at a big word that is really just a little word with a prefix added to the beginning and a suffix added to the end."

Underline *nation* in the sentence you have just written.

> The thinning of the ozone layer is an inter<u>nation</u>al problem.

"Who can tell me this word? Yes, that is the word *nation*. Now, let's look at the prefix that comes before *nation*."

Underline *inter*.

> The thinning of the ozone layer is an <u>inter</u>national problem.

"This prefix is *inter*. You probably know *inter* from words such as *interrupt* and *internal*. Now, let's look at what follows *inter* and *nation*."

Underline *al*.

> The thinning of the ozone layer is an internation<u>al</u> problem.

"You know *al* from many words, such as *unusual* and *critical*."

Write *unusual* and *critical* and underline the *al*.

> unusu<u>al</u> critic<u>al</u>

"Listen as I pronounce this part of the word."

Underline and pronounce *national*.

> The thinning of the ozone layer is an inter<u>national</u> problem.

"Notice how the pronunciation of *nation* changes when we put *a-l* on it. Now let's put all the parts together and pronounce the word—*inter nation al*. Let's read the sentence and make sure *international* makes sense."

Have the sentence read and confirm that ozone thinning is indeed a problem for many nations to solve.

> "You can figure out the pronunciation of many big words if you look for common prefixes, such as *inter;* common root words, such as *nation;* and common suffixes, such as *al.*"
>
> "In addition to helping you figure out the pronunciation of a word, prefixes and suffixes sometimes help you know what the word means or where in a sentence we can use the word. The word *nation* names a thing. When we describe a nation, we add the suffix *al* and have *national.* The prefix *inter* often means between or among. Something that is *international* is between many nations. The Olympics are the best example of an *international* sporting event."

This sample lesson for introducing the word *international* demonstrates how you can help your students see and use morphemes—meaningful parts of words—to decode polysyllabic words. A similar procedure could be used to model how you would decode a word that did not contain suffixes or prefixes. For the word *resources,* for example, you could draw students' attention to the familiar first syllable *re* and then point out the known word *sources.* For *geologic,* you might write and underline the *geo* in the known word *geography* and then point out the known word *logic. Policies* might be compared to *politics* and *agencies.*

Modeling is simply thinking aloud about how you might go about figuring out an unfamiliar word. It takes just a few extra minutes to point out the morphemes in *international* and to show how *policies* is like *politics* and *agencies.* But taking these extra few minutes is quickly paid back as your students begin to develop some independence in figuring out those big words that carry so much of the content.

The Nifty-Thrifty-Fifty

English is the most morphologically complex language. Linguists estimate that for every word you know, you can figure out how to decode, spell, and build meanings for six or seven other words, if you recognize and use the morphemic patterns in words. Activities in this section teach students how to spell a Nifty-Thrifty-Fifty store of words to decode, spell, and build meaning for thousands of other words. These 50 words include examples for all the common prefixes and suffixes as well as common spelling changes. Because these 50 words help with so many other words, we have named them the Nifty-Thrifty-Fifty.

The Nifty-Thrifty-Fifty words should be introduced gradually, and students should practice chanting and writing them until their spelling and decoding become automatic. The procedures for working with these words and their important parts follow:

1 Display the words, arranged by first letter, someplace in the room. Add four or five each week. You may want to use a bulletin board or hang a banner above a bulletin board and attach the words to it. The words need to be big and bold so that they are seen easily from wherever the students are writing. Using different colors makes them more visible and attractive. Many teachers use large colored index cards or write them with different colors of thick, bold permanent markers.

2 Explain to students that in English, many big words are just smaller words with prefixes and suffixes added to the word. Good spellers do not memorize the spelling of every new word they come across. Rather, they notice the patterns in words and these patterns include prefixes, suffixes, and spelling changes that occur when these are added.

3 Tell students that one way to practice words is to say the letters in them aloud in a rhythmic, chanting fashion. Tell students that although this might seem silly, it really is not because the brain responds to sound and rhythm. (That is one of the reasons you can sing along with the words of a familiar song even though you could not say the words without singing the song and also why jingles and raps are easy to remember.) Point to each word and have students chant it (cheerleader style) with you. After "cheering" for each word, help students analyze the word, talking about its meaning and determining the root, prefix, and suffix, and noting any spelling changes. Here is an example of the kind of word introduction students find most helpful:

> **composer**—A composer is a person who composes something. Many other words, such as *writer, reporter,* and *teacher,* are made up of a root word and the suffix *er,* meaning a person or thing that does something. When *er* is added to a word that already has an *e,* the original *e* is dropped.
>
> **discovery**—A discovery is something you discover. The prefix *dis* often changes a word to an opposite form. To *cover* something can mean to hide it. When you *discover* it, it is no longer hidden. *Discovery* is the root word *cover* with the added prefix *dis* and suffix *y.* There are no spelling changes.
>
> **encouragement**—When you encourage someone, you give them encouragement. Many other words, such as *argue, argument* and *replace, replacement,* follow this same pattern. The root word for *encourage* is *courage.* So *encouragement* is made up of the prefix *en,* the root word *courage,* and the suffix *ment.*
>
> **hopeless**—Students should easily see the root word *hope* and the suffix *less.* Other similar words are *painless* and *homeless.*
>
> **impossible**—The root word *possible* with the suffix *im.* In many words, including *impatient* and *immature,* the suffix *im* changes the word to an opposite.

musician—A musician is a person who makes music. A *beautician* helps make you beautiful, and a *magician* makes magic. *Musician* has the root word *music* with the suffix *ian*, which sometimes indicates the person who does something. None of the spelling changes but the pronunciation changes. Have students say the words *music* and *musician, magic* and *magician,* and notice how the pronunciation changes.

4 Once you have noticed the composition for each word, helped students see other words that work in a similar way, and cheered for each word, have students write each word. Writing the word with careful attention to each letter and the sequence of each letter helps students use another mode to practice the word. (Do not, however, assign students to copy words five times each. They just do this "mechanically" and often do not focus on the letters.) Students enjoy writing the words more and focus better on them if you make it a riddle or game. You can do this simply by giving clues for the word you want them to write:

a. Number 1 is the opposite of *discouragement.*

b. Number 2 is the opposite of *hopeful.*

c. For number 3, write the word that tells what you are if you play the *guitar.*

d. For number 4, write what you are if you play the *guitar* but you also make up the songs you play.

e. Number 5 is the opposite of *possible.*

f. For number 6, write the word that has *cover* for the root word.

After writing the words, have students check their own papers, once more chanting the letters aloud and underlining each as they say it.

5 When you have a few minutes of "sponge" time, practice the words by chanting or writing. As you are cheering or writing each word, ask students to identify the root, prefix, and suffix and talk about how these affect the meaning of the root word. Also have them point out any spelling changes.

6 Once students can automatically, quickly, and correctly spell the words and explain to you how they are composed, it is time to help them see how these words can help them decode and spell other words. Remind students that good spellers do not memorize the spelling of each word. Rather, they use words they know and combine roots, suffixes, and prefixes to figure out how to spell lots of other words. Have the students spell words that are contained in the words and words you can make by combining parts of the words.

Have each word used in a sentence and talk about the meaning relationships when appropriate. Note spelling changes as needed. From just the eight words—*composer, discovery, encouragement, hopeless, impossible, musician, richest,* and *unfriendly*—students should be able to decode, spell, and discuss meanings for the following words:

compose	encourage	music	dispose	enrichment
pose	courage	rich	discourage	uncover
discover	hope	friend	discouragement	richly
cover	possible	friendly	enrich	hopelessly

The Nifty-Thrifty-Fifty

(7) Continue adding words gradually, going through the above procedures with all the words. Do not add words too quickly, and provide lots of practice with these words and the other words that can be decoded and spelled by combining parts of these words. Because this store of words provides patterns for so many other words, you want your students to "overlearn" these words so that they can be called up instantly and automatically when students meet similar words in their reading or need to spell similar words while writing.

Nifty-Thrifty-Fifty Words and Transferable Chunks

			impression	im	sion
			independence	in	ence
			international	inter	al
			invasion	in	sion
antifreeze	anti		irresponsible	ir	ible
beautiful		ful (y-i)	midnight	mid	
classify		ify	misunderstand	mis	
communities	com	es (y-i)	musician		ian
community	com	y	nonliving	non	ing (drop e)
composer	com	er	overpower	over	
continuous	con	ous (drop e)	performance	per	ance
conversation	con	tion	prehistoric	pre	ic
deodorize	de	ize	prettier		er (y-i)
different		ent	rearrange	re	
discovery	dis	y	replacement	re	ment
dishonest	dis		richest		est
electricity	e	ity	semifinal	semi	
employee	em	ee	signature		ture
encouragement	en	ment	submarine	sub	
expensive	ex	ive	supermarkets	super	s
forecast	fore		swimming		ing (double m)
forgotten		en (double t)	transportation	trans	tion
governor		or	underweight	under	
happiness		ness (y-i)	unfinished	un	ed
hopeless		less	unfriendly	un	ly
illegal	il		unpleasant	un	ant (drop e)
impossible	im	ible	valuable		able (drop e)

The Wheel

The popular game show *Wheel of Fortune* is based on the idea that having meaning and some letters allows you to figure out many words. On *Wheel of Fortune*, meaning is provided by the category to which the word belongs. A variation of this game can be used to introduce big words and to teach students to use meaning and all the letters they know. Here is how to play The Wheel.

Remind students that we can figure out many words (even if we cannot decode all the parts) as long as we think about what makes sense and keep the parts that we do know in the right places. Ask students who have watched *Wheel of Fortune* to explain how it is played. Then explain how your version of The Wheel will be different:

1. Contestants guess all letters without considering if they are consonants or vowels.

2. They must have all letters filled in before they can say the word.

3. The word must fit in a sentence rather than in a category.

4. Vanna will not be there to turn letters!

Write a sentence on the board, and draw a blank for each letter of an important word. Here is an example:

> If you were to travel to Antarctica, you would be struck by its
> almost unbelievable _ _ _ _ _ _ _ _ _ _.

Have a student begin by asking "Is there a . . . ?" If the student guesses a correct letter, fill in that letter. Let the student continue to guess letters until he or she gets a "No!" When a student asks about a letter that is not there, write the letter above the puzzle and go on to the next student.

Make sure that all letters are filled in before anyone is allowed to guess. (This really shows students the importance of spelling and attending to common spelling patterns!)

For our example, a student might ask, "Is there an *r?*" ("Sorry, no *r!*") The next student asks for an *s*. One *s* is filled in.

> If you were to travel to Antarctica, you would be struck by its
> almost unbelievable _ _ s _ _ _ _ _ _ _.

The student who guessed correctly continues to ask for letters. "Is there a *t?*" ("Yes, one *t!*")

> If you were to travel to Antarctica, you would be struck by its
> almost unbelievable _ _ s _ _ _ t _ _ _.

The student asks for an *o*. Two *o*'s are filled in.

> If you were to travel to Antarctica, you would be struck by its
> almost unbelievable _ _ s o _ _ t _ o _.

Next, the student asks for an *i* and then for an *n*.

> If you were to travel to Antarctica, you would be struck by its
> almost unbelievable _ _ s o _ _ t i o n.

After much thought, the student asks for an *m*. Unfortunately, there is no *m,* so play passes to the next student, who asks for an *e,* an *a,* a *d,* and an *l* and correctly spells out *d e s o l a t i o n !* If there is time, play continues with another big word introduced in a sentence context.

Students who are introduced to vocabulary by playing The Wheel pay close attention to the letter patterns in big words. They also get in the habit of making sure that the word they figure out, based on having some of the letters, fits the meaning of the sentence in which it occurs.

Summary

Reading is a complex process in which you have to identify words from which you construct meaning. Writing is equally (if not more!) complex. Both reading and writing require that the most common words be read and spelled automatically—without thought or mediation—so that the brain's attention can focus on meaning. When children are first starting to read and write, their word identification and spelling will not be automatic. Teaching them how to read and spell high-frequency words and providing a lot of varied practice reading will help children develop fluency.

As they are learning high-frequency words and developing fluency, children also need to learn patterns so that they can quickly decode and spell words they have not yet learned. The patterns in short words are the *onsets*—commonly called beginning letters—and the *rimes*—spelling patterns. In big words, *morphemes*—prefixes, suffixes, and roots—are the patterns that allow readers to quickly decode and spell longer words.

Few instructional studies have compared different types of phonics instruction. After reviewing the research on phonics instruction, Stahl, Duffy-Hester, and Stahl (1998) concluded that there are several types of good phonics instruction and that there is no research base to support the superiority of any one particular type. The National Reading Panel (NRP) (2000) reviewed the experimental research on teaching phonics and determined that explicit and systematic phonics is superior to nonsystematic or no phonics but that there is no significant difference in effectiveness among the kinds of systematic phonics instruction. The NRP also found no significant difference in effectiveness among tutoring, small-group, or whole-class phonics instruction.

Newer approaches to teaching phonics often use guided and independent spelling activities to teach letter-sound relationships and their application (Stahl, Duffy-Hester, & Stahl, 1998). A number of studies have supported integrating phonics and spelling instruction with young children (Ehri & Wilce, 1987; Ellis & Cataldo, 1990). Juel and Minden-Cupp (2000) noted that based on their observations, the most effective teachers of children who entered first grade with few literacy skills combined systematic letter-sound instruction with onset-rime, compare-contrast activities instruction, and taught these units with applications in both reading and writing.

Phonics and spelling instruction in the upper grades has not been investigated much, but some understanding about the new words encountered in these grades provides some instructional direction. In 1984, Nagy and Anderson published a landmark study in which they analyzed a sample of 7,260 words found in books commonly read in grades 3 through 9. They found that most of these words were polysyllabic words and that many of these big words were related semantically through their morphology. Some of these relationships are easily noticed. For instance, the words *hunter, redness, foglights,* and *stringy* are clearly related to the words *hunt, red, fog,* and *string.* Other more complex word relationships exist between words such as *planet/planetarium, vicious/vice,* and *apart/apartment.* Nagy and Anderson hypothesized that if children knew or learned how to interpret morphological relationships, they would know six or seven words for every basic word. To move children along in their decoding and spelling abilities in the upper grades, instruction needs to focus on morphemes—prefixes, suffixes, and roots—and how they help us decode, spell, and gain meaning for polysyllabic words.

chapter 6

Building Vivid, Vital, and Valuable Vocabularies

R ead each of these three words, and think about what comes immediately to mind:

plastic   purple   racket

What did you think of for *plastic?* Did you image the multitude of plastic objects that make up everyday life? Did you experience negative feelings, such as "I hate using plastic knives, forks, and spoons," while simultaneously realizing that our current world would be very different if it weren't for the omnipresence of plastic? Did you worry because plastic biodegrades so slowly and is not good for the environment? Did you recall one of the most famous lines in movie history from *The Graduate?*

What did your brain do with the word *purple?* Did you picture something purple? Did you think "I hate purple" or "Purple is one of my favorite colors"? Did you imagine different shades of purple—orchid, lavender, lilac? Perhaps the word *purple* made you think immediately of someone you know who was in the military and earned a Purple Heart, and you wondered how this medal came to be associated with the color purple.

Did you picture a tennis or badminton racket for the word *racket?* Or did you think of all the racket being made by the construction across the street? Perhaps you were reminded about the shenanigans of your local government and thought, "It's all a racket!"

When we see or hear words, our brains make all kinds of connections with those words, depending on our past experiences. These connections include images and scenes from our own lives as well as from movies and television. We have emotional reactions to words. Words make us worry, celebrate, appreciate, and wonder.

What our minds don't do when they see or hear a word is think of a definition. Look up *plastic, purple,* and *racket* in any standard dictionary, and you will find definitions such as these:

> plastic—any of a large group of synthetic organic compounds molded by heat pressure into a variety of forms
>
> purple—a color made by mixing red and blue
>
> racket—a loud noise; a scheme for getting money illegally; an oval strung frame with a long handle used for hitting balls

When you see or hear words, your brain makes connections to those words. Your brain does not think of definitions.

Now think back to your elementary school days and recall your associations with the word *vocabulary.* Do you remember looking up words and copying their definitions? If a word had several definitions, did you copy the first one or the shortest one? Did you ever look up a word and still not know what it meant because you did not understand the meanings of the other words in the definition? Did you copy that definition and memorize it for the test, in spite of not understanding it? Do you remember weekly vocabulary tests, in which you had to write definitions for words and use those words in sentences?

Copying and memorizing definitions has been and remains the most common vocabulary activity in schools. It is done at all levels and in all subjects. This definition copying and memorizing continues in spite of research that shows definitional approaches to vocabulary instruction increase children's ability to define words but have no effect on reading comprehension (Baumann, Kame'enui, & Ash, 2003).

Vocabulary is critical to reading comprehension. If you are reading or listening to something in which you can instantly access the appropriate meanings for the words, you are well on your way to understanding. But when you are reading or listening to something and you don't have meanings for a lot of the words, your comprehension is severely impaired. Vocabulary is also crucial for writing. We all know that one of the challenges of writing well and clearly is "choosing just the right word."

Helping children build vivid and vital vocabularies is a crucial goal in helping all children become the very best readers and writers they can be. Vocabulary is one of the most valuable tools for literacy. In the next two chapters, we will describe specific strategies teachers use for teaching students to comprehend and to write clearly. A schoolwide, day-in-day-out vocabulary-building component in the curriculum provides the foundation on which specific comprehension and writing skills can be built.

How Do We Learn All the Words We Know?

How many words do you know?

5,000?
10,000?
20,000?
50,000?
100,000?

If you found it difficult to estimate the size of your vocabulary, you should be comforted to know that this seemingly simple question is a difficult one to answer. The first question is, of course, "What do you mean by *know*?" Is it enough to know that anthropoids are some kind of apes, or do you have to know the specific information that anthropoids are apes without tails, such as chimpanzees, gorillas, orangutans, and gibbons? The next question is, "How many meanings of the word do you have to know?" If you know the sports meaning of coach, do you also have to know the motorbus and "coach class" meanings to count this word in your meaning vocabulary? The other complication in counting the words you have meanings for is how to count the various forms of a single word. If *play, plays, playing, played, playful, replay,* and *player* count as separate words, your vocabulary is much larger than if these words count as one word, all related to the root word *play*. All these variables, word depth, multimeaning words, and how to count words with the same root, result in wide differences in the estimate of vocabulary size.

In spite of the difficulties of estimating vocabulary size, it is important for teachers to have an idea of what the meaning vocabulary development goal is. Biemiller (2004) estimates that entering kindergartners have meanings for an average of 3,500 root words. They add approximately 1,000 root word meanings each school year. The average high school graduate knows about 15,000 root words.

Other vocabulary experts (Graves, 2006; Stahl & Nagy, 2006) argue that Biemiller's estimate is way too low. They believe that words with multiple meanings should be counted as separate words and that many children do not recognize words with common roots. Furthermore, they believe that proper nouns—Canada, Abraham Lincoln, the White House—should be included in the total word count. When counted in this way, these experts argue that the average child learns 2,000 to 3,000 word meanings each school year and that the average high school graduate has meanings for 40,000 to 50,000 words. Regardless of which estimates you believe, the number of new words children need to add to their vocabularies each year is staggering.

Children differ greatly, however, in the sizes of their meaning vocabularies at school entrance and as they continue through the grades. Children who enter school with small vocabularies tend to add fewer words each year than children who enter with larger vocabularies. Since vocabulary size is so closely related to children's comprehension as they move through school, there is a sense of urgency about intensifying efforts to build more and deeper word meaning stores for all children.

To help you understand how we add words to our meaning vocabulary stores, consider the analogy that learning word meanings is a lot like getting to know people. As with words, you know some people extremely well, you are well acquainted with others, you have only vague ideas of still others, and so on. Your knowledge of people depends on the experiences you have with them. You know some people, such as family members and close friends, extremely well because you have spent most of your life in their company. You have participated with them regularly in situations that have been intense and emotional as well as routine. At the other extreme, think of people that you have only heard about as well as historical figures, such as Charles Darwin and Catherine the Great, and current public figures, such as politicians and entertainers. You have heard of them and seen pictures and videos of them, but these people are known to you only through the secondhand reports of others. Your knowledge of people that you know indirectly through secondhand information is limited in comparison to your knowledge of those you know directly through firsthand experience. Learning words—like coming to know people—varies according to how much time you spend with them and the types of experiences you share.

Now think of how you make new friends. Social gatherings, such as parties and meetings, are excellent opportunities for getting to know others. When you move through a gathering on your own, you strike up conversations and get to know new people, in part as a function of your motivation and your social skills. However, having a host, hostess, friend, or group of friends introduce you to people tends to expedite the process. And once you have made new contacts, you might get to know them better as you meet again in other settings. And don't forget the power of social networking: The more people you know, the more opportunities you have for helping each other out and meeting even more people.

The levels of knowledge about people and the dynamics of getting to know them are comparable in many ways to learning words. When given the opportunity, students learn new words on their own, depending on their motivation and literacy skills. Students also benefit from direct introductions to and intensive interactions with a few new words. As students learn new words, their opportunities for learning additional words increase exponentially.

Literacy experts all agree on the need for vocabulary building for all students at all grades. They disagree, however, about the best way to provide students with the valuable vocabulary tools they need. We know that you can teach specific vocabulary and that learning new words will improve the comprehension of text containing those words. But the teaching must be quite thorough and across several days and weeks, and thus, the number of words any teacher can directly teach is limited. Many of the words children add to their vocabularies each year are learned through reading. Thus, wide reading is often recommended for vocabulary development.

When you meet a word in your reading, you have two sources of information to help you figure out the meaning of that word. Consider the following sentence:

I wish I understood how they can colorize old movies.

If you had never heard the word *colorize* before, you probably figured out what it meant by using the context of the sentence and your morphemic knowledge about the root *color* and the suffix *ize*. Since you know that when you *modernize* something, you make it more modern; when you *categorize* things, you put them into categories; and when you *rationalize* something you have done, you make it rational (even if it really wasn't!), then you quickly realize that to *colorize* something is to make it have color. Of course, you know that old movies were black and white, and thus you can read the sentence, immediately understand the meaning of *colorize,* and wonder how they do that! Because we know that wide reading is associated with large vocabularies and that the clues available when you come to a new word in your reading are context and morphemes, some experts argue that the best way to help students build vocabulary is to promote wide reading and teach the use of context and morphemes.

Since we know that words can be directly taught and that wide reading—supported by context and morpheme detection—are both valuable ways of building vocabulary, the wise thing for most teachers to do is to "hedge their bets" and tackle the vocabulary challenge from "both fronts." In the remainder of this chapter, we will describe a variety of ways teachers can help all their students build vivid, vital, and valuable vocabularies.

Provide as Much Real Experience as Possible

We all learn best when we have real, direct experience with whatever we are learning. Most of the vocabulary learning children do before they come to school is based on real things and real experiences. Children first learn to name things—*table, chair, cat, dog.* Two-year-olds delight in pointing to the objects they can see and naming them. Put them in a new environment, such as the beach or the doctor's office, and they will almost immediately begin to point to things and ask, "What's that?" It is not only nouns that children learn through direct experience. Every young child knows the meanings of *run* and *walk* and has probably been told many times that you can't run in the parking lot! Children also learn emotion words through real experiences:

"I know you feel sad that your friend moved away. I would be sad too if that happened."

The words we know best and remember longest are those we have had real, direct experience with. Teachers who want to build students' vocabularies are always looking for ways to introduce words with "real things."

Bring Real Things into the Classroom and Anchor Words to Them

Look around your house or apartment, and identify common objects your students might not know the names of—even if they have the same objects in their houses or apartments! Here are some of the objects one teacher brought to school for Show and Talk:

- Vases in assorted sizes, colors, and shapes
- Balls—tennis, baseball, basketball, football, golf, volleyball, beachball
- Art—watercolors, oils, photographs in frames of different colors, materials, and sizes
- Kitchen implements—turkey baster, strainer, spatula, whisk, zester
- Tools—hammer, screwdriver, nails, screws, drill, wrench

In addition to the names of objects, of course, many descriptive words are used in talking about the objects and many verbs are used in talking about what you do with the objects. You may want to teach children a simple version of the game 20 Questions, in which you think of one of the objects, and the children see how many questions they have to ask you to narrow down which one it is.

"Mine" Your School Environment for Real Things

In addition to gathering objects from home and carting them to school, look around your school environment and think about what objects your students might not know the names for. They probably know the words *door* and *window,* but can they tell you that what goes around the door and window is the *frame?* Can they tell you that the things that allow the door to open and close are the *hinges* and that the thing you grab to open and close the door is the *knob?* They can turn the water in the sink off and on, but do they know that they use *faucets* to do that? Is your playground covered with *asphalt? Gravel? Grass? Sand?* What kind of *equipment* do you have in your *gymnasium,* and what can you do with it?

Seize Unexpected Events as Opportunities for Vocabulary Development

Clever teachers seize every opportunity to turn classroom occurrences into opportunities for vocabulary development. The misfortune suffered by a child who breaks his leg and arrives at school with his leg in a cast and walking on crutches can be "mined"for vocabulary development opportunities. The clever teacher will encourage the children to ask questions and share their own experiences with broken bones. He or she might take a photo of the child with the broken leg and write a few sentences summarizing that experience:

> Michael slipped on the ice and broke his leg. He went to the hospital in the ambulance. The doctor set the bone and put a cast on his leg. He has to walk with crutches and can't move very quickly.

Look for Real-Thing Connections for New Vocabulary Words

When you are reading to or with children and new words occur, think first of how you might connect those new words with things in their environment. When reading about a mountain ledge, the teacher might point out the window ledge and table ledge as examples of other kinds of ledges right there in the classroom. The word *pierce* can be connected with students' pierced ears. When encountering the word *unexpected,* the teacher can remind children of something unexpected that happened in the classroom.

Introduce Science and Social Studies Units with Real Things

As you are planning to introduce a new science or social studies topic, begin by collecting objects that are even vaguely related to that topic. Some museums have crates of objects related to commonly studied topics. Some school media centers collect and store things that many teachers need. In some schools, teachers take responsibility for gathering objects related to a particular topic and then teach those topics at different times so that everyone can use the same objects.

Send Students Looking for Real Things in Their Home Environments

Many of the objects you bring to school or identify in school to build vocabularies can also be found in the home environments of your students. Get in the habit of posing questions that will send students looking for and identifying similar objects in their homes:

> "Do you have tools (kitchen implements, balls, vases, picture frames, etc.) in your house? What do they look like? What do you use them for?"
>
> "How many faucets (hinges, knobs, ledges, door frames, etc.) do you have in your house? Count them and bring in the number tomorrow. We will add up all the numbers at the beginning of math."
>
> "Is there gravel (asphalt, grass, sand, etc.) anywhere in your neighborhood?"
>
> "Is there a playground or park near your house? What kind of equipment does it have?"

In addition to having children identify common objects in their home environments, encourage them to talk with family members about those objects. Children can tell them that they have the same things at school, too, and explain what they are for. Children can tell their families about how they are using batteries—like the ones they have at home—to learn about electricity in school.

Teachers are always looking for opportunities to make home-school connections. Having children take new vocabulary words they are learning into their home environments helps make school learning more relevant and extends each child's opportunities for vocabulary development.

Take Advantage of Media and Technology

Many young children have a concept for *mountain* even if they have never seen a real mountain. Most young children can recognize zebras, elephants, and monkeys even though they have never been to a zoo, circus, or other place with these animals. Many children who have never sailed or been in a canoe know what sailboats and canoes are. How did this learning occur? Did someone explain to them what a mountain was? Was the dictionary definition of the word *monkey* read to them? Did some adult attempt to explain or define a *canoe?* In most cases, when children have concepts for objects and realities they have never directly experienced, they have seen these objects or realities portrayed on television, in movies or videos, or in pictures or picture books.

The Internet makes providing visual images and simulated experiences a daily possibility in every classroom. Through the Internet, you can follow the progress of the latest space probe, find images of all the major deserts of the world, and see and hear Winston Churchill as he rallies the people of London during World War II. You and your children can take virtual field trips all over the world and back in time.

The saying "A picture is worth a thousand words" is definitely true when it comes to vocabulary. When you can't provide the real thing in your classroom, looking to the media for visual and auditory images is definitely the next best thing.

Simulate Real Experiences with Dramatization

Using word dramatizations is a powerful way to help students build vivid word meanings. Both skits and pantomimes can be used to help students "get into words." To prepare your students to do vocabulary skits, select six words and write them on index cards. Tell your students that in a few minutes, their group will plan a skit—a quick little play—to demonstrate the word they have been given. Choose a few students to work with you and model for them how to plan a skit. Talk with your group as the rest of the class listens in. Plan a scene in which you can use the word several times. When you have a plan, act out your skit using the target word as many times as possible. Have one member of your group hold up a sign containing the word every time it occurs in the skit.

Imagine, for example, that the word your group is acting out is *curious*. You decide that the skit will involve a dad and his 2-year-old son walking to the post office. The dad and the 2-year-old meet several people on their walk, and each time, the 2-year-old stops, points to the stranger, and asks these questions:

> "What's your name?"
>
> "Where are you going?"
>
> "What's that?"
>
> "What are you doing?"
>
> "What's in the bag?"
>
> "Why are you wearing that funny hat?"

The dad smiles each time and explains to the stranger that his son is curious about everything. The strangers answer the boy's questions and then remark, "He's the most curious kid I ever saw" as they walk on.

Perform the skit as the class watches. At the end of the skit, have the people in the skit ask the audience how the skit showed that the little boy was curious. Finally, you should ask if anyone in the audience has a story to share about a curious person.

Next, divide the class into five groups, putting one of the children who helped you in the skit in each of the groups. Give each group a card on which the word they will dramatize is written. Today, you are focusing on adjectives and give the groups the words *nervous, frantic, impatient, jubilant,* and *serene.* Help the groups plan their skits by circulating around and coaching them. Encourage the child in each group who helped in the original skit to take a leadership role and help boost the group's confidence that they can do this.

Each skit is acted out with one person in each group holding up the card each time the word is used. The group then asks the audience what they saw in the skit that made the word "come alive." You should ask if anyone in the class wants to share a personal experience with the target word. After the last skit, place the six word cards with others on a board labeled

GET YOUR ADJECTIVES HERE: COOL DESCRIBING
WORDS TO SPICE UP YOUR TALK AND WRITING

Pantomime is another form of dramatization that is particularly useful when the words you want to teach are emotions or actions. Imagine that you want to introduce the emotional adjectives *confused, disappointed, furious,* and *frightened.* Assign a pair of students to each word. Have the rest of the class watch the pairs pantomiming the words and try to guess which pair is acting out each word. The same kind of pantomime can be done with actions such as *swaggered, crept, sauntered,* and *scurried.* Adverbs are also fun to pantomime. Imagine four pairs of students walking to school: One pair walks *briskly.* One pair walks *cautiously.* One pair walks *proudly.* One pair walks *forlornly.*

For any kind of dramatization, it is important to conclude the activity by asking all the students to relate the word that was acted out to their own experience:

"When have you been *confused? Disappointed? Furious? Frantic?"*
"When have you *swaggered? Crept? Sauntered? Scurried?"*
"When would you walk *briskly? Cautiously? Proudly? Forlornly?"*

Acting out words in skits and pantomimes provides students with real experience with many words. They will remember these words because of this real experience and because they enjoyed acting and watching their friends act. Keep a list of words your class encounters that could be acted out in skits or pantomimes, and schedule 20 minutes for vocabulary drama each week. You will be amazed at how students' vocabularies and enthusiasm for words will grow.

English Language Learners

Using real concrete objects and experiences to build meaning vocabulary is important for all your students. It is absolutely essential for your English language learners whose vocabularies will grow in direct relationship to the amount of "comprehensible input" you provide them.

Increase Meaning Vocabularies through Reading

Reading is one of the major opportunities for vocabulary learning. Many words occur much more frequently in written text than in spoken language. As children listen to text being read aloud by the teacher and read independently, they will have lots of opportunities to add words to their meaning vocabularies. Unfortunately, many children do not pay a lot of attention to the new words they meet while reading, and thus, they miss many opportunities to increase the sizes of their vocabularies. Here are ways to help all children increase their meaning vocabularies through reading.

Teach Three Words from Your Teacher Read-Aloud

Teacher read-aloud is one of the major opportunities for children to learn new word meanings. Several studies have demonstrated the power of focused read-alouds on fostering vocabulary growth (Beck, McKeown, & Kucan, 2002; Juel et al., 2003). In each of these studies, the teachers went beyond just reading books aloud to children. Before they read a book aloud, they selected a few words that they felt many children would not know the meanings of. After the book had been read aloud and discussed, the teachers returned to those selected words and focused student attention on them. Use the following Three Read-Aloud Words activity to promote more vocabulary learning from your teacher read-aloud.

Using "Goldilocks" Words in Teacher Read-Alouds   Any good book is going to have many words you could focus your attention on. Narrowing the number of words you are going to teach to a reasonable number will increase the chances that all your children will learn them. Beck, McKeown, and Kucan (2002) divide vocabulary into three tiers. The first tier includes words generally known by almost all children. *Boy, girl, jump, sad, laugh,* and *late* are examples of tier-one words. The third tier includes uncommon, obscure, and technical words. *Languid, thrush, oblique,* and *catamaran* are examples of tier-three words. Tier-two words are words many students don't know but will need to know. *Despair, exhausted, catastrophe,* and *proceeded* are tier-two words. Beck and other experts suggest that teachers focus their time and energy on vocabulary development in teaching these words. Some people refer to these tier-two words as "Goldilocks" words because they are not too well known, not too obscure, but hopefully "just right" for children.

As you look at the book you are going to read aloud to choose your three Goldilocks words, you will probably find a lot more than three possibilities. Narrow the selection down to three by considering the usefulness and appeal of each word to your children and how well the word is defined by the context and pictures in the book. If you have more than three words that are useful, appealing, and well defined, consider how many times each word occurs. Your best choices for three words are useful, appealing, well-defined words that are central to the text and that occur many times.

Once you have chosen the three words, write them on index cards. Then follow these steps:

(1) *Read the text the first time, making no reference to the three chosen words.* The first time you read anything aloud should always be for enjoyment and information. Read the book to your children as you normally would, stopping from time to time to ask questions of the students that will engage them in the text but not doing anything particular about your chosen words.

(2) *Show the three words to your children.* After reading and enjoying the text, show your children the words one at a time. You may want to give a very brief meaning or sentence for each word, but don't do a lot of elaborate meaning building because you want the text to help you do that.

(3) *Reread the text and have children stop you when you read each of the words.* Put the index cards with your three chosen words where your children can clearly see them, and read the text to them again. On this second reading, do not stop to discuss pictures or engage the children with questions. When you come to one of the chosen words, some of the children will be sure to notice and signal you. Stop reading and use the pictures and context to explain each word. If the word is used more than once, let the children stop you each time and see if any new information is added to their understanding of the word.

(4) *Help children connect their own experiences to the three words.* Once you have finished reading the book, stopping each time one of the chosen words has occurred, focus again on each word and ask a question that helps children connect their own experiences to the text. Ask questions such as.

> "When have you felt . . . ?"
>
> "Have you ever experienced a . . . ?"
>
> "Where would you see a . . . ?"

(5) *Reread and have children retell, using the three words in their retelling.* On the next day after you did the first and second readings of the text, show the children the words once more and tell them that you are going to read the book to them one more time. This time, they are to listen to everything that happens in the text—paying special attention to the order in which things happen and to the three words. Tell them that after they read, they will try to retell the information to a partner and use the three words in their retelling. Reread the piece without stopping. Partner up the children and have them jointly try to retell the information, using the three words in their retelling.

(6) *Display the title and the three word cards somewhere in the room.* Once you have introduced these three words in the rich context of the book, helped your children connect these words to their own experiences, and given your children an opportunity to use these words to retell the text, display these words someplace in the room. You may want to copy the cover of the book and display the three index cards next to it. Tell your students that you and they are all going to be on the lookout for these words in books and conversations and will be trying to use the words at school and at home. Every time someone hears, reads, or uses one of these words, he or she can put a tally mark next to the word. The word with the most tally marks at the end of one week is the winning word! (Kids love competitions, especially if they cannot possibly be the loser!) Once you do this, contrive to use these words in your conversations with your children over the next several days. Congratulate them when they notice one of the words, and allow them to put a tally mark next to the word. Soon, you will notice the children trying to sneak these words into their talk— exactly what you are aiming for! Once the children are alert to these words, ask them to listen for them and to try to use the words in their home environments. Have the children report any instances of these words in their home environments, and add tally marks to the appropriate words.

Read-Aloud Words Posters

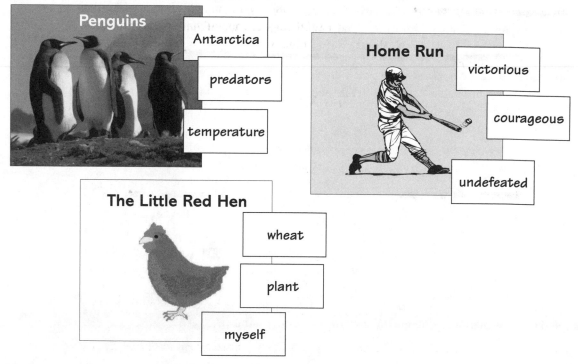

Use "Picture Walks" to Build Vocabulary

One resource constantly available to elementary teachers to build students' vocabularies is the variety of pictures in the books and magazines teachers read aloud and in the texts that students read. Get in the habit of taking your students on a "picture walk" before you read to them or they read to themselves, and you will find lots of opportunities to build meanings for words.

When you picture walk a text, do not stop on every page or take a long time to develop meanings. Children are going to read or listen to the text soon, and they will build more meanings for words as they read or listen. Your purpose before reading is only to alert children to the words and get them in the habit of "mining" the pictures for all the information they can.

Read and Create Alphabet Books

All books contain numerous possibilities for vocabulary building, but one particular kind of book is a "gold mine" for vocabulary development. Alphabet books are written on all kinds of topics, including animals, foods, and the ocean. Captivating pictures make real the words students are unfamiliar with and add depth to words they already know a little about. Reading and rereading alphabet books with young children can help them develop their letter name and sound knowledge and help build their vocabularies at the same time.

If you are reading a lot of alphabet books, you may want your children to create their own alphabet books, individually or as a class. Of course, you will have to brainstorm possible words for each letter of the alphabet. Just think of all the vocabulary development that will occur during that brainstorming!

Alert Children to New Words They Meet in Their Reading

If you are doing the Three Read-Aloud Words activity and taking your students on picture walks before reading, you are already doing a lot to help them be alert to new words in their own reading. Your students will be in the habit of looking at the pictures and thinking about what words in the text those pictures relate to. They will know how the context of what you are reading often clarifies the meaning of a word and that each time you meet the same word, the additional context often adds to your meaning for that word.

If you want to give children an additional nudge, however, to use what they know about learning word meanings from their reading, designate one day each week as a "Sticky-Note New Word Day." At the beginning of independent reading time, give each child one sticky note on which to write one word. Ask the children to be on the lookout for words that are relatively new to them and that they figure out the meanings based on the context and the pictures. Explain to them how you pick your three read-aloud words by looking for words that many of them don't know but that are useful and interesting words. Tell them that you also try to choose words where the context and pictures make the meanings clear and that are used more than once.

Ask each child to look for the perfect word to teach to the class in their reading and to write that word on the sticky note and place it on the sentence in which the word first occurs. When the time for independent reading is over, gather your students together and let four or five volunteers tell their words and read the context and/or share the pictures that helped them with the meanings of their words. Do not let all the children share their words because this would take more time than you have and you want your students to be excited about finding new words—not bored with having to listen to 25 explanations! Assure your students that you will give them more sticky notes next Thursday and that you will let other children share their finds with the class.

If you designate one day each week as "Sticky-Note New Word Day," your children will get in the habit of looking for interesting new words and using the pictures and context to figure out those words. Soon, they will be doing this in all their reading—even when they do not have blank sticky notes staring at them—and they will be on their way to adding exponentially to their vocabularies every time they read!

Another simple way to keep students alert for new words is to designate some space in your room as a vocabulary board. Supply your students with lots of colorful index cards and markers, and encourage them to add new words they find in their reading to the board. Each student should initial the card on which he or she writes the word so everyone can tell who found which words. Take a few minutes each day to note new additions to the vocabulary board and ask students where they found the words, what they mean, and why they thought everyone would want to learn these words.

Teach Morphemes, Context, and the Dictionary to Learn New Words

The activities already described in this chapter will help all your children build vivid, vital, and valuable vocabularies. Once your students are on the lookout for new words and convinced that words are wonderful, you can teach them some specific strategies to help figure out the meanings for new words. Good readers use morphemes, context, and the dictionary to help them refine the meanings of words.

Morphemes

You learned in the previous chapter that *morphemes* are prefixes, roots, and suffixes, which are meaningful parts of words. Look again at the Nifty-Thrifty-Fifty list on page 90. This list has an example word for each of the common prefixes and suffixes. You may want to teach students these words or help them collect other words from their reading that have these helpful parts.

Four prefixes—*un, re, in,* and *dis*—are the most common, and knowing them will help students figure out the meaning of over 1,500 words. Graves (2004) suggests teaching these four prefixes to all elementary students. You may want to focus on each of these for a few weeks. Begin a chart with some *un* words your students are familiar with, such as *unhappy, unlucky,* and *unlocked.* Help students notice the prefix *un* and that it changes the meaning of the root word to the opposite meaning. Encourage your students to be on the lookout for words in their reading in which *un* changes a word to the opposite meaning, and add these to the chart.

After a few weeks, make a chart for *re,* with the meaning of "back" or "again," and add such common words as *return, reboot,* and *replay.* The prefix *in,* which means "the opposite," can be spelled *in, im, il,* and *ir,* so you may want to start the *in* chart with the key words *insane, impossible, illegal,* and *irregular.* Your *dis* chart might begin with common words such as *dishonest* and *disagree.*

One problem with teaching students to look for prefixes and use them as clues to meaning is that many words start with *un*—such as *uncle, understand,* and *uniform*—but *un* is not the prefix and does not have the meaning of opposite. Graves (2004) provides the practical solution that for these simple prefixes, elementary children can be taught that a letter combination is not a prefix if removing it leaves a nonsense word. Thus, *un* is not the prefix in *uncle, understand,* and *uniform* because *cle, derstand,* and *iform* are not words.

When teaching morphemes to help students build meanings for words, it is probably best to begin with these four common prefixes because students will encounter many words in which these prefixes have these predictable meanings. Once students are comfortable with these prefixes, you may want to add some of the less common and less transparent ones from the Nifty-Thrifty-Fifty list.

Elementary students can also learn to notice base or root words and think about how words with the same roots are related. Again, you should start with the most common and predictable root or base words. The word *play* occurs in such related words as *replay, playground,* and *playoffs. Work* is part of many words, including *workers, workout,* and *workstation. Place* is another common base word, and students often know the meaning of *placemats, replace,* and *workplace.* Beginning a chart with common words and asking students to be on the lookout for other words containing those words will help them become attuned to root and base words in their reading.

Vocabulary experts disagree about teaching students Latin and Greek roots. Although it is true that these roots do contain clues to meaning, the meaning relationships are often hard to figure out, and students might get discouraged if they cannot "ferret out" the meaning of a word based on the meaning of the root. Perhaps the most sensible way for elementary teachers to approach Greek and Latin roots is to be aware of them and to point out relationships when they think these will be understandable to most of their children.

English Language Learners

Some words are similar in English and Spanish. Words derived from the same base or root word are called *cognates*. Here are some Spanish-English cognates:

piloto	pilot
exactamente	exactly
clima	climate
curioso	curious
familia	family
decidir	decide
hospital	hospital

Instruction in Spanish-English cognates should follow the suggestions given for teaching morphemes described in this chapter and the preceding chapter. Help your students become sensitive to the meaningful parts of words and get in the habit of deciding if two similar-looking words share meaning as well.

When encountering the word *spectacle,* for example, the teacher might point out that a *spectacle* is something you see that is quite striking or unusual. Furthermore, the teacher might point out that the root *spect* means "to watch" and invite the students to think about how words they know, such as *inspection* and *spectators,* are related to this meaning. The word *constructive* might be explained as "helpful" or "building up," as opposed to *destructive,* which is "unhelpful" or "tearing down." Students might be told that the root *struct* means "build" and asked to think about how other words they know, such as *structure* and *reconstruction,* are related to this meaning.

Context

If you are doing the Three Read-Aloud Words activity regularly and having students share how they figured out the meanings of sticky-note words in their own reading one day each week, then you are teaching them to use context to figure out the meanings of unfamiliar words. If you are taking your students on regular picture walks before reading, then you are teaching them how new words are often brought to life by the pictures in the text. This regular attention to how context and pictures make word meanings clear is probably the best instruction you can do so that your students get in the habit of and know how to use pictures and context.

One caution you may need to point out to students is that context does not always directly reveal the meaning of an unfamiliar word and can sometimes be misleading. Imagine that the only reference in the text to the word *incredulously* is in this sentence:

> Her dad listened incredulously.

This context does not provide much of a clue to the meaning of this new word. On the other hand, the text might continue with a much richer context:

> Her dad listened incredulously. "I find what you are telling me really hard to believe," he admitted when she had finished explaining how the accident had happened.

How much context helps with meaning varies greatly. If a word is important and the context is slim, students need to use the dictionary to figure out the meaning that might make sense in the context of what they are reading.

Context can sometimes be misleading in trying to determine a word's meaning. One student had put a sticky note on the word *grimaced* and explained that the word meant "yelled." The sentence in which the student had read the word was:

> The waiter in the crowded restaurant grimaced as the tray slid to the floor.

The teacher explained to the student that "yelled" would make sense here but that the waiter could have done many things and there really wasn't enough context to decide exactly what the waiter did. The child quickly looked up the word *grimaced* in the dictionary and shared its meaning with the class. The teacher had the whole class twist their faces into the grimaces they might make if they had just dropped a whole tray of food in a crowded restaurant.

As children are sharing their sticky-note words, you will have many opportunities to show them both how the context can be extremely helpful and how it can lead them astray. You can also model how a dictionary is best used—to clarify meaning and let you know if the meaning you inferred from the context is indeed the right one.

Dictionary

This chapter began with a discussion of unproductive dictionary use—looking up words and copying and memorizing definitions. There are, however, a variety of ways to promote active use of the dictionary to help students broaden their concepts and also teach them what a valuable resource the dictionary is. Students should learn to turn to the dictionary to find out about an unfamiliar word on a scavenger hunt list. The teacher should regularly ask one child to consult the dictionary when a new word occurs and the meaning of that word is unclear. A teacher who regularly says, "Let's see what the dictionary can tell us about this word" and sends one child to look it up is modeling the way adults who use the dictionary actually use it. (Did you ever see an adult look up a word to copy and memorize the definition? Maybe the reason so few adults use the dictionary is because that is the only way they have ever seen anyone use it!) If you have a dictionary on your classroom computers, model how useful this is by saying to a child, "See what our computer dictionary has to say about this word."

In many classrooms, helpers are appointed to jobs each week. Someone greets visitors, someone collects papers, someone waters the plants, and so on. Why not appoint a weekly "Dictionary Disciple"? This person gets possession of the dictionary and is always ready to be dispatched to the farthest corners of the wide world of words to seek and share facts about them.

Teach Children to Monitor Their Vocabulary Knowledge

One of the first steps in learning anything is recognizing that you don't already know it. Children need to notice when they come to words they don't have meanings for. Sometimes, young children get so focused on pronouncing a new word that they fail to realize they don't know what it means. Children can be taught to self-assess their vocabulary knowledge using a simple scale like this one:

1 = I never heard of that word.

2 = I heard the word but I don't know what it means.

3 = I think I know what that word means.

4 = I'm sure I know what that word means.

5 = I can make a good sentence with that word.

This scale could be used with any of the activities for teaching vocabulary. To make this quick and easy, consider using a five-finger, every-pupil-response system. Say the word you are focusing on, and ask everyone to show you the appropriate number of fingers. When you are focusing on a word for the first time, be sure that you positively acknowledge all the responses so that children do not get in the habit of showing you five fingers just so they "look good." Try acknowledging their vocabulary self-assessment with comments such as these:

> "I see lots of one and two fingers. That makes me happy because I know I chose a word you need when I chose *desperate. Desperate* is an important word and lots of you don't know it yet."
>
> "Some of you think you know the meaning of *desperate,* and some of you are sure you do. Can someone tell me what you think it means?"
>
> "I see someone with five fingers up. Todd, tell me your sentence that shows the meaning of *desperate.*"

After you have worked with the new vocabulary words for several days, ask children again to show you how well they know the meanings of these words and comment on how many people are showing four or five fingers. Many teachers display a chart, such as the one below, to help children remember the five-finger vocabulary self-assessment system.

"I never heard
of that word."

"I heard the word but I don't
know what it means."

"I think I know what
that word means."

"I'm sure I know what
that word means."

"I can make a good sentence
with that word."

Teach Children to Monitor Their Vocabulary Knowledge

Promote Word Wonder

Enthusiasm is contagious! Teachers who are enthusiastic about words project that enthusiasm by conveying their eagerness to learn unfamiliar words and by sharing fascinating words they encounter outside the classroom. Young children are usually enthusiastic about new words, repeating them over and over, enjoying the sound of language, and marveling at the meanings being expressed. Encourage the continuation of this natural enthusiasm. Open your class to wondering about words, to asking spontaneous questions about unfamiliar words, and to making judgments about the sounds and values of words.

We hope this chapter has increased your "word wonder" and that you see that the activities described are all intended to transmit the "Words are wonderful" message. In addition to the ideas already described, here are a few more "tricks of the trade" for turning all your students into "word wizards."

Display Words in Various Ways

Displaying words enhances learning by calling attention to particular terms and signaling the importance of learning them. We have already suggested some ways of displaying words in your classroom. The Three Read-Aloud Words can be displayed along with the cover of the book, and the children can add tally marks as they hear, read, or sneak these words into conversations at school and at home. The scavenger hunt words, along with their objects and pictures, can be displayed on a bulletin board created by the winning team. Words that are dramatized can be added to lists of other words dramatized in the past. Class books can be made both for general words and for specific science and social studies words. Vocabulary boards are effective tools for calling attention to words and their meanings. Words can be displayed on a word wall or bulletin board so that all students can see them. Once the words are up, students can visit and revisit them to learn their meanings.

Many teachers like students to keep vocabulary notebooks. If you do this, make sure your students see themselves as word collectors rather than definition copiers. In fact, most teachers do not allow students to copy any definitions into their notebooks. Rather, the students include the sentences in which they found the words and note their personal connections with the words. Students often enjoy illustrating the words in their collections with pictures and diagrams. Some older word sleuths like to include information about the words' origins.

RICH resources

Word Play

Brian Wildsmith's Amazing World of Words, by Brian Wildsmith (1997)

Double Trouble in Walla Walla, by Andrew Clements (1997)

Night Knight, by Harriet Ziefert (1997)

Tangle Town, by Kurt Cyrus (1997)

Read Books about Words to Your Students

Some books for children call special attention to words by presenting them in humorous or unusual ways. Countless children have delighted in Amelia Bedelia's literal attempts to dress a chicken and draw the drapes. Sharing books with children that celebrate and play with words is just one more way to show your students you are a serious word lover.

Designate a Weekly "Words Are Wonderful Day"

Choose a day of the week and designate it as "Words Are Wonderful Day." Do a variety of things to celebrate words that day. Read a wonderful word play book during your teacher read-aloud. Share a new word that you have come across in the last week. Find a crossword puzzle your children would enjoy, and let them work in teams to complete it.

Culminate this day by picking "One Wonderful Word." Let students nominate various words that have been highlighted throughout the past week, and let everyone vote for the most wonderful word. Display this word on some kind of trophy chart along with all the other wonderful words chosen in previous weeks.

the tech-savvy TEACHER

Word Wonder on the Computer

All your students probably love to do things on the computer, and your computer can help your students develop word wonder. These three sites have a variety of games and puzzles:

wordcentral.com

vocabulary.com

wordplays.com

Wordcentral lets your students build their own dictionaries. Wordplays.com has games and puzzles in many different languages.

Summary

As we try to close the achievement gap and make high levels of literacy possible for all children, we must pay renewed attention to the issue of meaning vocabulary. In 1977, Becker identified the lack of vocabulary as a crucial factor underlying the failure of many economically disadvantaged students. In 1995, Hart and Risley described a relationship between growing up in poverty and having a restricted vocabulary. In 2001, Biemiller and Slonim cited evidence that the lack of vocabulary is a key component underlying school failure for disadvantaged students. More and more of the children in U.S. schools are English language learners. The limited English vocabularies of many of these children is one of the major factors impeding their literacy development.

Researchers now agree that most meaning vocabulary is learned indirectly, probably through teacher read-aloud and independent reading. Research supports both the direct teaching of some words and the teaching of vocabulary learning strategies (Baumann, Kame'enui, & Ash, 2003; Blachowicz & Fisher, 2000; Graves & Watts-Taffe, 2002; NRP, 2000). All experts indicate that the number of words directly taught must be kept to a minimum because the words need to be thoroughly taught and students need to meet them in a number of different contexts across some span of time. The need for children to actively encounter the words in different contexts over an extended period of time led the NRP to recommend choosing many of the words for direct teaching from content-area subjects. In addition to the direct teaching of a limited number of useful, frequently occurring words, research supports teaching children word-learning strategies, including using context and morphemic clues to determine word meanings and learning to use dictionaries and other word resources.

The activities described in this chapter are designed to teach children some vocabulary directly and to maximize their learning of words from teacher read-aloud and their own independent reading. In addition, children will learn how context and morphemes give them clues to words and how to use dictionaries to clarify the meanings of words. Equally important, in vocabulary-rich classrooms, children learn how to assess their own vocabulary knowledge and develop a sense of word wonder that will propel them to continue to develop vivid, vital, and valuable vocabularies.

chapter 7

Developing Thoughtful Comprehenders

A myth about children who have difficulty with reading comprehension is that they "just can't think!" In reality, everybody thinks all the time, and some struggling readers who must take care of themselves (and often younger brothers and sisters) are especially good thinkers and problem solvers. If children can "predict" that the ball game will be canceled when they see the sky darkening up and can "conclude" that the coach is mad about something when he walks in with a scowl on his face, then they can and do engage in higher-level thinking processes. The real problem is not that they cannot think but that they do not think while they read. Why don't they think while they read?

Some children do not think while they read because they do not really know that they should! Imagine an extreme case of a child who had never been read to and had never heard people talking about what they read. Imagine that this child goes to a school in which beginning reading is taught in a "learn the letters and sounds" and "read the words aloud perfectly" way. This child would learn to read words just as you would read this nonsensical sentence:

He bocked the piffle with a gid daft.

You can read all the "words" correctly, and you can even read with expression, but you get no meaning. In your case, of course, you get no meaning because there is no meaning there to get.

For children who have limited literacy experience and who are taught to read in a rigid, phonics-first method with texts written to include only decodable words (*Tad has a tan hat*), the real danger is that they will not learn that thinking is the goal. The goal, to them, is sounding out all the words, which is what they try to do. Ask them what reading is, and they are apt to look at you as if you are a complete fool and tell you that reading is saying all the words right! The ability to decode is critical, but when we overemphasize accurate word pronunciation and only provide beginning reading materials in which all the words are "decodable," we can create readers who not only misread the purpose of reading but also do not comprehend the story.

Some struggling readers are unaware that they should be thinking while they are reading, and many have inadequate background knowledge for understanding the books and curriculum materials in their schools. Read the next two sentences and think about the implications for your teaching:

Current models do not allow expectancy-based processing to influence feature extraction from words. Indeed, most current models largely restrict expectancy-based processing and hypothesis-testing mechanisms to the postlexical level. (Stanovich, 1991, p. 419)

You are probably wondering why we would waste book space (and your time) on these two nonsensical sentences. In reality, these sentences are not nonsensical. They actually have meaning, and if you are a research psychologist, you can think and talk intelligently about them! For most of us, however, we can say these words, but we cannot really read them because we are unable to think as we say them. Background knowledge, which includes topically related vocabulary, is one of the major determinants of reading comprehension.

In addition to specific knowledge about the topic, knowledge about the type of text about to be read is called up as well. When you begin to read a story or a novel, a whole set of expectations based on other stories that have been heard or read are called up. You do not know who the characters are but you do expect to find characters. You also know that the story takes place in a particular time and place (setting) and that goals will be achieved or problems will be resolved. In short, you have a story structure in your head that allows you to fit what is read into an overall organization.

Imagine that you are going to read a *Consumer Guide* article on the newest car models. Again, you do not know what specific information you will learn, but you do have expectations about the type of information and how it will be related. You expect to find charts comparing the cars on different features and to find judgments about which cars appear to be the best buys.

Imagine that you are about to read a travel magazine article about North Carolina. You have never been there and do not know anyone who has, so you do not know too many specifics. However, you do have expectations about what you will learn and about how that information will be organized. You expect to learn some facts about the history of North Carolina, along with some descriptions of historical regions and locations in the state. You also expect to find information about places tourists like to visit, such as the coast and the mountains. You would not be surprised to find a summary of the cultural and sporting events that are unique to North Carolina. Information about the climate and the best times to visit different parts of the state, as well as some information on how to get there and places to stay, would also be expected. As you begin to read, you may create a mental outline, or web, that helps you understand and organize topic and subtopic information.

The different ways in which various reading materials are organized are referred to as *text structures* and *genres*. To comprehend what we are reading, we must be familiar with the way in which the information is organized. The fact that most children can understand and remember stories much better than informational text is probably because they have listened to and have read many more stories and thus know what to expect and how to organize the story information. To create readers who think about what they read, we must help them become familiar with a variety of ways that authors organize ideas in their writing.

Even with a clear understanding that reading is primarily thinking, sufficient background knowledge, and a familiarity with the kind of text structure being read, you cannot think about what you read unless you can identify a majority of the words. Try to make sense of this next sentence, in which all words of three or more syllables have been replaced by blanks:

> The _____ _____ fresh ideas for action and _____
> new _____ that will help the _____ _____ and the _____
> meet the challenge of _____ adult and _____ _____
> worldwide.

Now read the same sentence but put the words *conference, provided, generated, partnerships, literacy, community, association, promoting, adolescent,* and *literacy* in the blanks. To learn to think while you read, you must

1. Be able to quickly identify almost all the words.
2. Have sufficient background knowledge that you can connect to the new information.
3. Be familiar with the type of text and be able to see how the author has organized the ideas.
4. Have a mindset that reading is thinking and know how to apply your thinking in comprehension strategies.

Comprehension Strategies

The different kinds of thinking that we do as we read are referred to as *comprehension strategies*. As you read, your brain uses these thinking strategies:

- Calling up and connecting relevant prior knowledge
- Predicting, questioning, and wondering about what will be learned and what will happen
- Visualizing or imagining what the experience would look, feel, sound, taste, and smell like
- Monitoring comprehension and using fix-up strategies such as rereading, pictures, and asking for help when you cannot make sense of what you read
- Determining the most important ideas and events and summarizing what you have read
- Drawing conclusions and making inferences based on what is read
- Evaluating and making judgments about what you think: Did you like it? Did you agree? Was it funny? Could it really happen?

In teaching all these strategies, your big goal is for your students to use them not just during the lessons but to become automatic at thinking strategically whenever and wherever they are reading. To do this, you will want to provide lots of modeling in initial lessons and then gradually turn over the responsibility for thinking to your students. This gradual release of responsibility model of instruction suggests that for any learning task, responsibility should shift slowly and purposefully from teacher-as-model, to joint responsibility, to independent practice and application by the learner (Pearson & Gallagher, 1983). The teacher moves from assuming all of the responsibility to having the students assume all of the responsibility. Depending on the complexity of the task, this gradual release may occur over a day, a week, a month, or even a year. It may help you to conceptualize this by thinking about this sequence.

I do, you watch. (Teacher models.)

I do, you help. (Teacher models and invites suggestions from students.)

You do, I help. (Students work on strategy in small groups with teacher support as needed.)

You do, I watch. (Students apply strategy independently; teacher observes and assesses.)

Many different, engaging, and research-supported ways can be used to carry out comprehension lessons, and there are three compelling reasons to use a large variety of lessons. First, comprehension is primarily thinking, and thinking involves many complex processes, so no one type of comprehension lesson can teach all the different kinds of thinking. Second, comprehension of story text and informational text requires different kinds of mental organizing. Third, children differ on all kinds of dimensions, including the types of comprehension lessons that engage their attention and help them learn how to think while reading. We organize our comprehension lessons into four categories: literate conversations, think-alouds, informational text lessons, and story text lessons. As you use the different lesson frameworks across the year, follow the gradual release of responsibility model and your students will become more strategic and thoughtful readers.

Literate Conversations

Asking your students questions after reading may provide you with a quick assessment of student understanding, but traditional question and answer sessions do not offer much in the way of comprehension strategy instruction. When your students engage in conversations about what they read, their understanding improves (Fall, Webb, & Cudowsky, 2000). So how do you get good conversations going in your classroom?

A good first step is to modify the questions you do ask so that you are asking more open-ended questions. *Open-ended questions* are those that can have multiple correct responses. For instance, after reading you might ask:

Is there anything you want to know more about?

Is there anything you are wondering about?

Does this remind you of anything else you have read?

What did you think about . . . ?

Has anything like this ever happened to you?

Were you surprised by anything you read?

Did anyone in the book remind you of someone you know?

Each of these open-ended questions allows for a range of responses. Open-ended questions serve to begin a conversation about the material read. In many respects, the goal is to create the kind of conversation that adults typically engage in when discussing something they have read. Adults do not interrogate each other. They do not ask each other the types of questions that teachers typically have asked. Instead, they discuss, they converse. The goal is to share understandings and through this to gain an even better understanding of the material read.

One way to think about creating classroom conversations is provided by Keene and Zimmerman (1997). The framework they provide focuses on helping children think about three types of connections:

1. Text to self (Do any of you have a pet that is creating problems like the one in the story?)
2. Text to text (What other book have we read where a child was brave?)
3. Text to world (Has anyone ever ridden on a subway? Tell us what it was like.)

It is just these kinds of connections that good readers make as they read. It is these kinds of connections we make as we discuss something we have read with a friend or colleague.

Some students find responding to open-ended questions easier than others do. Some find it easier to make connections. To help all your students develop and refine their ability to engage in literate conversations, you can model making connections after a read-aloud activity. In other words, after a read-aloud you might say, "This story reminds me of *The Little Engine That Could* because the boy in the story just wouldn't give up." Next, you might share a personal incident of persistence in your life and ask your students to make the same connections.

In addition to modeling (I do, you watch) and inviting your students to share (I do, you help), you will want to move the responsibility for conversations about reading to your students (you do, I help). Literature circles are a good venue for conducting these small-group conversations. The typical literature circle has three to seven members, all reading the same text on a common schedule. Each group is reading a different book but the books are connected by theme (courage), genre (biography), or topic (the Civil War). Research by Day, Spiegel, McLellan, and Brown (2002) found that comprehension instruction organized in literature circles fostered:

- Greater opportunities for children to talk
- More natural contexts for conversation
- Ability to find texts all members of the group can and want to read
- Greater choice of books for all students
- Cooperation and collaboration
- Personal responsibility

In addition to giving students multiple opportunities to develop thoughtful literacy by engaging them in conversations guided by higher-level questions, there are two other types of activities you can use to ensure that your students engage in literate conversations. In "Questioning the Author," you and your students raise questions that you would like to discuss with the author. In the "Oprah Winfrey Interview," you and your students become interviewers—like Oprah—and you interview characters from the books you have been reading.

Questioning the Author (QTA)　When we read, we do not just understand what the author is saying; rather, we figure out what the author means. This might sound like a picky distinction, but helping struggling readers put this distinction into practice as they read makes a huge difference in their comprehension. If you have ever taught students who read a passage carefully and then tell you they cannot answer the questions because the passage "didn't say!," you have experienced the reason students need to have their reading guided by a constructivist strategy such as Questioning the Author (QTA).

The word *constructivist* is currently in danger of death from overuse, but it names a simple and powerful concept. When we read, we use the author's words to construct meaning. The meaning is more than what the author has written. Authors cannot tell us everything. They assume we know some things that we will connect to what they are telling us. They assume that we will form some opinions based on what they tell us and what we know. Our initial assertion—that reading, at its heart, is thinking—means that reading is a constructive activity. Readers construct meaning by understanding what the author is saying, figuring out what the author means, and forming opinions based on the author's meaning and what the reader already knows.

Several things distinguish QTAs from other comprehension-fostering formats. The most important differences to us are that the instruction goes on not before students read or after students read but as students are reading, and that the teacher's job is to pose queries that foster meaning construction, not to ask questions to assess if that meaning construction took place. To plan a QTA lesson, the teacher carefully reads the text and decides (1) what the important ideas are and what problems students might have figuring out these ideas, (2) how much of the text to read in each segment before stopping for discussion, and (3) what queries to pose that might help students construct meaning from the text. A clear distinction is made between *queries,* which lead the students to think and construct, and *questions,* which usually assess whether students have been able to think or construct. The teacher's job in a QTA is to pose the types of queries that can help

RICH resources

Literate Conversations

This description of QTA is based on an excellent book by Isabel Beck, Margaret McKeown, Rebecca Hamilton, and Linda Kucan (1997) that gives detailed examples of QTA lessons, suggestions for planning and implementing QTA lessons, and results of QTA use in several classrooms. If our brief description intrigues you, we highly recommend you read their practical and clearly written book.

students use what they know and figure out what the author means. Having decided on important ideas and segmented the texts, teachers plan both initiating and follow-up queries. The following example is adapted from Beck and colleagues (1997) as students are about to read and construct meaning for a social studies passage on how Pennsylvania was formed.

The teacher and students are seated in a circle or horseshoe shape so that they can all see each other. They all have copies of the book open. For this lesson, the teacher has decided that the first segment to be read is just the first sentence. She tells the students to read the first sentence to themselves:

The shape of the land in North America has changed over millions of years. (p. 51)

And then she poses a typical initiating query:

"What do you think the author is telling us?"

Initially, students may want to respond by just reading the sentence aloud, but the teacher responds by saying,

"Yes, that's what the author says, but what is the author trying to tell us?"

The teacher then poses the follow-up query designed to help them connect information learned in previous chapters.

"What have we already learned about the different kinds of shapes land can have that we need to connect here?"

The second segment contained many sentences and ended the paragraph. It is important to note that the segment division is not determined by paragraphs but by ideas. (Sometimes you want to make sure students are constructing meaning from a single sentence, and sometimes you may want them to read several paragraphs.) The teacher segments the text so that students stop at points where they need to construct important meanings. This segment developed the concept of glaciers, and after students had read this segment to themselves, the teacher initiated the query:

"What is the author telling us about snow and ice and glaciers?"

The QTA continued with the teacher telling the students how much to read and posing both initiating and follow-up queries until students had shared their thinking to construct meaning for this difficult and complex text.

Children often think that authors are infallible! In doing QTAs with your students, you can point out that authors are not perfect! Sometimes authors do not write clearly. Sometimes they assume we know lots of things that we do not know, and they leave out important facts. When you and your students engage in regular QTAs, they learn that when you are reading, you try to figure out what the author means—not just remember what the author says. With this epiphany, your students are set on the path to constructing meaning and active reading.

The Oprah Winfrey Interview   The Oprah Winfrey Interview is another technique that fosters literate conversations. To model what you want students to do, you play the role of Oprah in the first several lessons and interview characters in a book (your students) about their lives and roles. For instance, after reading *Anastasia at Your Service*, assign students the roles of Anastasia, Mrs. Bellingham, and her granddaughter, Daphne. (You could also add Mr. and Mrs. Krupnik, Sam, and perhaps the surgeon or the maid.) Now, just like Oprah, invite the students to appear on your "show." Arrange chairs alongside your desk, facing the rest of the class. Seat the "guests," with Anastasia next to your desk, and welcome them. Start your interview with some broad question:

> "Tell me a bit about yourself, Anastasia."
> "What seemed to be the problem?"

Then move to other characters for verification:

> "Do you agree with her, Daphne?"
> "What else would you add, Mrs. Bellingham?"

Next, turn to the audience (your other students) for questions.

Basically, like Oprah, you let your guests tell their stories. Ideally, readers transform themselves into the characters, taking on mannerisms and speech patterns that seem appropriate. You may want to model this transformation yourself by letting a student take Oprah's role while you become Mrs. Bellingham or another character. This activity can be brief (3 to 5 minutes is all most guests get on talk shows!) and takes little time to set up once your students understand the interview format.

Of course, when you have modeled what Oprah and guests do, you will want to turn over the Oprah and other roles to your students. If students are reading different books in their literature circles, each group can plan and "perform" their Oprah show. Students who have read other books become the audience and, just as on the Oprah show, they get involved by asking questions.

Literate Conversations

Literate conversations mimic the conversations real readers in the real world have about real books they really want to talk about! The key to good literate conversations is to help your students learn to ask and think about the questions real readers ask each other and friends who have read the book. Real readers do not interrogate each other about books. They do not ask "Who were the main characters?" or "What year did the conflict break out?" Rather, they ask and converse about the big ideas—and particularly their reactions to and feelings about what they have read. To promote literate conversations in your room:

1. Conduct your discussions with your readers as conversations—not interrogations. Ask them higher-level questions that require reactions and responses—questions to which you don't know the answer because there isn't one right answer.

2. Model for your students the types of connections readers make—text to self, text to text, and text to world. If your comments and questions regularly focus them on these connections, your students will get in the habit of making these connections when reading on their own.

3. Arrange for students to have literate conversations in small groups. Literature circles is one format for organizing small-group conversations.

4. For variety, use Questioning the Author and the Oprah Winfrey Interview to increase the number of people with whom your students can have conversations. Be sure to model what you want students to do before handing over the responsibility for these conversations to them.

Think-Alouds

Think-alouds are a way of modeling or "making public" the thinking that goes on inside your head as you read. To explain think-alouds to your students, tell them that two voices are really speaking as you read. The voice you can usually hear is your voice reading the words but inside your brain is another voice telling you what it thinks about what you are reading. In think-alouds you can demonstrate for your students how we think as we read.

Across your lessons, try to include all the thinking strategies. Show your students you are making connections by starting sentences like these:

> "This reminds me of . . . "
> "I remember something like this happened to me when . . . "
> "I read another book where the character . . . "
> "This is like in our school when . . . "
> "Our country doesn't have that holiday, but we have . . . "

Demonstrate how your brain predicts, questions, and wonders:

> "I wonder if . . . "
>
> "I wonder who . . . "
>
> "I think I know what is coming next . . . "
>
> "He will be in trouble if . . . "
>
> "I think we will learn how . . . "

Stop periodically and summarize the most important ideas or events:

> "The most important thing I've learned so far is . . . "
>
> "So far in our story . . . "
>
> "So far I have learned that . . . "

Share the conclusions and inferences you are making based on the facts you have read:

> "It didn't say why she did that, but I bet . . . "
>
> "I know he must be feeling . . . "

Demonstrate how you monitor meanings and use fix-up strategies:

> "I wonder what it means when it says . . . "
>
> "I don't understand . . . "
>
> "It didn't make sense when . . . "
>
> "I'm going to reread that because it didn't make sense that . . . "

Share the images, pictures, and visualizations your brain creates:

> "Even though it isn't in the picture, I can see the . . . "
>
> "Mmm, I can almost taste the . . . "
>
> "That sent chills down my spine when it said . . . "
>
> "For a minute I thought I could smell . . . "
>
> "I could hear the . . . "
>
> "I can imagine what it is like to . . . "
>
> "I can picture the . . . "

Share your opinions, judgments, and evaluations:

> "My favorite part in this chapter was . . . "
>
> "I really liked how the author . . . "
>
> "What I don't like about this part is . . . "
>
> "It was really interesting to learn that . . . "
>
> "I am going to try this out when I . . . "
>
> "I wish I could . . . "
>
> "If I were her, I would . . . "

To help you remember these thinking strategies, we have created an acronym:

CIPCOMS: Connect Imagine Predict Conclude Opine Monitor Summarize

Teachers use think-alouds in a variety of ways, but the most efficient and effective use of time is probably to read and think-aloud the first quarter or third of a selection the children are about to read. In addition to hearing you think your way through the text, children get introduced to the selection, including characters, setting, type of writing, and important vocabulary. After listening to you think-aloud your way through the first part of the text, children collaborate in small groups, finish reading the selection, and share the thinking voices inside their brains.

The following example of a think-aloud is based on the first part of *Missing: One Stuffed Rabbit* by Maryann Cocca-Leffler (1999). The think-aloud begins with the cover of the book. The teacher reads aloud the title, *Missing: One Stuffed Rabbit,* and looks at the picture, saying something like what follows:

> "This is an intriguing illustration on the cover of the book. A girl is reading from a notebook labeled Coco, and she looks very unhappy. The two children listening look surprised and upset. Because the title of the book is Missing: One Stuffed Rabbit, I bet the unhappy and surprised looks have something to do with the lost rabbit. I wonder who lost the rabbit and who the rabbit is and what the notebook has to do with it?"

The teacher turns the page and thinks aloud about the picture on the first two pages:

> "I see a teacher holding a stuffed rabbit and reaching into a fishbowl to pull out a slip of paper. The children in the class are all watching her. They all look happy and excited. In the other picture is the stuffed rabbit and the notebook labeled Coco. I bet Coco is the name of the stuffed rabbit."

The teacher then reads aloud the text on these two pages, which explains that Coco is indeed the stuffed rabbit and that the teacher is pulling the name of one student who will get to take Coco home for the weekend. She pulls out a slip of paper and the lucky winner is Janine!

> "I bet Janine is the girl in the front in the glasses. She is also the unhappy-looking girl on the cover, reading from Coco's notebook."

The teacher turns the page and thinks aloud first about the pictures.

> "There's Janine looking very happy and hugging Coco and his notebook."

The teacher reads the text aloud and we discover that the notebook is Coco's diary. Each student gets to take Coco home overnight and write Coco's thoughts about the adventure in his diary.

> "I used to have a diary when I was younger. I wrote in it every night."

The next two pages have some of the diary entries written by children who have already taken Coco home and helped him write about his adventures. We learn that Coco fell off the monkey bars while playing with Danny, went to Matthew's soccer game and cheered when Matthew got a goal, and went to the skating rink with Christina. The teacher makes these comments:

> "I love how the author showed the diary pages. I can tell different children wrote them because you can see the different handwriting. I can't wait to see what Janine does with Coco and what she writes in the diary."

The pictures and text on the next two pages show Janine and Coco being picked up by Janine's mom and heading home. They stop to visit with Janine's Nana. On this page the teacher models self monitoring:

> "It says Nana cut some carrots for Coco. Nana is a funny name. I wonder who she is?"

The following pages show Janine and Coco having a good time together. Janine reads Coco a bedtime story and gives him a ride on the back of her bike. After reading these four pages, the teacher comments:

> "They seem to be having such a good time. But I am worried. I remember how unhappy Janine looked on the cover, and the title of the book says a stuffed rabbit is missing. I hope Janine is not going to let Coco get lost!"

Think-Alouds

The next four pages show the family shopping at the mall and, sure enough, as they are having lunch, Janine realizes that she cannot find Coco! She thought she put him in one of the bags, but he is not there. Coco is missing!

> "I can just imagine how Janine must be feeling. She looks like she is going to cry, and I feel like crying too! How could she have lost him? Will she find him? What will the other kids—and the teacher!—say if she doesn't find him?"

At this point in the book, the teacher stops reading and thinking aloud and turns to the children, asking them what they think will happen. They share some ideas and the looks on their faces show how concerned they are. The teacher quickly reviews the pages read and reminds the children that she shared her thinking with them about the pictures and the words. Next, the teacher forms small groups of three or four students and tells them that it is now their turn to read and share their thinking. She chooses one group to model for the others what they will do, and, with the teacher's help, this group shares their thinking about the pictures and words on the next two-page spread. The teacher tells them that when they read, little voices inside their heads tell them what their brains are thinking. "When we do think-alouds," says the teacher, "we let that little voice talk out loud so that we can hear what all our different brains are thinking."

The groups form and begin reading. The teacher circulates to the various groups and helps them take turns and verbalize their thinking. She also writes down some of the most interesting thoughts to share with the whole group when they reconvene after reading to react to the story and "debrief" their thinking.

English Language Learners

Modeling and having students engage in think-alouds and literate conversations are important for all your students. Think about how much more important they are for your students who are learning English as they learn to comprehend. When you are modeling and inviting children to join in the modeling, your English language learners can watch, listen, and learn without being required to produce any language. Of course they do need to learn how to produce language but much of this production (talk) is done within the "safe" context of a small group, rather than in front of the whole class.

Many teachers, when they first hear about think-alouds, are afraid to do them because they do not know exactly what they are supposed to think! We hope that our example shows you that your brain is thinking as you read, and if you tune into that thinking and learn how to communicate your thinking to children, think-alouds are not difficult to do. It is important to read the selection and plan what you are going to say as you think aloud. Many teachers find it helpful to attach sticky notes with reminders to the appropriate pages. We try to use as many different ways of expressing our thinking as we can and try to have it match as closely as we can the thinking actually engendered by the text.

Although we normally invite participation, it is important not to let the children "chime in" as you are thinking. If you use the procedure of beginning the selection with your think-aloud and finishing the selection with the children sharing their think-alouds, they are usually willing to let you have your turn! Some teachers tell the children that they are to pretend to be invisible while the teacher is reading and thinking. They get to hear the teacher thinking, but they are invisible and should not let the teacher know they are there! You want to signal the children when you are reading and when you are thinking. Many teachers look at the book when they are reading and then look away from the book—perhaps up toward the ceiling—when they are thinking. Other teachers use a different voice to signal their thinking. They read in their "reading voice" and think in their "thinking voice."

Think-Alouds

The goal of comprehension instruction is that children learn how to think as they read on their own. Think-alouds help children see what good comprehenders do. If you do your think-aloud based on the first part of the selection they are going to read, you give them a "jumpstart" into the selection. To do think-alouds,

1. Choose a selection that truly causes you to think.

2. Decide how much of that selection you will read aloud.

3. Look at the pictures and read the selection before you do the think-aloud. Look for places where you actually use different thinking strategies—CIPCOMS . Think about how you will explain your thinking to your children. Write your thoughts on sticky notes and attach to the pages.

4. Do the think-aloud as the "invisible" children watch and listen. Comment on pictures first; then read the text, stopping at appropriate places and sharing your thoughts.

5. Put your students in groups to share their thinking as they finish the selection or read another selection.

Two wonderful sources just full of examples to teach children to think and share their thinking are *Strategies That Work* (Harvey & Goudvis, 2000) and *Mosaic of Thought* (Keene & Zimmerman, 1997).

Informational Text Lessons

Most children are much better at comprehending stories than at comprehending informational text. If your students have difficulty with informational text, they approach reading informational text with less confidence and enthusiasm. Engage your students in KWL lessons and teach them how to construct a variety of graphic organizers and they will become better and more enthusiastic readers of informational text.

KWL

One of the most flexible and popular ways of guiding students' thinking is KWL (Carr & Ogle, 1987; Ogle, 1986). The letters stand for what we *know,* what we *want* to find out, and what we have *learned.* This strategy works especially well with informational text.

Imagine that you are planning to have your students read about Washington, D.C. Have your students locate Washington, D.C., on a map and ask if any of them have ever been there. Let any students who have been to Washington, D.C., share their experiences with the rest of the class. Next, begin a KWL chart.

Washington, D.C.		
What we know	**What we want to find out**	**What we learned**

Have students brainstorm what they know about Washington, D.C., and write their responses in the first column.

Washington, D.C.		
What we know	**What we want to find out**	**What we learned**
Capitol White House president lives there lots of drugs azaleas in spring cold in winter near Virginia near Maryland		

Next, direct your students' attention to the second column and ask them what they would like to find out about Washington, D.C. List some of their questions in the second column:

Washington, D.C.		
What we know	**What we want to find out**	**What we learned**
Capitol	How old is it?	
White House	How big is the White House?	
president lives there	What else is in D.C.?	
lots of drugs	Where is the FBI?	
azaleas in spring	What kind of government does D.C. have?	
cold in winter		
near Virginia	Why do so many people visit D.C.?	
near Maryland	How many people live there?	
	What do the people do who aren't in the government?	

After the questions are listed, have students read to find out which questions were answered and to find other interesting "tidbits" they think are important. After reading, record any answers to questions and other interesting facts in the third column. Put a question mark next to any information that is not clear or disputed by other members of the class.

When all the initial recalls are recorded, let your students go back to the text to clarify, prove, or fill in gaps. Have students read the relevant part aloud and help them explain their thinking. When the information on the chart is complete and accurate, point out how much was learned and how efficiently the chart helped to record it. Inevitably, some questions are not answered in the reading. Challenge your more inquisitive students to find the answers to these questions.

Graphic Organizers

Another way you can help your students better comprehend informational text is to use a variety of graphic organizers. Webs are the most commonly used graphic organizers at the elementary level and they help your students summarize and organize information.

Imagine that your class is going to read an informational selection about birds. You might begin a web to help them organize the information they will be learning. As you set up each spoke of the web, have your students predict what they might expect to find out: "What are some ways you already know that birds move? What do you already know that birds eat? What body parts do birds have?" Have your students read to find out more about birds. After reading, the children reconvene and complete the web.

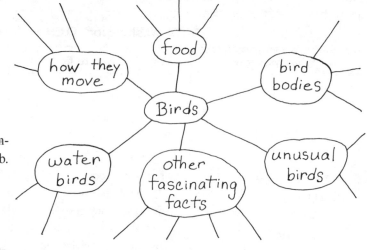

Webs are efficient graphic organizers for topic and subtopic information, but many other ways to show types of relationships exist. A feature matrix helps students organize information about several members of a category. Imagine that your students are reading a selection that compares and contrasts many different types of birds. This information would be better organized in a feature matrix than in a web. Here is what that feature matrix skeleton might look like:

Birds						
	fly	swim	build nests	lay eggs	have feathers	molt
robins						
whippoorwills						
penguins						
ostriches						

Before reading, talk with your students about the birds listed and the categories. Have them make predictions based on what they know about which birds fly, swim, build nests, and so forth. Point out the four blank lines and tell your students that in addition to robins, whippoorwills, penguins, and ostriches, four other birds will be described. Their job is to decide which features apply to the four birds listed on the matrix and to the four other birds they will add after reading. Once everyone has read the selection, lead them to fill in a yes/no or a +/– for each feature.

Data charts are another way of helping children organize information that compares and contrasts members of the same category. Rather than indicate whether something has a feature, children fill in particular facts. Here is a data chart used in a science classroom:

Planets in Our Solar System			
Name	Size (1 = biggest)	Distance from sun	Earth days in year
Earth	5	92,960,000 mi.	365
Mars			
	1		
		3,660,000,000 mi.	
			60,188

To begin this chart, you might partially fill in the chart for the students, talking as you write about what is needed in each column:

"Earth is the fifth-largest planet. Its mean distance from the sun is 92,960,000 miles. The year is the number of days it takes a planet to orbit the sun, and the Earth year is 365 days."

Now you point to the second row and have students explain what they will try to put in each column about Mars. For the third row, help them notice that because you put a 1 in the size column, this planet has to be the biggest planet. The fourth row must be completed for the planet that is 3,660,000,000 miles from the sun. The planet that takes 60,188 Earth days to orbit the sun goes in the fifth row. The remaining rows are filled in with the remaining planets.

Webs, feature matrices, and data charts are the most popular graphic organizers used in elementary classrooms, but they are not the only possibilities. Here are two other types of graphic organizers:

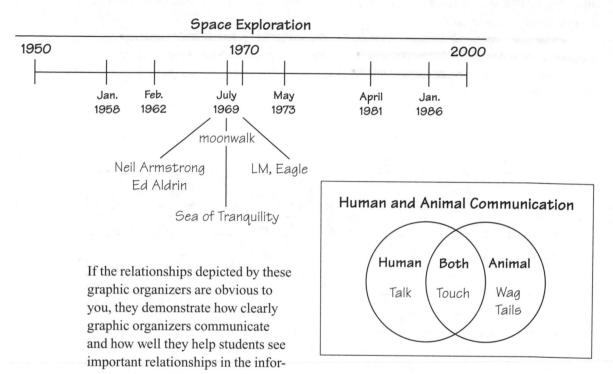

If the relationships depicted by these graphic organizers are obvious to you, they demonstrate how clearly graphic organizers communicate and how well they help students see important relationships in the information they are reading. In the Venn diagram (which children like to call a "double bubble") children compare and contrast how animals and humans communicate. The time line is an excellent device to use when order or sequence is important—for instance, in history, historical fiction, and biography. Students fill in the important space exploration events that occurred on each date and a few details about each. A variation is to give students a time line of events and have them fill in the dates.

English Language Learners

Using a variety of graphic organizers to help your students organize information they are reading provides the "comprehensible input" necessary for your students learning English to build concepts and add to their English vocabularies.

Informational Text Lessons

KWL

KWLs help your students connect what they know to new information.

1. Before beginning the chart, lead a general discussion of children's experiences with the topic. By letting your students discuss these experiences (e.g., "My uncle lives in Washington"; "We're going to go to Washington some summer"), you avoid having to put these "experiences" in the known column.

2. After the discussion of experiences, ask children what they know about the topic and list these in the K (*known*) column. If children disagree about a fact, put it in the W (*want*) column with a question mark. ("Washington is in Virginia." "No, it's not!" Record this exchange as *Is Washington in Virginia?*)

3. When you have all the known facts recorded, show the children what they will read and ask them to come up with questions they think that text will answer. If their questions are too specific, help make them broader.

4. After reading, begin with the questions first and add answers to the L (*learned*) column. Then add other important facts.

5. If they are going to continue reading about the topic for another day, ask them whether what they have read so far has helped them think of more questions that the remaining part might answer. Add these to the W column.

Graphic Organizers

Graphic organizers help children organize and summarize information.

1. Look at the text and decide how the information can best be organized. If the text structure is topic/subtopic/details, you probably want a web or a data chart. If the text compares two or more things, a feature matrix, data chart, or Venn diagram works well. Time lines help your students focus on sequence.

2. Let your students see you construct the graphic organizer skeleton. Use this time to discuss the words you are putting there because these are apt to be key vocabulary from the selection.

3. Have students read to find information to add to the organizer.

4. Complete the organizer together.

5. When your students understand and can complete the various organizers, have them preview the text and decide what kind of graphic organizer works best, and have them help you construct the skeleton.

Story Text Lessons

Children understand stories better than informational text, but they still need instruction in story comprehension. Story maps, the Beach Ball, and "doing" the book are three activities that help children understand story structure and develop independent story comprehension strategies.

Story Maps

Story maps are popular and effective devices to guide students' thinking when they are about to read a story. There are many different ways of creating story maps, but all help children follow the story by drawing their attention to the elements that all good stories share. Stories have characters and happen in a particular place and time, which we call the *setting*. In most stories, the characters have some goal they want to achieve or some problem they need to resolve. The events in the story lead to some kind of solution or resolution. Sometimes stories have implicit morals or themes from which we hope children learn. The story map here is based on a model created by Isabel Beck (Macon, Bewell, & Vogt, 1991). Here is the story map filled in for *The Three Little Pigs:*

Story Map

Main Characters:

Setting (Time and Place):

Problem or Goals:

Event 1:

Event 2:

Event 3:

Event 4:

Event 5:

Solution:

Story Theme or Moral:

Story Map

Main Characters: Mother Pig, three little pigs, Big Bad Wolf

Setting (Time and Place): Woods, make-believe time and place

Problem or Goals: Pigs wanted to be independent and have their own houses.

Event 1: Mother Pig sends three little pigs out to build their own houses.

Event 2: First little pig gets some straw and builds a straw house. Big Bad Wolf blows the straw house down.

Event 3: Second little pig gets some sticks and builds a stick house. Big Bad Wolf blows the stick house down.

Event 4: Third little pig gets some bricks and builds a brick house. Big Bad Wolf cannot blow the brick house down.

Event 5: Big Bad Wolf runs off into woods (or gets scalded coming down the chimney, depending on how violent the version of the story is).

Solution: Pigs live happily ever after in strong brick house.

Story Theme or Moral: Hard work pays off in the end!

When using story maps to develop a sense of story structure, follow the gradual release of responsibility model. Model how you fill one out based on a familiar story. As you complete the map, think aloud about your thought processes to make them visible to your students. Let your students share the responsibility by helping you fill one out based on another familiar story.

Once your students understand the story map elements and how to fill them in, have them complete story maps in small groups and then independently. Once the story maps are completed, let students retell the story using the completed map as their guide.

The Beach Ball

You can also use a beach ball to help your students develop their ability to understand and retell stories. Write these questions in black permanent marker on each colored segment of the ball:

> Who are the main characters?
> What is the setting?
> What happened in the beginning?
> What happened in the middle?
> How did it end?
> What was your favorite part?

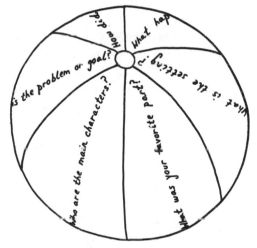

After reading a story, form yourself and your students into a large circle. Toss the ball to one of your students. That student catches the ball and can answer any question on the ball. Have each student toss the ball back to you and then you toss the ball to another student. The next student can add to the answer given by the first student or answer another question. The ball continues to be thrown to various students until all the questions have been thoroughly answered. Some questions, such as, "What happened in the story?" and "What was your favorite part?" have many different answers.

English Language Learners

Toss the beach ball to your English language learners first. They may not have enough English to be able to elaborate about the story events but they can surely tell you who some of the main characters are and they love telling you their favorite part.

The Beach Ball is a favorite comprehension activity for children in all the classrooms, including children in intermediate grades. As children read a story, they begin to anticipate the answers they will give to the questions on the various colored segments. If you organize your comprehension lesson with the Beach Ball activity once every week or two, your students will develop a clear sense of story structure, and their comprehension (and memory) for important story elements will increase.

"Doing" the Book

Children who "do" the book become more active readers. Characters, setting, events, dialogue, conclusions, mood, and motivation become important, and children pay more attention to them when they have to interpret and re-create the drama. This activity greatly increases story comprehension. Doing the book can take a variety of forms, from performing a play, to acting out stories, to concentrating on re-creating a single scene of a play.

Do a Play   Children of all ages enjoy being in a play, and some wonderful stories for children are already written in play format. Recasting a story as a play can also be a powerful reading/writing activity, especially if your older students create the script and stage directions from the original story.

When having your struggling readers do a play, remember that doing repeated readings is a powerful way to help children develop oral reading fluency and an understanding of characters. It helps their reading more if they do not memorize lines but rather read and reread their parts until they can read them fluently.

Some teachers do not do plays because there are not enough parts for everyone, or they do not know what to do with the children who are not in the play while the players are preparing. Most children enjoy preparing to do the play and then watching each other do it. For example, if you have a play that requires 7 actors and you have 24 children in your class, divide your class into three groups of eight, putting a director and seven actors in each group. Let all three groups prepare and practice the play simultaneously. Then let each "cast" put on the play for the others.

If you have children do plays, remember that the purpose of this activity is for them to become more active readers, to visualize characters, to do some repeated readings, and to transfer their enjoyment from being in the play to reading. "Doing it" is what matters, not how professionally it is done. Props, costumes, and scenery should be nonexistent or very simple. Take the "process attitude" (the play helps develop important reading processes) rather than a "product attitude," and you will develop a new appreciation for plays.

Some teachers find that letting children make a simple mask to hide behind (using a paper plate and Popsicle stick) can help diminish shyness and stage fright.

English Language Learners

English language learners particularly seem less self-conscious and more comfortable speaking when they have something to hide behind.

Act Out a Story Acting out a story is another way to help children think actively and to visualize as they read. The best stories for acting out are the ones that you can visualize as plays. Everyone should have a part, as they did in the plays. Many teachers write down on little slips of paper the characters' names along with a number to designate acting cast:

First Little Pig 1	First Little Pig 2	First Little Pig 3
Second Little Pig 1	Second Little Pig 2	Second Little Pig 3
Third Little Pig 1	Third Little Pig 2	Third Little Pig 3
Mama Pig 1	Mama Pig 2	Mama Pig 3
Wolf 1	Wolf 2	Wolf 3
Man with sticks 1	Man with sticks 2	Man with sticks 3
Man with straw 1	Man with straw 2	Man with straw 3
Man with bricks 1	Man with bricks 2	Man with bricks 3
Director 1	Director 2	Director 3

The teacher then explains to the students that three groups will be acting out the story and that they will all have parts. She explains what the parts are and that she will pass out the slips after the story is read to determine what parts they will have. She encourages them to think about what all the characters do and feel because they might end up with any of the parts.

After the story is read and discussed, the teacher hands a slip of paper to each child randomly. (This procedure of letting chance determine who gets starring roles and who gets bit parts is readily accepted by the children and easier on the teacher, who will not have to try to decide who should and could do what. Sometimes, the most unlikely children are cast into starring roles and astonish everyone—including themselves!) The children then form three groups, and whoever gets the director slip in each group helps the others act out the story. The teacher circulates among the groups, giving help and encouragement as needed. After 10 to 15 minutes of practice, each group performs its act while the other groups watch. Just as they enjoy doing a play, children generally enjoy acting out

Story Text Lessons

The goal of comprehension instruction is to have children learn how to independently do the strategies as they read on their own. Story maps, the Beach Ball, and "doing" the book activities will help your students use all the thinking strategies to enjoy a wide range of stories.

Story Maps

1. Decide on a story map skeleton that will work best for your children.

2. Choose a familiar story and model how to complete a story map. Share your thinking as you complete it.

3. Choose another familiar story and let students help you complete a second story map.

4. Have students complete story maps in small groups and use the maps as guides to retell the story.

5. When all students understand how to complete a story map, let students choose a story and compete the story map independently.

The Beach Ball

1. Model answering the beach ball questions using a familiar story.

2. Choose another familiar story and let students help you answer the questions for the colored segments of the ball.

3. Form small groups of students and have them read a story and decide together what answers they will give for the questions on the beach ball.

4. When all students understand the questions and how to answer them, let them choose a story and then use the beach ball segments to guide their retelling of that story to the class or a small group.

"Doing" the Book

1. Include plays in your reading repertoire. Have children read and do plays, and have older children turn stories into plays by writing scripts for them.

2. Have children do some impromptu acting out of stories—no scripts, props, or costumes needed. Children should read the story several times, parts should be chosen, and children should "do their thing." To include more children, have several casts performing the same story.

3. Have children act out scenes from longer stories. Let small groups choose different scenes; then have each group perform in order of scenes. All the groups not in a particular scene become the audience for that scene.

a story. Teachers who keep their focus on the process children go through as they read and act out stories enjoy this activity and do not worry too much about the product. Acting out stories is designed to turn the children into avid readers, not accomplished actors.

Make a Scene!   Whereas full-blown plays may seem a bit daunting for children and teachers (and take time), a variation on this theme is often easier for children and can be quickly incorporated into many lessons. Rather than acting out a full play, have your students re-create a single scene. Scenes can be done by individuals, pairs, or small groups. They simply require the readers to select a scene, transform it into a script (not necessarily written out), briefly rehearse it, and then present it—no props, no costumes, just reenactment! The scene can be as short as a single exchange between characters or can even be a single sentence delivered in the appropriate voice. Children who can literally become Richard Best from *The Beast in Ms. Rooney's Room* or the sassy little brother in *Island of the Blue Dolphins* demonstrate an understanding of the story and the characters.

Summary

Comprehension—thinking about and responding to what you are reading—is "what it's all about!" Comprehension is the reason and prime motivator for engaging in reading. What comprehension is, how comprehension occurs, and how comprehension should be taught have driven hundreds of research studies in the last 30 years. Reading comprehension—and how to teach it—is probably the area of literacy about which we have the most knowledge and the most consensus. It is also probably the area that gets the least attention in the classroom.

In 1979, Dolores Durkin published a landmark study demonstrating that little, if any, reading comprehension instruction happened in most classrooms and that the little bit that did occur was "mentioning," rather than teaching. Having children answer comprehension questions to assess their reading comprehension was the activity most often seen. This finding shocked the reading community and probably propelled much of the reading comprehension research that has occurred since. Unfortunately, more recent research (Beck, McKeown, & Gromoll, 1989; Pressley & Wharton-McDonald, 1998) has indicated that reading comprehension instruction is still rare in most elementary classrooms.

Duke and Pearson (2002) reviewed the research and summarized what good readers do as they comprehend text:

Are active and have clear goals in mind.
Preview text before reading, make predictions, and read selectively to meet their goals.

- Construct, revise, and question the meanings they are making as they read.
- Try to determine the meanings of unfamiliar words and concepts.
- Draw from, compare, and integrate their prior knowledge with what they are reading.
- Monitor their understanding and make adjustments as needed.
- Think about the author of the text and evaluate the text's quality and value.
- Read different kinds of text differently, paying attention to characters and settings when reading narratives and constructing and revising summaries in their minds when reading expository text.

Previous chapters of this book described a variety of activities for building word identification, fluency, and vocabulary, all of which are required for comprehension. This chapter described a variety of activities designed to teach children how to think as they read and how different kinds of text require different kinds of thinking.

Developing
Ready, Willing, and Able Writers

Imagine that you come upon someone who is sitting, pen in hand or fingertips poised over a keyboard, staring at a blank page or blank screen. When you ask, "What are you doing?," the person will often respond, "I'm *thinking!*" Continue to observe, and you will see the person move into the writing phase eventually, but this writing will not be continuous. There will be constant pauses. If you are rude enough to interrupt during one of these pauses to ask "What are you doing?" the writer will again probably respond, "I'm *thinking!!!*"

Eventually, the writer will finish the writing, or rather the first draft of the writing. The writer may put the writing away for a while or may ask someone, "Would you take a look at this and tell me what you think?" Later, the writer will return to writing to revise and edit. Words will be changed, and paragraphs will be added, moved, or deleted. Again, the writer will pause from time to time during this after-writing phase. If you ask what the writer is doing during this phase, you will get the familiar response: "*I'm thinking!*"

We offer this common scenario as proof that the essence of writing is thinking and that even the most naive writer knows this basic truth. Because writing is thinking and because learning requires thinking, students who write as they learn will think more and thus will learn more.

In addition to the fact that writing is thinking, writing is hard! It is complex. There are many things to think about at the same time. There are such big issues as:

- What do I want to say?
- How can I say it so that people will believe it?
- How can I say it so that people will want to read it?

In addition to these big issues, there are a host of smaller but still important issues:

- How can I begin my writing in a way that sets up my ideas and grabs the reader's attention?
- Which words will best communicate these feelings and thoughts?
- What examples can I use?
- Do I need to clarify here or include more details?
- How can I end it?
- Now, I have to think of a good title!

As if these grand and less grand issues are not enough, there are also a number of small details to worry about. Sometimes, these are taken care of during the after-writing phase, but often writers think about them as they write. Some examples include:

- I wonder if this sentence should begin a new paragraph?
- Do I capitalize the word *state* when it refers to North Carolina?
- How do you spell *Beijing?*
- Does the comma go inside or outside the quotation mark?

We do not offer this sampling of a few of the "balls" writers have to keep in the air as they perform the difficult juggling act of writing in order to discourage you. Rather, we offer them to convince you that students need instruction, guidance, support, encouragement, and acceptance if they are going to be willing and able participants in writing.

To become the very best writers, children need two kinds of writing instruction. First, all children need to engage in some writing in which they select the topics and decide how they will write about those topics. Most teachers organize their classrooms in a Writer's

Workshop fashion to provide children with opportunities to write on their self-selected topics and help them learn how to write, edit, revise, and publish. Second, children need to know how to write particular forms and genres, including letters, reports, descriptions, and narratives. To teach children how to write these forms and genres, teachers carry out focused writing lessons, in which all the children are writing on the same topic and/or in the same form or genre. The remainder of this chapter will describe ways successful teachers organize their instruction to do both Writer's Workshop and focused writing.

Starting the Year with Writer's Workshop

Writer's Workshop (Calkins, 1994; Graves, 1995) is the term most commonly used to describe the process of children choosing their own topics and then writing, revising, editing, and publishing. In Writer's Workshop, you try to simulate as closely as possible the atmosphere in which real writers write and to help children see themselves as "real authors."

Usually, Writer's Workshop begins with a mini-lesson during which you model writing. Next, the children write. As the children write, you conference with them and coach them on how to revise, edit, and publish. Writer's Workshop usually concludes with an Author's Chair, in which children read their writing and get responses from the other "writers" in the room.

Writer's Workshop can be done in all elementary grades. Although the basic principles are the same, the focus for the mini-lessons and the amount of revising, editing, and publishing will be quite different. Regardless of grade, if you want to create willing writers, you must begin the year by emphasizing meaning and deemphasizing mechanics and perfection. Because writing is hard and complex, children who see the goal as producing a certain number of perfect sentences will not write willingly and will only do the bare minimum needed to get by.

English Language Learners

If you have ever tried to learn a second language, you know that learning to read a different language is hard and learning to write it even harder. Knowing that you care more about their ideas than about the correctness with which they can write them frees up all your children to write. Your students who are learning English will attempt writing if you respond with enthusiasm to their ideas. Being willing to write in your classroom is especially important for these children because writing is one more avenue for them to learn and become literate in English.

You want to establish in the first few weeks of school that the most important thing about writing in your classroom is what the writing says—not how perfectly it says it. To demonstrate this, teachers begin each school year by doing mini-lessons in which they focus on how you choose a topic and how you write the first draft as best you can. After the 8- to 10-minute mini-lesson in which the teacher writes what he or she "wants to tell," the teacher asks the students to write what *they* want to tell. As the children write, the teacher circulates and encourages them by making comments such as:

"Did you really go to camp this summer? I went to camp every summer when I was your age. I think I will write about that one day soon."

"Oh, you are interested in dinosaurs. I bet lots of the other students like dinosaurs, too. They will be eager to hear what you have learned about them."

"I watched that TV program last night, too. It is one of my favorites."

When a child writes one sentence and has an "I wrote a sentence—that's all I know" attitude, the teacher barrages him or her with questions related to the sentence. If the child has written

I got a dog.

The teacher might ask:

"Do you really have a dog?"

"Is your dog a male or a female?"

"What's her name?"

"Is she a big dog or a little dog?"

"What color is she?"

"Do you take her for walks?"

"Where did you get her?"

Let the child tell you the answers to these questions, but do not wait for the child to write them. Just leave the child by saying something like:

"You sure have a lot to tell about your dog. I bet other kids will wish they had thought of writing about their dog."

As you circulate, remember the message you are trying to convey to your students:

"The most important thing about writing in this classroom is *what* you write. I am eager to hear what you are telling me in your writing. Your classmates will also want to know about what you are writing."

Inevitably, as you circulate, someone will ask you to spell a word. How you respond to this request will determine the progress you can make in your Writer's Workshop for the rest of the year. If you spell words for children now, you will never be able to pull away from them and use the time while they are writing to hold conferences with individuals and groups about their writing. Consider the following responses to the "Can you spell *dinosaurs?*" request:

> "Yes, I can now, but I couldn't when I was your age and I don't want you to get too hung up on spelling when you're doing your first-draft writing. I want you to write what you want to tell—not just what you can spell. Let's stretch out *dinosaurs* together and put down the letters you think are there. You will be able to read it, and that's all that matters now. In a few weeks, we will start publishing some of our best pieces, and then we will fix up all the spelling to make them easy for everyone to read."

> "I'm sorry, but teachers aren't allowed to spell words for kids when they are first drafting, but I can help you stretch it out."

> "Dinosaurs—hmmm . . . I think I see the word *dinosaurs* in the title of that book over there."

However you accomplish it, make it clear to your students that you will help them stretch out words and point them to places in the room where they can find words, but on first draft, you cannot spell words for them. At the same time, assure them that if these are pieces they choose to publish, you will enthusiastically help them "fix" the spelling.

Limit the amount of time your children write for the first few weeks of school. Eventually, you want them writing for 15 to 20 minutes, but it is better to start with a smaller amount of time, perhaps 6 or 7 minutes, so that they do not get too discouraged and bored if they are not particularly good writers. Some teachers use a timer and increase the amount of time in one-minute intervals as the children become more able to sustain their writing.

When the time is up, circle your students and ask who wants to read or tell about what they have written. You may want to single out some of the children with affirming statements such as:

> "Carl has a big dog named Tammy. Carl, tell us more about Tammy."

> "Josh is a big dinosaur fan. He hasn't finished writing all he wants to about dinosaurs, but perhaps he will tell or read what he has written so far."

> "Jamal and I like the same TV show. I wonder how many of you like it, too."

Be sure you let your students read or tell what they are writing. Some children do not like to write but they almost all like to "tell," and soon they will be writing eagerly so they have a chance to tell during the sharing time. Again, keep in mind your goal for getting Writer's Workshop off to a successful start. You want the children to look forward to the writing time (which does not last too long!), and you want them to see writing as a way of telling about themselves and the things that are important to them.

Tips for Starting the Year with Writer's Workshop

The Mini-Lesson

Begin each Writer's Workshop with an 8- to 10-minute mini-lesson in which you write and the children watch. Include mini-lessons in which you model and think aloud about how you decide what to write about:

- "When I saw Carl writing about his dog Tammy, it reminded me of the dog I had when I was your age. I think I will write about Serena today."

- "Yesterday, we were reading about the pioneers. I am going to write what I think it would have been like to be a pioneer."

- "In science yesterday, we did that experiment with balloons. I think I will write about that."

- "Just before the buses came yesterday, we had that huge thunderstorm. My cat hates thunderstorms. I will tell you what my cat does when it thunders."

- "I went to the football game at Wake this weekend. I saw several of you there. I am going to tell you what I liked best about the game."

- "I have a lot of things I want to tell you about, and I think I might forget some of them. Today, instead of writing about one thing, I am going to make a list of all the things I might want to write about." (Refer to your "Things I want to write about list" over the next several weeks before you write, and add to it when you get good ideas from what your students are writing. Encourage your students to make their own lists, if they want to.)

Also model for students what you do about spelling:

- Look up at your word wall periodically, and model how using it helps you spell.

    "*Because* is a tricky word. I am glad we have *because* on the word wall."

    "*Brook* rhymes with *look*, so I can use *look* to help me spell it."

    "*Talked* is our word wall word *talk* with *ed* on the end."

- Use other print in the room to spell words.

    "I can spell *Wednesday* by looking at the calendar."

    "*Hydrogen* is on our science board."

    "*Pioneers* is on the cover of the book I read to you this morning."

- Stop and stretch out a word, putting down the letters you think are there.

    "I can spell *ridiculous* now, but let me show you how I would have stretched it out when I was your age."

- Model for students how you add on to a piece you have not finished:

    "Yesterday, I was telling you about my two grandmothers, and I only had time to describe my mama's mother. I am going to reread what I wrote yesterday to get my thoughts back and then tell you about my dad's mother."

    "This is the third day I have been writing about our trip to the museum. I am going to reread what I wrote the first two days and hope I can finish this up today."

The Students Write

- Increase the time gradually, starting with a small amount of time that all your students can handle. Many teachers use a timer and increase writing one minute at a time.
- Circulate and encourage your writers by "oohing" and "aahing" about their topics. Ask questions of students who have just written a sentence or two. Comment regularly that they have "given you a good idea for your writing." If you are keeping a writing topics list, go right over and add it to your list.
- Do not spell words for students but help them stretch them out and use the word wall and other print in the room to find words.

The Students Share

- Let volunteers tell or read what they have written.
- Spotlight some children who you interacted with as they were writing.
- Let children ask questions of their fellow writers.
- Point out children who are going to be "adding on" to their writing tomorrow.
- Encourage children to find writing topics during this sharing by asking questions of one another. How many of them have dogs? Grandmas? Went to the football game? Ever broke a bone?
- Add topics to your writing list, inspired by what they share.

Make a point of asking some of your students to share writing they have not finished yet. Tell them that during Writer's Workshop, we do not usually start writing a new piece every day and that sometimes it takes a week or more to finish a piece if we are writing about something we really care about or know a lot about.

Adding Editing to Writer's Workshop

Early in the year at every grade level, we have three major writing goals we want to accomplish. We want children to get in the habit of writing each day and coming up with their own topics, based on what they want to tell. We want them to learn to use the supports for spelling words displayed in the classroom and how to stretch out the big words they need to be able to write what they really want to tell. Finally, we want them to realize that they can take several days to write a piece if they have a lot to tell and that in order to add on, they need to read what they have already written.

When all the children are writing willingly, if not well, we begin teaching them how to edit their writing. Here is how one teacher described the first editing lesson.

One Teacher's First Editing Lesson

As I was getting ready to write one morning, I told the children that soon we would be publishing some of their best pieces and before we did so, we needed to know how to edit. I then wrote on a sheet of chartpaper:

Our Editor's Checklist

1. Do all my sentences make sense?

I explained to the children that one thing editors always read for is to make sure that all the sentences make sense. Sometimes, writers leave out words or forget to finish a sentence, and then the sentences don't make sense. I told the children, "Each day, after I write my piece, you can be my editors and help me decide if all my sentences make sense." I then wrote a piece and purposely left out a word. The children who were, as always, reading along as I wrote and often anticipating my next word, noticed my mistake immediately. When I finished writing, I said, "Now let's read my piece together and see if all my sentences make sense. Give me a 'thumbs up' if my sentence makes sense." The children and I read one sentence at a time, and when we got to the sentence where I had left out a word, we decided that the sentence didn't make sense because my mind had gotten ahead of my marker and I had left out a word. I wrote the word in with a different-colored marker and thanked the children for their good editing help.

After I wrote my piece, the children all went off to do their own writing. As they wrote, I circulated around and encouraged them. When the writing time was up, I pointed to the editor's checklist we had just begun. I said, "Be your own editor now. Read your paper and give yourself a 'thumbs up' if each sentence make sense. If you didn't finish a sentence or left a word out, take your red pen and fix it." I watched as the children did their best to see if their sentences made sense and noticed a few children writing things with their red pens.

Every day after that when I wrote, I left a word out or didn't finish a sentence. The children delighted in being my editor and helping me make all my sentences make sense. Every day when their writing time was up, I pointed to the checklist and they read their own sentences for sense. They didn't find every problem, but they all knew what they were trying to do. After a few weeks, I noticed almost everyone picking up their red pens and glancing up at the checklist as soon as the writing time ended.

Now, I am about to add to our checklist a second thing to read for. I will add:

2. Do all my sentences have ending punc?

From now on, the children will read my sentences and give me a thumbs up if the sentence makes sense and another thumbs up if it has punc (more fun to say than punctuation!) at the end. When the writing time is up, I will remind them that we are at the "thumbs up" editing stage and that they should read their sentences for sense and ending punc just as they read mine.

Build Your Editor's Checklist Gradually

The items on the editor's checklist are not just there so that children will find them as they edit. The goal is that by focusing on the checklist items as children check the teacher's writing at the end of mini-lessons and by asking children to do a quick self-edit of their own writing each day, children will begin to incorporate these conventions as they write their first drafts. The question of when to add another item to the checklist can be answered by observing the first-draft writing of the children. If most of the children, most of the time, apply the current checklist items as they write their first drafts, it is time to add another item to the checklist.

Developing your editor's checklist is easy if you let your observations of children's first-draft writing determine what is added, the order in which it is added, and the speed with which it is added. Here are two examples of editors' checklists—one for primary and one for intermediate grades:

Our Editor's Checklist

1. Do all my sentences make sense?
2. Do all my sentences have ending punc?
3. Do all my sentences start with caps?
4. Are the words I need to check for spelling circled?
5. Do names and places start with caps?
6. Do all my sentences stay on topic?

Editor's Checklist

1. Do all the sentences make sense and stay on topic?
2. Do all the sentences start with caps and end with correct punc?
3. Are the words I need to check for spelling circled?
4. Do names and places start with caps?
5. Do words in series have commas?
6. Do quotes have correct punc?
7. Is there a beginning, middle, and end?

Teach Children to Peer Edit

Once children have had lots of experience editing the teacher's piece each day, they can learn how to edit with partners. You can introduce this by choosing a child to be your partner and role-playing how he or she will help with the editing. Here is how one teacher taught students to peer edit.

Adding Editing to Writer's Workshop

A Peer-Editing Mini-Lesson

I began by telling the class that we would soon start choosing some of their best pieces to publish and that once they had each chosen a piece, the first step in the publishing process would be to choose a friend to help with the editing:

> "Boys and girls, we are going to pretend today that I am one of the children in the class. I am getting ready to publish a piece, and I will choose one of you to be my editor."

I then wrote a short piece on the overhead as the children watched. Instead of letting the whole class read the sentences aloud and do "thumbs up or down," as we had been doing, I chose one child to be my editor. As the children watched, my editor and I read my sentences one at a time and edited for the four things on the checklist. As we read each sentence, we decided if it made sense and had ending punc and a beginning cap. Next, we looked at the words and decided if any of them needed to be circled because we thought they were not spelled correctly. Here is what the edited piece looked like:

Polar Bears

Polar bears live in the arctic which is one of the coldest places on earth. Polar bears are the largest bears. Male polar bears are about 10 feet tall and weigh 1,100 pounds. Polar bears are fast movers. They can run 30 miles an hour. They are good swimmers too. Polar bears have a lot of fur and blubber to keep them warm. Polar bears eat fish, seals, careboo berries and seaweed. People used to hunt polar bears. They were almost extink. only about 5,000 were left. Now, there are laws against hunting polar bears and there are about 40,000. Polar bears are amazing animals.

English Language Learners

Take special care in thinking about who to partner with your English language learners. Choose your most nurturing students and help them understand the supportive and encouraging role you want them to take when helping their English language learning peers to edit their writing.

For the next several days, I followed the procedure of choosing a child to be my editor and doing the partner editing in front of the children. When I thought most of the children understood how to help each other edit for the items on the checklist, I partnered them up, assigning partners of similar writing ability to work together, and had each pair choose a piece and edit it together. I had several more peer-editing practice sessions before turning the children loose to peer edit without my supervision.

Editing Tips: Editing = Fixing Up Your Writing

- Don't begin editing instruction until children are writing willingly and fluently—if not well!

- Observe children's writing to decide what mechanics and conventions they can do automatically and what things you need to focus on.

- Begin your checklist with one item. Let children edit your piece for this one item every day.

- When the writing time is up, ask students to be their own editors. Praise their efforts at self-editing, but don't expect them to find everything.

- Add a second item when most of your students do the first item correctly most of the time. In your mini-lesson, sometimes make a #1 error and sometimes a #2 error—but do not make more than two errors total.

- Continue to add items gradually, using the same procedure to teach each.

- Teach children to peer edit by role-playing, and then provide supervised practice as children peer edit with writers of similar ability.

Adding Conferencing, Publishing, and Author's Chair to Writer's Workshop

After your students understand how to edit and partner edit with an editing checklist and are writing for about 15 minutes each day, you may want to add conferencing, publishing, and Author's Chair to your Writer's Workshop. (You should not wait until the editor's checklist is complete before beginning this, and, in fact, you will continue to add items to the checklist and do mini-lessons on editing conventions all year long.) Once publishing begins, you will spend the writing time holding conferences with your students to help them get their pieces ready to publish. (Since you cannot be in two places at one time, this means you will no longer be circulating and encouraging children as they write. Do not begin publishing until almost all your children are coming up with topics, spelling words for themselves, and writing willingly.)

Author's Chair

When children begin publishing, most teachers also shift from the informal circle sharing that has been happening each day at the end of Writer's Workshop to an Author's Chair format. One-fifth of the children share each day. They can share anything they have written since their last day in the Author's Chair. Of course, when they have published a piece, they share that. But they can also share a first draft or work in progress. After each child has read, he or she calls on class members to tell things they liked about the piece. The author can also ask if anyone has any questions and elicit suggestions to make the piece better. During Author's Chair, the focus is exclusively on the message that the author is trying to convey.

Here again, the role of the teacher model is extremely important. Useful comments include:

> "I love the way you described . . . "
> "I wondered why the character . . . "
> "Your ending really surprised me."
> "The way you began your story was . . . "
> "I could just imagine . . . "
> "I thought this was a true story until . . . "

When assigning children to days to share in the Author's Chair, you may want to assign one of your best and one of your most struggling writers for each day. The best writer might get an extra minute to share because these children often write longer, more complex pieces. Take a minute before Author's Chair each day to check in with your struggling writer and make sure he or she has selected something to share and is prepared to read or tell about it.

English Language Learners

If your children who are just learning English are hesitant to share in the Author's Chair, offer to be their voice. Let them tell you what they were writing and then use your voice to share this with the whole class.

Publishing

Most elementary teachers tell children that they can choose a piece to publish when they have written three or four good pieces. They then teach mini-lessons in which they role-play and model choosing a piece to publish and taking it through the process. Once the publishing part of the Writer's Workshop has been established, students will be at all different stages of the writing process each day. Those children who have just finished publishing a piece will be working to produce new first drafts, from which they will pick another one to publish. Other children will have picked a piece to publish and will be editing it with a friend. Some children will be having a writing conference with the teacher. Other children will have had their piece "fixed" during the writing conference and will be busy copying, typing, and illustrating the final product.

Since you can't help everyone publish at the same time, you may want to begin the publishing cycle by choosing five or six children to publish. This will allow you to conference with these children while the others continue to produce first drafts. Once these children are at the copying/typing/illustrating stage, you can continue to choose more children to begin the publishing process, until all the children have published something. From then on, the children will know that they can choose a piece to publish when they have three or four good first drafts. Many teachers post a chart like this to remind children of the publishing steps:

Steps for Publishing

1. Pick one piece that you want to publish.
2. Choose a friend and partner edit your piece for the items on the checklist.
3. Sign up for a writing conference.
4. Work with your teacher in a conference to edit your piece and fix spelling.
5. Copy or type your piece, making all the corrections.
6. Illustrate your piece.

Adding Conferencing, Publishing, and Author's Chair to Writer's Workshop

The Writing Conference

Be sure that each child edits his or her piece with a friend before signing up for a writing conference with you. Children, of course, are at all different stages of understanding about writing and how to edit, and some children are much better editors than others. Peer editing for the checklist items is not perfect, and teachers often find things that should have been changed that weren't (and things that were changed that shouldn't have been!). But all the children become much better at being editors of their friends' and their own pieces as the year goes on, and they get in the habit of trying to edit before they publish and not leaving all the work for the teacher.

After the piece has been edited with a friend using the checklist, you should hold an individual conference with the writer and "fix everything!" Your goal in publishing is to have children experience the pride of being authors and having others read and enjoy their writing. This cannot happen if the final piece is not very readable. So, before the child goes to the publishing phase, sit down with that child and do a final edit. Fix the spellings of words, add punctuation and capitalization, clarify sentences that do not make sense, delete sentences that are totally off the topic, and do whatever else is necessary to help the child produce a "masterpiece" of writing!

You can generally do the "fixing" right on the first draft with a different-colored pen. To make this easier, have children write all their first drafts using every other line on the paper, leaving blank lines so that editing can occur. (Of course, some children can't write on every other line but most can, and they all get better at it as the year goes on.) If something must be inserted and cannot be clearly written between the lines, write it on a separate piece of paper and mark the insertion point. You should read each edited piece with each child, making sure he or she can read anything inserted and stopping to notice where to add punctuation, change spelling, and make other needed changes.

Give Additional Support to Your Most Struggling Writers

In almost every class, once you begin publishing, you will have a few children whose writing is really not "editable." (Like love, this is hard to describe, but you will recognize it when you see it!) You generally should not begin publishing until almost all of the children are writing something "readable"—but *almost all* leaves a few children whose pieces are collections of letters with a few recognizable words and very few spaces to help you decipher the letters from the words! You might say these children simply aren't ready to publish and that they should just continue producing first drafts. But the message that these children will get from being left out of the publishing process is that, just as they thought, they "can't write!" Once you begin publishing, you need to include everyone in the process. Some children will publish more pieces than others. Some authors are more prolific than others! The goal is not for everyone to have the same number—and in fact, you should not count or let the children count. The goal is, however, for everyone to feel like a real writer because he or she has some published pieces.

Once you begin publishing, you should work with the most avid writers first, but when most of them have pieces published and are on their second rounds of first drafts, you should gather together the children who have not yet published anything. Help them choose pieces they want to publish and then give them the option of reading or telling what they want to say. Then, sit down individually with these children and help them construct their pieces. Get them to tell you again what they want to say. As they tell, write down their sentences by hand and later type them on the computer. After these children's sentences have been written, read the sentences with them several times to make sure they know what they have said. Then cut the sentences apart and have the children illustrate each one and put them all together into a book! They —like everyone else—are now real published authors, and they will approach their second round of first-draft writing with renewed vigor—confident that they, too, can write!

It is important to note here that you would not give this kind of support to the majority of your children. If more than a few children need this support, you are not ready to pull away during their writing time to hold individual and group conferences. But when most are ready and only a few lag behind, the solution just suggested works quite well in most classrooms and provides a big boost for your most struggling writers.

English Language Learners

The procedure just described is exactly what you will want to use to help your children learning English publish their writing and feel proud of their products.

Keep the Publishing Process Simple

There are numerous ways to publish, but you don't want to spend too much of your or your children's time in publishing. In many schools, groups of volunteers create "skeleton books" for children to publish in. They cut sheets of paper in half and staple or bind them with bright-colored covers into books of varying numbers of pages. Children write (or type on the computer and cut and tape) their sentences on the pages and add illustrations. In other classrooms, the pieces are typed on the computer (by the child or an assistant/volunteer) and then illustrated (with drawings, photos, or clip art) and displayed on the writing bulletin board. A variety of computer programs are available that make the publishing process a much less onerous one and help children produce professional-looking products. In many classrooms, children publish their pieces on the Web to share with the larger world.

Tips for Publishing, Conferencing, and Author's Chair

- Don't begin publishing until most children are writing "editable" pieces and can edit for the items on the checklist.
- Don't let students publish every piece. Most of the learning in Writer's Workshop takes place as children participate in the mini-lesson and write their first drafts. Publishing is the "icing on the cake."
- Be sure that each student chooses a friend and edits for the items on the checklist before conferencing with you.
- During the conference, fix whatever needs fixing—including things not yet on the checklist. Every child should produce a readable published piece to be proud of.
- Everyone does not need to publish the same number of pieces, but everyone does need to publish some pieces. Provide extra support so that your struggling writers can be proud of their writing and their status as authors.
- Let one-fifth of your children share each day in the Author's Chair. Model positive comments and good questions, and allow each author to choose one classmate to ask a question and one classmate to tell something he or she liked.

Adding Revising to Writer's Workshop

Editing is "fixing" your writing. *Revising* is making good writing *even* better! Because learning to do some basic editing is easier than learning to revise, teachers usually teach some editing rules first and then teach some revising strategies. After teachers have taught some revising strategies, students should revise their pieces before editing.

When you begin to teach revising, make sure your students understand that revising is not editing. *Editing* is fixing mistakes and making the writing easy for the reader to read. *Revising* is making the writing better—clearer—more interesting—more dramatic—more informative—more persuasive—more *something!* When a writer revises, he or she looks again at the writing, asking the essential question:

"How can I make this piece of writing *even better*?"

The word *even* in this question is important because it implies that the writing is good but can be even better! Using the phrase *even better* is part of the attitude adjustment your students may need to make about revising, since many children think that having to revise means you did not do a good job to begin with. All successful writers revise, and all published writing has been revised. Writers always begin revising by rereading their writing and thinking about how to make it *even better*.

Once they decide what is needed to make the meaning or clarity of their drafts even better, writers make revisions by adding, replacing, removing, or reordering. Sometimes they add, replace, or remove one or more words or phrases, or they reorder some words or phrases. Sometimes they add, replace, or remove one or more sentences or paragraphs, or they reorder some sentences or paragraphs. Occasionally, a writer will add, replace, or remove an entire section or reorder the sections that are already there.

To teach children how to revise, use the general revising strategies of adding, replacing, removing, and reordering. This will help them understand what revision is, how it is different from editing, and where to begin when trying to make the meaning of a selected piece of writing even better. As with editing, begin your revising instruction by teaching mini-lessons in which you select one of your writing pieces and revise it in front of the children. Of course, you want students to learn how to help each other revise, so you should teach some mini-lessons in which you pick a student to be your revising helper and role-play this peer revising as the other students watch. Next, partner up children with writers of similar ability and give them practice peer revising.

As with editing, revising strategies should be taught gradually, and when students have been taught only one strategy, they should be expected to use only that one strategy. As you conference with children getting ready to publish, remind them of the revising strategies you have taught so far and give them help implementing some of these with their pieces.

Steps for Publishing (Including Revising)

1. Pick one piece that you want to publish.
2. Choose a friend to help you revise.
3. Check your revisions with your teacher.
4. Partner edit your piece for the items on the checklist.
5. Have a conference with your teacher to do a final edit.
6. Copy or type your piece, making all the corrections.
7. Illustrate your piece.

Teaching the Adding Revising Strategy

Adding is the easiest revising strategy, and thus you should teach it first. Children are often impressed with themselves when they write a long piece—and adding makes it even longer and more impressive! By starting with the adding revising strategy, you can capitalize on your students' affinity for length and start them off with a positive attitude toward revising.

If you have been writing on every other line on your transparency or chart and having your children write on every other line on their first drafts, adding just a word, phrase, or sentence will be easy to do and be seen right on the original piece. Adding longer sections will require cutting and taping—something children love to do and that also helps improve their attitude toward revising.

For your first adding mini-lesson, you may want to show students how adding words or phrases can make the meanings of their pieces clearer and more vivid. To do this mini-lesson, choose a piece you wrote recently. Tell the children that you want to revise this piece before you publish it and that one way to revise is to add a few words or phrases that will make the meaning clearer. Use a bright-colored marker and show children how you put a ^ and then insert a word or phrase in the empty line above at two or three different places to make what you have written better. Over the next several days, demonstrate adding words or phrases to revise with a few more of your pieces.

When you have done enough mini-lessons to be sure that most of your students understand how to revise by adding words or phrases, partner them so that children of relatively equal ability are working together. Ask each pair to choose pieces of their own writing and suggest words or phrases to each other that will make their writing clearer and more vivid. Give them brightly colored pens and christen them "revising pens." Collect the pens when children have finished revising their two papers and reserve them only for revising. The children will enjoy using these special pens, and this, too, will have a positive effect on their attitude toward revising.

As the children revise, go around and help the partners who seem to be having trouble adding words and phrases, as you have taught them in your mini-lessons. As you move around the room, monitoring and helping the partners, be on the lookout for particularly good additions. At the beginning of Author's Chair, take a few minutes and share some of the best revisions you have noticed.

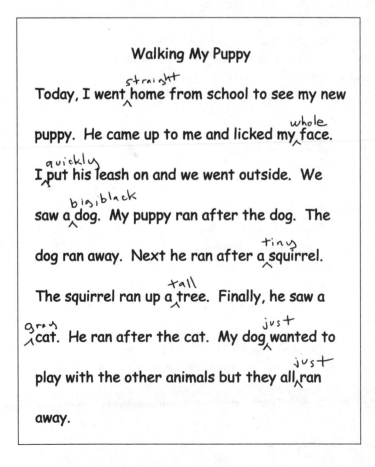

Walking My Puppy

Today, I went ^straight home from school to see my new puppy. He came up to me and licked my ^whole face. I ^quickly put his leash on and we went outside. We saw a ^big, black dog. My puppy ran after the dog. The dog ran away. Next he ran after a ^tiny squirrel. The squirrel ran up a ^tall tree. Finally, he saw a ^gray cat. He ran after the cat. My dog ^just wanted to play with the other animals but they all ^just ran away.

Another way of making writing clearer and more vivid is to add dialogue. Again, take one of your pieces and use it as the first example. (You might want to plan ahead and write a piece with no dialogue but that would be improved by a few exact words so that you have a good example to use.) Tell the children that you want to revise this piece because after you wrote it, you realized that adding some dialogue—the words people or characters actually said—will make it "come alive." Use the same procedure that you used with adding words and phrases, and include a brief explanation of how quotations are punctuated.

Depending on the age and writing levels of your children, you may want to teach them how to revise by adding a missing part. To do this, write a first draft in which you purposely leave out some important information. Bring that piece out on the following day, and explain to the students that you realized you failed to include some very important information. As the students watch, cut your transparency, write the new part on another transparency, and then tape it between the two parts of the original transparency. Students of all ages will be intrigued by this idea that you can cut your writing piece and tape in a missing part. Encourage them to look at their own first drafts and find one that would be "even better" if it had more information. Then turn them loose with scissors and tape!

Teaching the Replacing Revising Strategy

Replacing is another revising strategy all writers use. While the adding strategy makes writing better by making it more elaborate and complete, the replacing strategy makes writing better by improving the quality of what is already there. As with adding, you can replace words, phrases, sentences, or a whole chunk of text. When replacing a small amount of text, use the special revising pens to cross out the text you want to improve and then write the new text clearly above it. When replacing large chunks in order to improve them, use the cut-and-tape procedure.

To prepare for your first replacing mini-lesson, write a first draft in which you purposely use as many "boring, tired, and common" words as you can. Don't tell the children your intent ahead of time. Just write it as you normally write during a mini-lesson. When you finish, have the class read it with you, and ask if they can think of any ways you can make your writing even better. Since you have already taught several lessons on revising by adding, children may suggest some words or phrases for you to add. It is all right to quickly add a few of the words suggested, but if no one suggests replacing some of your "overused" words, you will need to suggest it yourself in order to move your mini-lesson from the adding to the replacing strategy:

> "I notice that I have some common words here that don't create very vivid pictures. *Good,* for example, doesn't even begin to describe how wonderful the cookies were. I think I will cross out *good* and replace it with *scrumptious.*"

Continue replacing some of your boring, overused, or inexact words, eliciting suggestions from your students about which words need replacing and what you can use to replace them.

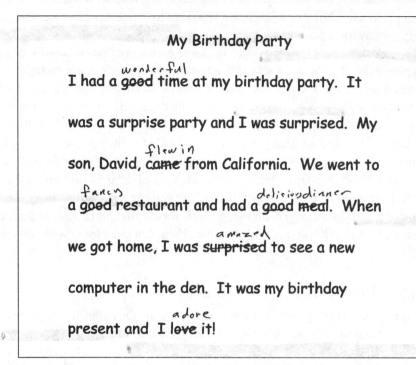

My Birthday Party

I had a ~~good~~ *wonderful* time at my birthday party. It

was a surprise party and I was surprised. My

son, David, ~~came~~ *flew in* from California. We went to

a ~~good~~ *fancy* restaurant and had a ~~good~~ *delicious dinner* ~~meal~~. When

we got home, I was ~~surprised~~ *amazed* to see a new

computer in the den. It was my birthday

present and I ~~love~~ *adore* it!

Just as with revising by adding, you probably will need to do several mini-lessons on replacing words or phrases before asking your students to use this strategy in their own papers. Again, when students try to apply this strategy to their own writing, have them work with partners as you move around helping individuals who are having trouble. Look for good examples of revision to share with everyone afterward.

"Show, don't tell" is a basic guideline for good writing. Unfortunately, many children (and adults!) are not sure what this guideline means. To teach your students what it means, you have to practice what you preach and *show* them how to "Show, don't tell," instead of taking the far easier road of *telling* them to "Show, don't tell!"

To teach children to replace *telling* words with words and sentences that *show,* you can use many of the procedures already described in this chapter. Write pieces in which you purposely tell rather than show, and then revise these pieces in mini-lessons with the children's help. You can also use paragraphs from the children's favorite authors as examples and rewrite them in mini-lessons by replacing the showing words with telling words and sentences. After identifying the places where the children wish the writer had shown them rather than told them, read the original and compare the telling version with the showing version. After several mini-lessons, partner the children and ask them to help each other find examples in their writing where they could make the writing come alive by replacing some of their telling words with showing words and sentences.

When my Grandpa died, I ~~was sad~~ moped around for a week. One day,

my mom asked me to take my Grandpa's dog

for a walk. He ~~was happy to see me~~ jumped up and wagged his tail when he saw me. We went

for a long walk and ended up at the river. I

threw sticks into the river and he swam in

after them. When I took him back home,

Grandma ~~was happy~~ smiled and thanked me. I took Champ for a walk

every day *and I felt better*. Walking Champ made me feel better and was ~~was fun and~~ something I could do for Grandpa!

When the children understand how to replace boring and telling words with more interesting and showing words, you may want to teach them how to replace whole parts of their pieces. For most children, the first revision they do that replaces a chunk of text is when they make the beginning of that piece noticeably better. Your students need to understand that many authors routinely revise the beginning of a piece because once they have written the middle and ending, they realize what the beginning lacked.

Any writer can tell you that a good ending is hard to write! Children often solve the problem by stopping when they can't think of anything else to say and writing "The End." Teaching students to revise by replacing the ending will help almost all of them to write better and more interesting endings.

Tips for Revising Beginnings and Endings

How to Make Your Beginning *Even Better*

- Include the background knowledge needed to understand the middle and end.
- If your piece is a story, be sure to describe the setting—time and place.
- Grab your reader's attention with an interesting question.
- Start with a real-life example.

How to Make Your Ending *Even Better*

- Answer any questions you posed in the beginning.
- Tie up all the "loose ends."
- Pose a question for your reader to think about.
- End with a surprise—but one that fits the rest of your piece.

To teach students to revise by changing the ending or beginning, you should once again contrive to write a piece in your mini-lesson that has a boring or noninformative beginning or ending. For the next day's mini-lesson, pull out your piece again, and tell your students that after writing the piece, you realized how you needed to begin it—or you thought of a much better ending. Let them watch as you reread your ending or beginning, write a replacement, and then cut and tape the new part to the original piece. (If you are fortunate enough to teach in a classroom in which you can write on the computer and have it projected on the screen, use the "Cut" and "Paste" functions on your computer to show your students how easy it is to replace with the help of a word-processing program!)

Teaching the Reordering and Removing Revising Strategies

Revising by *reordering* should not be taught until students can revise by adding and revise by replacing. Moreover, children cannot learn to revise by reordering until they have a firm sense of sequence and logical order, which many children do not develop until third grade.

Just as children like to add to their writing because it makes their pieces longer, they don't like to remove anything because they worked hard to write it and doing so shortens their pieces. Students are usually more willing to replace something than remove it. This is the reason that *removing* is the last of the four general revising strategies you should teach.

Often, however, when we finish writing something, we realize that something we included does not really add anything to our writing or distracts the reader from the point we are trying to make. None of us likes to delete the wonderful words we have written, but deleting or removing off-topic and distracting sentences or paragraphs is an essential revising strategy.

When your students are comfortable with revising by adding and replacing, you can teach reordering and removing just as you taught adding and replacing. Write some first drafts in which you purposely arrange things not in their logical sequence or include some extraneous information. Let students watch as you cut and reorder or remove sentences or paragraphs. Send them on a hunt for places in their writing they could make even better by reordering and removing, and provide guided practice with partners in using these strategies.

Revision is not an easy skill to learn, and although you want to teach children to revise and make sure they know how, you shouldn't expect a great deal of revision—particularly from first- and second-graders. The goal of revising should be to have children understand that meaning comes first—that authors often add, delete, or change things to make their writing more interesting, clear, or dramatic and that they should make whatever meaning changes they are going to make before they edit.

Revising Tips: Making Your Writing *Even Better*

- Look again at your writing. Pick a friend to look with you.

- Use special revising pens or cut and tape.

- Add: Words that make the writing more vivid or clearer
         Dialogue that makes the writing come alive
         Missing information

- Replace: Boring words
           Telling with showing
           Beginnings that don't set up your piece or don't grab the reader's attention
           Endings that don't provide closure or are not very engaging

- Remove: Sentences or paragraphs that don't stay on topic or distract the reader

- Reorder: Sentences or paragraphs that are not in the right sequence

Focused Writing

During Writer's Workshop, children choose their own topics as well as the type of writing they want to do. They come to think of themselves as writers and develop writing fluency and confidence. You do, however, need to teach children how to write specific forms. In addition to stories, children need to learn how to write short reports, business and friendly letters, and essays. Many children enjoy writing poetry, and various types of poetry do not have to rhyme. In a large number of states, children are tested on their ability to do specific writing—narrative, descriptive, persuasive, and so on—at specific grade levels.

Demonstration is once again the most effective teaching strategy for teaching children specific forms. The following section is a sample focused writing lesson in which children learn to write a friendly letter.

Modeling and Demonstration

The teacher of this class has a good friend who is teaching in a faraway state. The two teachers talk regularly on the phone and have both been concerned about giving their students "real" reasons to write. One of them remembers having a pen pal whom he never met but with whom he corresponded for years. The two teachers decide that, although this is a rather old-fashioned idea, their children may still enjoy having their own pen pals. The class is indeed excited about the idea; this is their first letter-writing experience. The teacher wants them to learn the correct form for a letter while also making sure the emphasis is kept on the message to be communicated.

The lesson begins with the teacher asking the children what they would like to know about their pen pals. He records these questions on large index cards:

How old is he/she?

What is school like there?

Do they have a gym?

Do they have a lot of homework?

Do they have a soccer team?

Does he/she play soccer?

Does he/she play baseball? football? other sports?

Is it cold all the time?

Does everybody ski?

What does he/she like to eat?

Do they have video games?

Do they have a mall?

It is clear that the children would like to know many things about their new pen pals. The teacher then helps them organize their questions by beginning a web like the following:

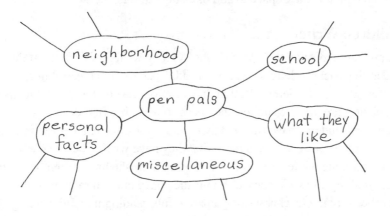

The children help decide where their questions should go and then come up with more questions that also are written on index cards and put in the correct places.

On the following day, the teacher and the children review the web, and the teacher points out that the things they would like to know about their pen pals are probably also the things their pen pals are wondering about them. He explains that they cannot possibly include all this information in the first letter but that they will be writing back and forth all year. As the year goes on, they will share and learn about these things and many things they have not even thought of yet.

The teacher then goes to the overhead and leads the children through the process of writing the first letter. He explains that the letter will be read not only by their pen pals but probably also by many other people, so each letter must be as correct and readable as possible. Today's task is to begin a good first draft that they can edit and recopy or type later. The teacher then explains and models for the children how and where to put the inside address, date, and greeting. The children watch as he does each step at the overhead. They then do the same on their papers.

Once these formalities are covered, the teacher leads them to look at the web and decide what to write about in the first paragraph. The class decides they should write about their personal facts. The teacher agrees and has them put their pencils down to watch as he writes a paragraph that communicates some personal facts about himself.

Revising and Editing as You Go

After writing this first paragraph, the teacher reads it aloud, changing a word and adding another word, to model for the children that when we write, we read and change as we go along. He points out the paragraph indentation and that his paragraph has four sentences.

The teacher then instructs the children to write their own first paragraphs, telling some personal facts about themselves. He reminds them to write on every other line in these first drafts so that they have space to add or change things later.

The Children Write

The children begin to write their paragraphs. As they write, they glance at the web on the board and at the teacher's letter on the overhead. Even though these children are not very sophisticated writers, the demonstration they have observed along with the displayed web and letter clearly provide the support they need to write the first draft of a paragraph.

When most students have finished their paragraphs, the teacher reminds them that good writers stop occasionally and read what they have written before moving on. He then waits another minute while each child reads what he or she has written. He is encouraged to see them making a few changes/additions they have noticed in their own rereading.

The process of the teacher writing a paragraph, reading it aloud, making changes and additions, and then giving the children time to write their own paragraphs continues that day and the next as the teacher and the children construct paragraphs with information from the categories on the web. After each paragraph, the children are reminded to reread and make any changes or additions they think are needed. The teacher is encouraged to notice that when they get to the fifth paragraph, many children are automatically rereading and changing without being reminded to do so. Finally, the teacher suggests possible closings and shows the children where to put the closing. As they watch, he writes a closing on his letter; then they write closings on theirs. This completes the first drafts of the letters.

Revising to Publish

The next day, the teacher helps the students polish their letters. He puts them into sharing groups of four children and has each child read her or his letter to the others. Just as they do for Author's Chair, this sharing is totally focused on the message. Listeners tell the author something they liked, and the author asks them whether anything is not clear or whether they have suggestions for making it better. When everyone in the group has had a chance to share, they make whatever additions and revisions they choose. Children can be seen crossing things out and inserting additional information. As they do this, it becomes apparent why writing the first draft on every other line is useful.

A Final Edit

Now that the letters are revised and the children are satisfied with their messages, it is time to do a final edit. During Writer's Workshop, the children are accustomed to choosing a friend to help them edit a draft that they are going to publish, so they just tailor this process to letters. They refer to the editing checklist displayed in the classroom and decide that the editing items are still valid, but that they need to add an item to correspond with letter editing. They add "Address, date, greeting, closing." The children then pair up with a friend and read for each item on the checklist together. When they have finished helping each other edit, they conference with the teacher for a final editing.

Publishing the Letter

On the following day, the children choose some stationery from a motley collection (contributed by parents or purchased from bargain bins) and copy the letters in their most legible handwriting. Finally, the teacher demonstrates how to put the address and the return address on the envelope. (Even though he intends to mail them all to the pen pals' school in one big envelope, he wants children to learn how to address an envelope and knows the pen pals will feel they are getting real letters when they come sealed in real envelopes.) The letters are mailed, and the writers eagerly await their replies. Next week, in a faraway city, this process begins again as the teacher's friend takes her class through the same steps of learning to write letters so they can write back.

The procedure just described is not difficult to carry out, but it does take time. Most classes would spend at least five 45-minute sessions going through brainstorming, webbing, modeling, first drafting, revising, and editing. When you get the letters sent off, you may think, "Never again!" But keep in mind that the first time you do anything is always the hardest—for you and the children. A month later, when the children have received their letters and are ready to write again, the process will be much easier and will go much more quickly. After three or four letters, most children know how to organize information and can write an interesting and correctly formed letter with a minimum of help. By the end of the year, they will be expert letter writers and will have gained a lot of general writing skills in the process.

Other Examples of Focused Writing Lessons

The procedure just described for learning to write friendly letters can be used for any writing format you want children to learn. Imagine, for example, that you think they would enjoy writing cinquain poetry. Cinquains can be created in many different ways. Perhaps the easiest way for elementary children is the form shown here:

> Teachers
> Smiling, worrying
> Smart, busy, perky
> They love their children.
> Teachers

As you see, the first and last lines are the same word—the subject of the poem. On line 2, you write two *-ing* words. On line 3, you write three adjectives. On line 4, you write a four-word sentence or phrase.

To teach children how to write a cinquain, draw lines to show the form of the cinquain. Duplicate this on paper for the children and on an overhead for your use:

Decide on a subject for the cinquain. (They make very impressive Mother's Day cards, but do expand the concept of mother to include a grandmother, an aunt, or whoever the primary female caretaker is!) Let children watch you write the noun on the first and last lines. Have them write the same noun on their first and last lines.

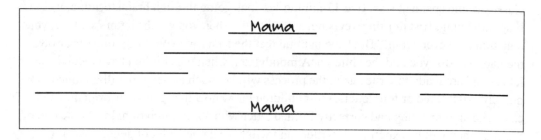

Next, have them brainstorm words that end in *-ing* and tell what mothers do, and list these on the board:

working	talking	driving	cooking	baking
thinking	worrying	fussing	cleaning	singing

Choose two of these *-ing* words and write them on your second line. Tell children to write two *-ing* words on their second line. Tell them that they can choose from the brainstormed list or can come up with any two on their own.

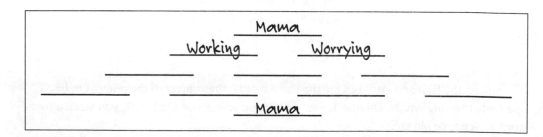

Next, brainstorm descriptive words for line 3, and write these on the board:

busy	pretty	sweet	soft	perky
smart	organized	lonely	worried	careful
tall	short	Black	proud	perfect

Write three descriptive words on your third line. You may want to use one or two words that are not on the brainstormed list to be sure your children understand that the list is just to give them ideas, not to limit their ideas.

                               __Mama__

             __Working__   __Worrying__

   __Busy__   __Black__   __Beautiful__

   _____   _____   _____   _____

              __Mama__

For the fourth line, have children brainstorm four-word phrases or sentences:

> She works too hard.
>
> She loves you best.
>
> My mama is best.
>
> I love her best.
>
> She makes me laugh.
>
> Always in the kitchen.
>
> Some kids have two!

Write one of these or write another four-line phrase or sentence on your fourth line and have the children write one on theirs.

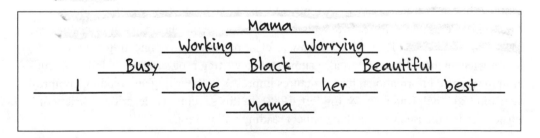

The cinquains are now complete. Let several children read theirs aloud. They will be amazed to discover that, although the topic was the same and they all worked from the same brainstormed list, each poem is different. When each child has written one cinquain, let the students make up another one on the same topic. You may then want them to choose one to use as the text on a Mother's Day card. If so, have them share, revise, and edit in the usual manner.

To get reluctant writers involved, oral histories and personal memoirs are wonderful long-term writing projects because they tell about the children's families or themselves (familiar topics). To begin, you want to locate an oral history to share with the class or invite a member of the community (the principal?) to be your subject for a class oral history project. Interview the subject, tape record the interview, take notes, and have the children take notes also. After the interview, create a group summary using your notes, the children's notes, and the tape if a dispute arises. Memoirs abound in children's literature. Elizabeth Fitzgerald Howard's *Aunt Flossie's Hats (and Crabcakes Later)* and Cynthia Rylant's *When the Relatives Came* are two wonderful examples of this genre. Again, after reading and discussing these published memoirs, teachers may create their own or perhaps create a class memoir based on a collective experience. Now children can begin to plan their own memoirs.

English Language Learners

Because of the vocabulary and syntactic support you provide in focused writing lessons, your English language learners may be more successful in these lessons than they are in the more open-ended Writer's Workshop. This is yet another reason to include both kinds of writing experiences across the year.

Focused Writing Connected to Reading

Children who write become better readers. One of the most powerful connections you can make is through reading and writing (Spivey, 1997). Children who read something knowing that they will write something are more likely to read with a clear sense of purpose. Children who use information from their reading to write produce better writing because they have more to say. Research has shown a clear benefit from connecting reading and writing (Shanahan, 1988). It has also shown that a writing program that includes instruction in specific informational text structures improves both writing and reading comprehension (Raphael, Kirschner, & Englert, 1988). In this section, we describe a variety of structures for focused writing that connect reading and writing.

Graphic Organizers   Chapter 6 described a variety of ways to guide children's reading so they can learn how to think about different types of reading. One type of guided reading lesson involved having students construct or fill in various types of graphic organizers. The webs, charts, diagrams, time lines, and so on that you and the children constructed to organize the information learned from reading are marvelous springboards for writing. Here is a character web about Amanda.

When the web is complete, you can have the children use the information in the web to create a character summary for Amanda. To demonstrate how you do this, choose one of the adjectives that best describes her and let the children listen and watch as you create a paragraph on the board or on chart paper. When teachers think aloud as they model writing in front of the class, they provide powerful lessons about the writing process.

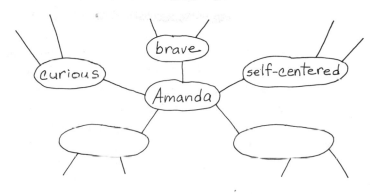

Amanda is a very curious little girl! She always wants to know everything about Miss Morgan One day she followed her home to find out where she lives and what her house looks like. She is also positive that Miss Morgan will marry Mr. Thompson who teaches next door. Miss Morgan isn't sure what she thinks about that! Who knows what Amanda will try and find out next!

Here is a paragraph describing Amanda as a curious person. The children watched as the teacher wrote this paragraph. Using this paragraph as a model but using their own ideas, each child then chose the adjective he or she thought best described Amanda and wrote a descriptive paragraph.

After the children watch you write and listen to you think aloud about how best to combine your ideas, point out to them the features of your paragraph that you want them to use:

- The paragraph is indented.
- All sentences begin with capital letters and end with a period.
- The name *Amanda* is always capitalized.
- The first sentence tells the most important idea—that Amanda is curious.
- The other sentences are details that show how curious she is.

Now each child should write a paragraph about Amanda, choosing any one of the remaining adjectives on the web (or an adjective that is not on the web that they think best describes her). Their paragraphs will all be different but should follow the form demonstrated in your paragraph.

This type of guided writing—in which children use the information they obtain from reading and record it on some type of graphic organizer and who then follow a model they watch the teacher create—is extremely effective for struggling readers. Almost all children will produce interesting, cohesive, well-written paragraphs and be proud of what they produce. With enough lessons such as this one, all children can learn how to construct paragraphs. This ability to create well-formed paragraphs is the basis for all different types of writing.

Almost any information recorded in graphic organizer fashion can be used for reading/writing lessons. In the previous chapter, you saw a web that children can use to organize the information read in an article about birds.

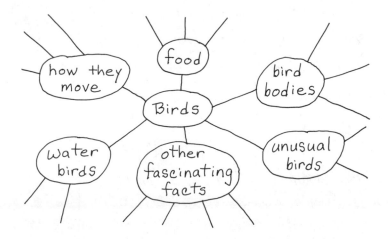

You also saw how information about birds could be recorded in a feature matrix.

Birds						
	fly	swim	build nests	lay eggs	have feathers	molt
robins						
whippoorwills						
penguins						
ostriches						

When these graphic organizers are completed, you can use them to have the children write about birds. Based on the web, the teacher would model how to write a descriptive paragraph about the different foods birds eat. Each child would then choose another one of the subtopics—bird bodies, ways birds move, and so forth—and would write a descriptive paragraph about that topic. Based on the information about particular birds from the feature matrix, the teacher would model how to write a paragraph about one of the birds and then let each child choose one of the other birds and write and illustrate a descriptive paragraph about it. After each child writes about one of the birds, the children might work in groups to revise, edit, and produce a book about birds.

English Language Learners

Lessons in which graphic organizers are constructed and then used as a basis for writing are particularly important and effective for children whose first language is not English. Watching the teacher use the information from the graphic organizer to write something and then using the model they have watched the teacher write to construct their own piece of writing is an extremely powerful way for these children to increase their control of the English language. If your class contains many children whose English is limited, you should use lessons such as these on an almost daily basis.

Response Logs Many teachers find that an easy and natural way to connect reading and writing is to have students keep literature response logs. Children are encouraged to take some time after reading each day and record their thoughts, feelings, and predictions. From time to time, the children can be asked to share the responses they have written. This is often a good basis for promoting a discussion of divergent responses to the same story. However, Sudduth (1990) reported that many of her third-graders did not really know what to record in their literature logs. This was especially true of those children who were finding learning to read difficult. She outlined the step-by-step instructions that she took them through:

1. Have the students read the same book. They can read the book silently, with a partner, listen to a tape recording, or listen to a teacher read aloud.

2. Stop at specific points in the reading and help the children verbalize what they are thinking and feeling.

3. On chart paper or the overhead, record some of the students' responses and have them copy the ones they agree with into their logs. Use "frames" such as:

> I was surprised when _____.
>
> Since _____ and _____ happened, I predict that _____ will happen next.
>
> The story reminds me of the time _____.

4. As students understand the various open-ended ways in which they can respond to literature, move them toward independence. Continue the discussions but don't write down what they say. Rather, have them write their own personal entries following the discussions. Have the class brainstorm a list of log topics and frames, and display these so that students can refer to them when they need a "starter."

5. Have students choose the books they want to read and do their own response logs. Divide the time available for self-selected reading into reading time and log-writing time, perhaps 20 minutes to read and 10 minutes to write. Once children are reading individual books, provide a time each week when they can share what they have written in a small-group format.

Summary

Writer's Workshop is a powerful and versatile structure for teaching children to write. Beginning each day with a mini-lesson in which children watch you write allows you to model, demonstrate, and think aloud about all the "big" and "little" components that constitute good writing. In your mini-lesson, focus on just one aspect—choosing a topic, what to do about spelling, how to edit your writing, how to revise by replacing, or any of the other things writers must learn to do. As children write, encourage them in their writing or conference with them about how to make their writing better and more readable. Beginning your Writer's Workshop with only the mini-lesson, children writing, and sharing steps allows all children to get off to a successful start in writing. When the children are writing willingly (if not well), you can add editing to your workshop and then conferencing, publishing, and Author's Chair. Because learning to edit is easier than learning to revise, you should teach some editing rules before teaching revising strategies. When the children know some revising strategies, make sure they revise their pieces before doing any editing.

In Writer's Workshop, children are usually writing on topics of their own choosing in whatever form or genre they choose. After the children have achieved some comfort level with Writer's Workshop, begin to include some focused writing lessons. Building on the basics required by all good writing taught in Writer's Workshop, focus your students' attention on particular topics, forms, or genres. Teach mini-lessons in which you model the particular kind of writing you are focusing on, and then guide children through the steps of the writing process to produce published pieces. Children who engage in both Writer's Workshop and focused writing lessons throughout their elementary years will become ready, willing, and able writers.

In reviewing the research on writing, Hillocks (1986) found that natural process writing instruction is effective and that what has been called *environmental writing instruction*, in which students engage in various writing activities designed to teach them to learn and apply specific writing strategies and skills, is more effective still. The key to teaching writing, including the conventions of writing, appears to include being consistent with a developmental sequence that recognizes the commonalties of children as they move from early emergence to sophisticated ability (Dyson & Freedman, 2003; Farnan & Dahl, 2003; Hodges, 2003). Effective writing programs will look very different grade by grade and will have expectations for children at each grade that are appropriate to their development as writers. The best writing instruction teaches students how to plan, compose, revise, and edit their own pieces of writing, all within the context of inquiry, self-assessment, and self-regulation fostered by interaction with teachers and peers.

chapter 9

Reading and Writing across the Curriculum

How many minutes across the day are your students actually reading and writing? Do your good readers read and write more than your struggling readers? Regardless of what grade you teach, your good readers read much more than your struggling readers. Good readers don't waste a minute of their independent reading time. They quickly grab a book when they finish an assignment in your classroom and they spend some time reading at home. Your good writers write more than your struggling writers (who are often the ones asking you how many sentences they have to write). If asked about the relationship between how much students read and write and their attitude toward reading and writing, most of us would explain that good readers and writers read and write more because they *like* to read and write, and struggling students read and write less because they *don't like* to read and write.

Consider the possibility that the cause-effect relationship between how much students enjoy literacy activities and how much time they spend in these activities might also flow in the opposite direction. Students who read and write more become more fluent in their reading and writing. Reading and writing are "easier" for them and so they feel more successful and enjoy reading and writing. Struggling students, on the other hand, don't read and write enough to become fluent, and every reading and writing encounter is a challenge for them. If we accept the fact that some students just don't like to read and write and will engage in these literacy activities only when forced to, students who are behind in their literacy development will stay behind. So accepting the "they don't like to do it and so they will do less of it" idea will doom our efforts to help all our students achieve their highest literacy potential.

So, how can you get your students—*all* your students—to increase the volume of reading and writing they do every day in your classroom? The answer is to view every subject you teach as an opportunity to add reading and writing. This reading and writing time does not need to be lengthy or to occupy all the time you allocate to teaching these subjects. Imagine that your students are engaged in a reading or writing activity for 30 minutes twice each week during science and social studies and once each week during math. At the end of the week, you have added 150 minutes of literacy engagement. Get all your students reading more, and all your students will read better than they would without this additional time. This chapter will suggest a variety of engaging literacy activities you can merge into existing curriculum plans.

Use Shared Reading to Teach Your Students How to Read Informational Text

Imagine that you are on an airplane going to some exotic destination and you peruse the airplane magazine. You page through several articles and then get engaged in an article about endangered animals. Next to the title of the article—"How You Can Save Us"—is a photo of a penguin stranded on a floating piece of ice. There are several other visuals on the page, captioned photos of polar bears, mountain gorillas, and manatees; a bar graph showing the increase in the number of endangered species in the last decade; and a world map with a key that shows which animals are currently most endangered on different continents.

Before beginning to read the text in the article, you read the title and study all the graphics. As you think about the information conveyed by the graphics, you call up prior knowledge and make connections. The title and graphics also spur you to do some higher-level thinking. Listen to your brain talking to you and you might hear statements such as:

> "I had no idea the number of endangered species was growing at this astronomical speed."
>
> "North America has the largest number of species but the number is growing fastest in Africa and Antarctica."
>
> "We have to do something about this. But what?"

As you read the article, you continue to think about what is happening and what part you might play in saving these animals. Your concern, your comprehension focus, and indeed your decision to read this article were all primed by the visual information.

Regardless of what grade level you teach, if you decide to expand the amount of reading your students do during science and social studies, the very first thing you need to teach your students is that we read informational text very differently from the way we read stories. Stories may have pictures but the pictures enhance the words; they do not carry a lot of the information. When reading a story, you glance at the picture and begin reading the connected text. When reading informational pieces, you always begin by "mining the graphics." Photos and illustrations often have labels or captions and you begin by reading this "quicktext" and studying the pictures. Most informational pieces have other visuals—maps, graphs, diagrams, charts—that good readers know will give them a lot of information with very few words. Your students need to learn that when reading information, the connected text is the last thing you read and that your comprehension of that connected text will be much greater when you have mined the graphics to build your background knowledge and vocabulary.

English Language Learners

All your students will benefit from learning to mine the graphics for everything they can learn from all the visuals. If you have children who are learning English, the visuals are a gold mine. The photos and illustrations accompanied by captions and labels will allow them to add multiple words to their English vocabularies. Once they learn how to interpret maps, graphs, diagrams, and charts, they can gain a huge amount of information from a very small number of words. All your students will comprehend what they read better if they always study the visuals first. English language learners may not yet be able to read the connected text in science and social studies texts but they can learn from these texts if you show them how huge amounts of information are portrayed by the visuals.

Even some of your students who are otherwise good readers may have trouble reading science and social studies textbooks. In addition to illustrations with captions, maps, charts, diagrams, and graphs, many informational books have a table of contents, a glossary, and an index. If your students do not know what to do when they encounter these foreign elements in their books, they probably skip over them. Guiding your students' thinking about the special features of informational books is difficult when your students are looking at individual copies of books. Imagine a scenario in which all your students have individual copies of a book and you are giving instructions such as this:

> "Everyone turn to page 28. Look at the diagram in the top left corner of the page. What do you see in the diagram? Begin at the arrow in the top left corner. Where is that arrow pointing? Follow your eyes around the arrows and see how the cycle works."

This step-by-step direction sounds simple enough, but careful observation of your students will show that many eyes are not focused on the diagram and still fewer eyes are following the arrows. Moreover, even those children who are focused on the diagram may not be thinking about how this diagram graphically portrays the water cycle. (A few children may not even be on the right page!)

To teach your students how to read information text, find some informational pieces that are large enough for all your students to see and engage them in shared reading of this text. Depending on your resources, you might use an informational big book, big-picture editions of children's newspapers, or informational text displayed on a screen with a projector.

Using one piece of text that everyone can see allows you to focus your students' attention on what you are teaching them. You can use a pointer, highlighting tape, or other attention getters to make sure everyone's eyes are in the right place! You can cover the connected text with large sticky notes and not reveal it until you have mined all the graphics for everything you can find out. You can lead students to read the title and headings and turn these into questions and then read the text to see if their questions were answered. You can direct their attention back and forth between the table of contents or index and the pages on which information they are seeking can be found. You can help them find the bold words on the page and turn to the glossary to build meanings for these words before reading the text containing

RICH resources

Informational Text for Shared Reading

There are numerous sources for informational text large enough for your whole class to see. Newbridge and National Geographic have a wide variety of science and social studies titles for all grade levels. Many of the *Magic School Bus* books come in a big-book edition. *Time for Kids* includes a big-picture edition with each classroom set ordered. *Weekly Reader* subscriptions include a digital edition that you can project onto a screen.

those bold words. You can point out the pronunciation (pro-nun-see-A-shun) guide in parenthesis after uncommon large frightening words and show them how easily they can pronounce these strange words if they use this handy guide. Use big books or projected text to teach your students these tips for reading informational text:

Tips for Reading Informational Text

1. Preview the text to see what it is all about and what special features it has.
2. Use the table of contents and index if you are looking for something specific.
3. Look for words in bold type and see if you can find the meanings for these important words in a glossary.
4. Look for pronunciations (pro-nun-see-A-shuns) of unfamiliar big words in parentheses after these bold words and use them to figure out how to say the words.
5. Read the title and turn it into a question to focus your mind on a big purpose for reading.
6. Read the pictures and all the labels and captions that go with them and see how much you can learn.
7. Study the maps, charts, graphs, and diagrams and try to figure out what they tell you.
8. Finally, read the text, turning each heading into a question and seeing if you can answer that question.

Help Your Students Transfer Their Comprehension Strategies When Reading Science and Social Studies

When the subject you are teaching is reading, do you lead your students to make KWL charts or create webs, data charts, Venn diagrams, or other graphic organizers to help them organize and remember new information? Do you use think-alouds to model all the different thinking strategies your brain uses to make sense of text? How many of your students do you think bring these comprehension strategies with them to science or social studies class? Probably not many! One of the quickest and easiest things you can do to help your students get more out of their reading in science and social studies is to take them through some lessons using the very same formats you have used during reading instruction.

> "Class, who can tell me what we did to help us connect what we knew about Washington, D.C., and organize the new information we learned in reading about it? Yes, we made a KWL chart. Today in science, we are going to be reading about how plants grow and reproduce. We already know a lot about plants. Let's make a KWL chart to organize our old and new knowledge about plants."

"Boys and girls, watch what I am drawing on the board and tell me how it helped us compare and contrast the ways humans and animals communicate. Yes, this is a Venn diagram or 'double bubble.' Today in social studies, we are going to read about the jobs people did in communities 100 years ago and compare them with the jobs we do today. We can use a double bubble to show how jobs have changed and the ways they are still the same."

"Remember last week, when we read *Missing One Stuffed Rabbit* and listened to what our brain was telling us? I read the first half and you listened to my brain talking to me and then you read the last part and I came around and listened in on your brains. Your brain talks to you when you read science, too. Today we are going to read about some endangered animals and share our thinking. I will read the first part and tell you what my brain is thinking. Then you will read with your reading partner and share with your partner what your brain is thinking."

Glance back at Chapter 7 and think about how you can use the lesson formats there as you teach the different subjects. Do you see some opportunities to have your students create webs, time lines, feature matrices, and data charts to organize information they are reading about in science? Could you use the Oprah Winfrey Interview to have your students interview people they are learning about in social studies who lived in a different location or historical period, or famous inventors or scientists? Would your students like to use the beach ball to retell the story of how the Pilgrims came to America? Would your students enjoy creating a play or reenacting a scene from some biographies they are reading in social studies?

As you help your students transfer their comprehension strategies to reading in all subject areas, remember to provide the modeling and support they need to succeed and then gradually release that responsibility to your students.

I do, you watch.

I do, you help.

You do, I watch.

You do, I help.

Spotlight Vocabulary in Science, Social Studies, and Math

The content areas of math, science, and social studies have their own special vocabularies your students must understand and use if they are to read and write well in these subjects. Fortunately, you do not need to develop a whole new set of activities for teaching content-area vocabulary. Most of the ideas described in Chapter 6 can be used not only during language arts time but also during math, science, and social studies. Think about the possibilities in all the different areas of your curriculum to build vocabulary using some of these activities.

- Use real things both from the school environment and collected from various places.
- Take advantage of media and technology—especially Internet images, videos, and simulations.
- Use pictures and picture walks—even from textbooks that may be too hard to read all the text but that contain illustrations and other graphics for important concepts.
- Use dramatization, especially in social studies, where many of the concepts involve interactions among various groups of people.
- Do the Three Read-Aloud Words activity with informational books related to your science and social studies topics.
- Provide topic-related materials for students to choose to read independently.
- Read and develop alphabet books related to topics being studied.
- Have students use context and pictures to figure out meanings of unfamiliar words during math, science, and social studies.
- Point out morphemes in math, science, and social studies vocabulary: *triangle, re-group*, *international, reconstruction, translucent, transparent.*
- Create class math, science, and social studies dictionaries with illustrations and examples of key terms.
- Once words have been introduced, display them in some way to keep them in front of your students and to remind you and them to use and notice these words.

Link Vocabulary Development to Comprehension Lessons

In addition to all the ideas presented in Chapter 6, there are three lesson frameworks that simultaneously build vocabulary and promote comprehension. Here are some example lesson frameworks for *Anticipation Guides*, *Preview-Predict-Confirm,* and *Ten Important Words*.

Anticipation Guides (Guess Yes or No)

Anticipation Guides (which we call "Guess Yes or No") require your students to predict before they read whether some statements are true or false. To prepare for this lesson, read the text your students will soon be reading and write 10 statements, some of which are true and some of which are false. For the false statements, write them so that students can change a word or two and turn them into true statements. When writing the statements, include key vocabulary your students may not be familiar with so that you can introduce them to that key vocabulary before they read. Make copies and distribute these to your students.

Guess Yes or No: Japan

_____ 1. Japan is on the continent of Europe.

_____ 2. Mt. Fuji is a volcanic mountain in Japan.

_____ 3. Japan has the highest life expectancy in the world.

_____ 4. Japan is made up of thousands of islands in the Atlantic Ocean.

_____ 5. Rice, fish, and seaweed are common foods in the Japanese diet.

_____ 6. Most people in Japan live in large houses out in the country.

_____ 7. The capital of Japan is Tokyo.

_____ 8. Karaoke is a very popular activity in Japan.

_____ 9. Japan is the world's largest economy.

_____ 10. Japan's national sport is Sumo wrestling.

Hand out the Guess Yes or No sheet and explain to students that they will soon be reading about Japan. Before they read, they will guess whether each statement is true or false. While they are reading, they will determine how good their guesses were and they will change all the false statements into true facts. For the first several lessons, your students may be hesitant to guess and will protest that "they don't know!" Assure them that they are not supposed to know and that is why we call this activity GUESS Yes or No. The guesses before reading are just guesses and it doesn't matter how many they guess right. What matters is that they can turn them all into true statements and show what they have learned from reading about Japan.

Because you are teaching key vocabulary with these sentences, have everyone read each sentence chorally with you and talk about the key vocabulary.

    1. Japan is on the continent of Europe.

After reading the first sentence, ask vocabulary-building questions such as: "Who knows how many continents there are in the world? Can we name them?" Lead the students to name as many as they can and then ask them to write their guess for whether Japan is on the continent of Europe on the line next to the statement. Wait until everyone has written "yes" or "no" on the line before going to the next sentence. Remind your hesitant students that it doesn't matter now whether their guess is right or wrong and that different people have different guesses. Assure them that as they are reading, they will have the chance to turn all the statements into true statements.

When everyone has committed themselves to a guess, have the second sentence read chorally.

> 2. Mt. Fuji is a volcanic mountain in Japan.

Again, take time to discuss the sentence and build vocabulary. What is a volcanic mountain? Do we have any volcanic mountains nearby us? Help the children make the morphemic connection that a volcanic mountain is a mountain that was formed by a volcano. Wait for all students to commit to a guess before proceeding to the next sentence.

When all the statements have been read and all the key vocabulary developed, have students read the text. Ask them to erase and change any "no" answers they guessed that are really "yes" answers, and to change a few words in the false statements to make them also true. Tell them that in turning false statements into true statements, they cannot use the word *NOT.* In other words, "Japan is not the world's largest economy" is not an acceptable way of turning sentence 9 into a true statement.

When your students have read the selection and made all the statements true, have the statements read again and let different students share how they changed the false statements to make them true. (Remember adding *NOT* is NOT allowed!)

Guess Yes or No: Japan
Yes   1. Japan is on the continent of ~~Europe.~~ Asia
Yes   2. Mt. Fuji is a volcanic mountain in Japan.
Yes   3. Japan has the highest life expectancy in the world.
Yes   4. Japan is made up of thousands of islands in the ~~Atlantic~~ Pacific Ocean.
Yes   5. Rice, fish, and seaweed are common foods in the Japanese diet.
Yes   6. Most people in Japan live in ~~large houses out~~ apartments in the ~~country.~~ city
Yes   7. The capital of Japan is Tokyo.
Yes   8. Karaoke is a very popular activity in Japan.
Yes   9. Japan is the world's second largest economy.
Yes   10. Japan's national sport is Sumo wrestling.

Although some of your students may be reluctant to commit themselves to a guess when they don't know, it is important to insist that they make the guess before letting them read. Once they make a guess, they will be more actively engaged in the text. It is human nature, once we have made a guess, to be eager to see how we did! Lead your students through some Guess Yes or No activities and watch how eagerly they read the text!

Preview-Predict-Confirm

Another activity that combines vocabulary and prediction is Preview-Predict-Confirm (Yopp & Yopp, 2004). To begin your PPC lesson, put your students in groups of three and show them pictures from the informational book or magazine article they are about to read. If possible, scan these pictures into a PowerPoint presentation and project them one at a time, giving your trios of students 30 seconds to talk with each other as they look at each image. Alternately, you can gather your students close to you and show them pictures from the actual text, making sure to cover all words on the pages so that only the pictures are visible to the students.

When they have viewed all the images and have had half a minute to talk together about each, give each trio 30 to 40 small slips of paper and tell them they will use these to write words they think will occur in the text they are about to read. Hand the small slips of paper and a pen to the most fluent writer in each group. Send the trios to far corners of the room to do this and ask them to use their "secret" voices so that no other group can hear the words they are guessing. Give them no more than 10 minutes to record words and then stop them and ask them to lay out all their words and put them into some groups. Give them five or six minutes to discuss and group the words.

When the students have had five or six minutes to discuss and group the words, hand each trio three large index cards. Have the recorder in each group label one index card with the letter *C* for *Common*, one *U* for *Unique* and one *I* for *Interesting*. Give the trios a few minutes to talk about their group of words and to choose one word they think all the other trios will have, one word they think is unique that no other trio will have thought of, and one word they think is a really interesting word that they hope to learn more about when reading the book. The recorder should write these words on the large index cards big

English Language Learners

Think about all the vocabulary your students learning English will be adding as they discuss the pictures with two of their classmates. If you spread your English language learners out in groups of three and provide them with empathetic, supportive peers, they will feel secure and comfortable in using their English speaking skills.

enough for everyone to see. Remind the trios to continue to use their "secret" voices so that no other groups can hear which words they are choosing.

Gather your students together and have each group show the word they have chosen as common, as unique, and as interesting. As the different words are shown, help the students determine how well they predicted which of their words were common to many other trios and unique to their trios. Ask each trio to explain their reasoning for which of their words was most interesting.

Now that you have used the pictures to build background knowledge and get your students talking and thinking about the words they might encounter in the text, have the trios read the text together and put an asterisk (*) or star on each word that actually occurred. Finally, have them choose five or six words they should have guessed but didn't. End the lesson by leading the students in a discussion about which words did occur and their reasons for choosing five or six words they wished they had guessed.

Here are some words one trio guessed after viewing some penguin pictures. Which groups would you put these in? Which word do you think was common to all groups? Which word might be unique? Which word interests you the most?

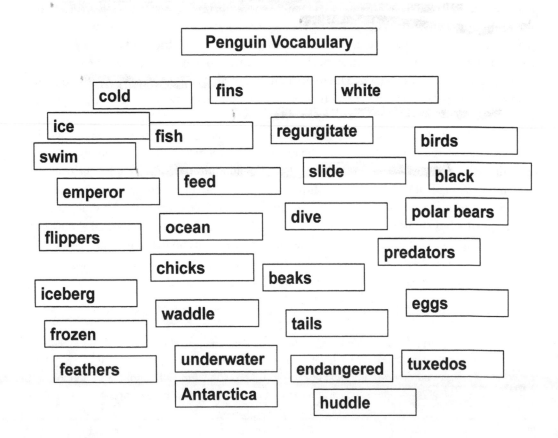

Penguin Vocabulary

cold · fins · white · ice · fish · regurgitate · birds · swim · slide · black · emperor · feed · polar bears · flippers · ocean · dive · predators · chicks · beaks · iceberg · eggs · waddle · tails · frozen · feathers · underwater · endangered · tuxedos · Antarctica · huddle

Ten Important Words

Another clever vocabulary strategy created by Ruth and Hallie Yopp (2007) is called Ten Important Words. This lesson format is designed to help students learn to determine which words in a text are the most important words. In informational text, when your students have chosen the most important words, they have simultaneously identified the major concepts or main ideas.

Just as in PPC, begin the lesson by arranging your students into groups of three, making sure to include a range of abilities in each trio and providing supportive peers for your English language learners or other students who need good peer role models. Give each group 10 small sticky notes and tell them that their job is to read the text together and place the sticky notes on what they think are the most important words. The piece they are reading should be relatively short, such as three or four pages of a textbook chapter or a two-page spread in a *Weekly Reader, Scholastic News,* or *Time for Kids* magazine. In this example, they are reading an informational piece on endangered sea turtles.

As they read, if the children decide other words are more important than the ones they have already designated with sticky notes, they may move the notes around. When the reading time is almost up, stop them and tell them that they must now make their final decisions and write these 10 words—one to a sticky note.

When the trios have made their choices, gather the students together and create a class tally. Ask each trio to tell you one of their ten words and then have the other trios show you how many of them also included this word. Write that word and the number of trios that chose it on your list and then ask a second trio for one of their words and get a count of the number of trios that included that word. Continue going around to the different trios until all the words included by any trio are tallied. Look at the tally completed in one classroom after the class had read a selection on *Sea Turtles* (page 192). This class of 25 students was divided into seven trios and one quartet so the largest number of votes a word could get was eight. The top 10 words from the article on endangered sea turtles are: *sea turtles, endangered, ocean, shells, migrate, swim, nests, reptiles, flippers,* and *eggs.*

Once the top 10 list is compiled, you can engage the students in a variety of tasks that require them to talk about, write about, draw or act out these words. Give two of the 10 important words to each trio and have them do two things that demonstrate each word. You might want to post of list of possibilities including:

1. List synonyms and antonyms.
2. Create three good sentences that use the word in different ways.
3. Draw two pictures that illustrate the word.
4. Act out the word.
5. Return to the text and find sentences and pictures in the selection that further explain the word and put sticky notes on them.

sea turtles	~~||||~~ |||	8
ocean	~~||||~~ ||	7
migrate	~~||||~~		6
endangered	~~||||~~ |||	8
shells	~~||||~~ ||	7
swim	~~||||~~		6
plankton	||||	4
plastron	|||	3
carapace	|||	3
nests	~~||||~~		6
reptiles	~~||||~~		6
flippers	~~||||~~	5
eggs	~~||||~~	5
Hawksbill	||	2
Loggerhead	||	2
Leatherback	||	2

Completing these two tasks for the two words will cause your students to talk with one another and further develop their meanings for the words. After 10 to 15 minutes, gather your students together and let them share their products.

Ten Important Words can be used with any informational text. Depending on the length of the text and the age of your students, you may want to adjust the number up or down a few words. In addition to providing your children multiple opportunities to actively engage these words, this strategy, if used regularly, will help your students with the important but difficult task of identifying key vocabulary in their own reading.

Writing to Learn

When your classroom schedule says "Writing," what are you trying to accomplish with your students during that time? When you read this question, did your brain talk to you and say, "DUH! I'm teaching them to write, of course." Most of the time, when we spend time having students write in our classrooms, improving writing skills is our goal. But, writing can also be the means to an end—the route to increased learning. When students write about what they are studying in science, social studies, or math, their brain uses all the thinking processes used to comprehend. They do all the CIPCOMS (connect, imagine, predict, conclude, opine, monitor, summarize). Writing down three things you think you know about Antarctica before you read about Antarctica requires you to make connections. Looking only at the visuals in the text about Antarctica and writing down questions prompted by these visuals helps you predict or anticipate the information you will soon be learning. Writing a letter to friends describing Antarctica requires your brain to use language and images that will allow your friend to imagine what you are experiencing in this very different environment. In addition to describing Antarctica, your letter will likely include your summary of some of Antarctica's most important features, some conclusions you reached about life in Antarctica, and your personal opinions and evaluation of Antarctica compared with the place you and your friends live in. As you are writing, you may realize that you don't fully understand something or are confused about something you are trying to explain. Your brain monitors what you are writing and it may send a message to stop writing and use fix-up strategies, including rereading and consulting other sources to clear up any confusions.

Writing requires thinking; that is the reason some people call writing "thinking made public." When you engage your students in writing tasks as part of your social studies, science, and math instruction, your students will think more about what they are learning. More and higher-level thinking will result in more learning. Just as with reading, when you include writing across your day, your students will write more. The more they write, the more fluent they will become in writing. As we described in the previous chapter, writing is always a difficult and complex task. Writing never really becomes easy, but, like anything else, with more practice, it becomes *easier*.

As with comprehension lessons, you can incorporate many of the writing lessons described in the previous chapter into your content-area instruction. When students know the letter-writing format, they can write letters to describe places they are visiting during social studies and imaginary journeys to various destinations in the solar system. It is easy to take the cinquain and other poetry formats you have taught them and have students use them to write poems that incorporate information they are learning in any subject area. Graphic organizers you create to focus their reading can become the fodder for constructing well-structured paragraphs and short reports. Your students can keep content journals in math, science, and social studies and record their learning using words, pictures, charts, graphic organizers, and diagrams.

Think-Writes

Another kind of writing you can easily incorporate into your content-area instruction are short, quick bits of writing you lead students to do to help them focus and clarify their thinking. These quick bits of writing are often completed in two minutes and never take more than five minutes. We call these quick bits of writing "think-writes" to distinguish them from other more formal, extended writing experiences. Because think-writes are written not for others to read but for the writer to help clarify thinking, think-writes are not published and thus they do not require revising and editing. To make it very clear to your students that think-writes are writing they are doing just for themselves, have your students do think-writes on scrap paper, sticky notes, or index cards. The think-write activities described here are adapted from *What Really Matters in Writing: Research-Based Practices across the Elementary Curriculum* (Cunningham & Cunningham, 2010).

Connection Think-Writes

Before your students begin to learn about a new topic in science or social studies, do you ask them to share what they already know about that topic? When you pose the "What do you know about . . . " question, do the same hands always go up—and the same hands never go up? Do you wonder why some students' hands almost never fly into the air? Equally problematic (and more annoying!) are the students whose hands always fly up and then when they are the first person you call on, they ask, "What was the question?"

Connection think-writes can make your efforts at prior knowledge activation more productive for all your students. Imagine that your learning focus for today's lesson is on presidents. You begin your lesson by saying,

> "Today we are going to start learning about some of our nation's presidents. Take a piece of scratch paper and write down everything you know about presidents. If you think you know something but you aren't sure, write it down anyway and we will try to find out. You have two minutes. Go!"

Your students grab scratch paper you have recycled from the copying room, torn into quarters and placed in small baskets at each table, and begin writing. You stand in front of the class and watch the clock, timing the students for exactly two minutes. Many of your students write as fast as they can, trying to "beat the clock" and write down many things.

The children no longer ask you to spell things—as they did the first few times you did these think-writes—because they know what the answer will be:

> "Spell it as best you can. This writing is just for you to get your thoughts down. No one else needs to read it, so as long as you know what you wrote, we're good."

When exactly two minutes have passed, you say,

> "Stop! Pens down! Who has something they want to share?"

Every hand is raised. You call first on a student who may not have much prior knowledge and that student proudly responds, "George Washington."

> "Good thinking! George Washington was our first president."

You continue to call on students and affirm their responses.

> "Yes, the president is the head of our nation."
> "Yes, presidents get elected every four years."

Sometimes, you ask a follow-up question.

> "Yes, Abraham Lincoln was a president. Does anyone know how Abraham Lincoln died?"
>
> "The president does live in the White House. Who knows where the White House is? Have any of you ever been to the White House?"
>
> "Good thinking. We did have two presidents named George Bush. We also had two other presidents with the same name. Does anyone have an idea who they might be?"
>
> "Yes, Barack Obama was our first African American president. Does anyone know where his father was born?"

Another student volunteers "George Washington" and you remind everyone that we need to listen and not repeat ideas and then ask that student if he has anything on his list that hasn't been said. When students volunteer information that is clearly incorrect, you correct that information but affirm the response of the student.

> "Benjamin Franklin was never president but he played a very important role in our government. Can anyone tell us what Benjamin Franklin did?"

When no more hands are raised, you congratulate your students on how much they already know about presidents and tell them that they will be learning many more interesting presidential facts and trivia in the coming days.

Think-writes to activate prior knowledge increase student engagement and motivation. Your most able students see it as a kind of race and they want to write as many ideas as they can in the two minutes. Your struggling students who may be reluctant to raise their hands are much more confident when they have had two minutes to think and when you are affirming of even a wrong answer or a misconception. Using think-writes forces you to do something we all know we need to do—but often find ourselves not doing. When we give students two minutes to write down ideas, we are forced to "wait" while they write. Both the quantity and quality of the responses you get will increase when you give your students wait-time. Two-minute think-writes make students think and teachers wait!

Once you start using think-writes, you will wonder how you taught without them. You can use think-writes to activate prior knowledge during math.

> "We are going to be learning more about measurement this week. You have two minutes to write everything you think you already know about measurement. Go!"

> "Our new math topic is fractions. I know you already know a lot about fractions. Take a piece of scratch paper and write down what you know. You have two minutes. Go!"

Science topics also can be introduced with two-minute think-writes.

> "Our new science topic is on natural resources. Do you know any? What do you think you know about natural resources? You have two minutes. Go!"

> "Rocks is our science topic for the week. I know you know things about rocks. Let's see how much rock knowledge you can write down in two minutes. Go!"

You may even uncover some science misconceptions that are part of your students' prior knowledge. If someone tells you something you are sure is incorrect, make a mental note of that and respond by saying something like,

> "A lot of people think that—but we are going to find out that it actually works quite differently."

Here are some two-minute think-writes used to access prior knowledge in social studies.

> "What holiday do we celebrate in November? Right! Thanksgiving will soon be here. I know you know a lot about Thanksgiving. Grab some scratch paper and get those brains thinking. You have two minutes. Go!"

> "Immigration is our social studies topic. I am not sure how much you know about immigration but we will soon find out. You have two minutes. Go!"

For all these connection think-writes, the students are recording their ideas on scratch paper. This scratch paper is essential to successful two-minute think-writes for several reasons. First, it often takes a whole class of students more than two minutes to "get out a piece of paper." In two minutes, the think-write is done. Second, scratch paper is unintimidating. No one asks if they need to "head their paper" or if "this counts for the grade" when jotting down thoughts on a small scrap of paper. Finally, we are recycling paper that would have been thrown away and not wasting a perfectly good whole piece of notebook paper!

It is also important to specify and stick to the time limit. Two minutes is plenty of time for students to recall and jot down most of what they know. Students who don't know much don't get too squirmy in two minutes and students who know a lot enjoy racing to write down an impressive array of facts before the time is up.

Abe Lincoln
George Bush
George Washington
Vise president
com ander and chief
first pitch

George Washington
white house
Jimmy Carter
election
air force
Lincoln

Prediction Think-Writes

Prediction is another thinking process you can engage all your students in using think-writes. You will find numerous opportunities across your school day to use prediction think-writes. Science is a fertile area for prediction. In fact, prediction is one of the science processes we want all students to do regularly. Imagine that you are teaching a science unit on magnets and electricity and want your students to make some predictions and then test those predictions.

> "Boys and girls, we are going to continue our unit on magnets and electricity today. In just a few minutes, you are going to get into your teams and test some materials and see if they will attract or repel the magnets. Before we test them, let's make some predictions. Grab a sheet of scratch paper and number it from 1 to 6. Next to number 1, write *ruler*. Then write either "*attract*" or "*not attract*" to show your prediction. Will the ruler be attracted to the magnet?"

The prediction think-write continues as you hold up each object your students are going to test. Students write the name of the object and their guess of "attract" or "not attract" next to each. Some students are hesitant to guess and claim they don't know. You push them, however, by saying something like:

> "You're not supposed to know. That's what a guess is. When you test them, you will change any guesses to the correct answers. Make your best guess. I'm not going to let you join your team to test the objects until you have made a prediction for each."

Prediction is a powerful motivator but students are often afraid of being wrong. When they learn that you don't care if they are wrong or right and that they are expected to change incorrect guesses to correct answers, and if you make it clear they will not move forward in the activity until they have some guesses, they will put something down. Once they have a prediction, human nature kicks in and they are eager to "see how they did." Think about the science units you teach and the science activities your students engage in and you will quickly envision many prediction think-write possibilities.

> "Which objects will sink and which will float?"
>
> "Will more water in the glass make the pitch higher or lower?"
>
> "When we roll all these round objects down the ramp, which one will hit the ground first?"
>
> "Today, we are going to test clay soil, loamy soil, sand, and pebbles to see how quickly water flows through them and how much water is absorbed.

Take a piece of scratch paper and order these four from slowest movement to quickest movement. Then order them from absorbs most water to absorbs least water."

In math, we also want students to learn to predict and we refer to these predictions as *estimates*. Teachers often ask their students to give oral estimates before doing math activities. Having the students write their predictions on scratch paper increases the participation and engagement for all students.

"We are continuing to work with measurement today and we are going to measure and compute some areas and perimeters. We will use our metric rulers, so our answers will be in centimeters. As I show you each object you are going to measure, write down the name of the object and your guess of the perimeter and area of that object, making sure your guess is in centimeters."

Prediction think-writes also work well in social studies, although they take a very different form from those done in science classrooms. This chapter began with the suggestion that you use shared reading to teach your students to mine the graphics—photos, illustrations, maps, charts, and graphs—before reading the connected text. Once you have modeled this a few times with enlarged text, you can use a prediction think-write to provide your students opportunities to practice this on their own. The prediction think-write we use to help students learn to "mine" the graphics is very similar to that used in the two-minute think-write we use to help students access prior knowledge and make connections. Instead of two minutes, we give them three minutes. Imagine that you are about to read a piece on Ecuador in your *Time for Kids, Scholastic,* or *Weekly Reader*

"We are going to read a short piece about Ecuador today. Before we read, I am going to give you exactly three minutes to "mine" the graphics. Look at all the graphics—photos, illustrations, maps, charts, graphs, anything visual—and write down as many things as you can that you think we are going to learn about Ecuador. You can use the labels, captions, and other quicktext that go with the graphics but don't waste your three minutes reading the longer pieces of text. Take a piece of scratch paper and get started. You have three minutes to write down as many things as you can about Ecuador. You may start now!"

When the three minutes is up, you have your students put the text out of sight and ask them to volunteer what they learned about Ecuador from the graphics. Just as in the connection think-write, you accept their answers and ask expanding or clarifying questions as appropriate.

> "Yes, Ecuador is on the equator. Does anyone remember what the equator is?"
>
> "Yes, bananas are a major crop. Do you think they keep all the bananas they grow there or export them?"
>
> "Right, Ecuador is about the size of Nebraska. Do you think that makes it larger or smaller than our state?"

As your students share information and think about your expansions on their ideas, they are going to want to return to the piece again and point out more information from the graphics. You explain that they will be reading the whole piece soon but until then you want them to focus on how much they were able to glean from the graphics in just three minutes. If you catch someone sneaking a peek, you remove the text from that student and return it when it is time to read. You adhere firmly to your "no sneak peeks" rule during the first several three-minute prediction think-writes, knowing that your students will learn to make maximum use of their three minutes in future lessons.

> Ecuador
> equator
> South America
> mountains
> borders Peru +
>   Colombia
> jungle
> Pacific Ocean

Think-Writes for Summarizing, Concluding, Evaluating, and Imagining

Connection and prediction think-writes are usually done before students read. You can also use think-writes to help your students do the thinking processes they use while they are reading. Imagine that you gave your students three minutes to mine the graphics and write down what they thought they were going to learn about Ecuador as described in the previous section. Next, your students will read the text. Before letting them reopen the text, give each student three sticky notes for marking the three most important facts they learn about Ecuador. Show them how to write a brief sentence or phrase telling what they think is important and place the sticky note right on the place where they found that information.

The first time you do this with your students, they will probably use their sticky notes quickly and ask for more. Make it clear that there is a lot of information about Ecuador in this short piece and that they can't sticky-note everything. Their job is to pick three important facts they think everyone should know about Ecuador. Don't give them any additional sticky notes. Letting them cover the piece with sticky notes would defeat your purpose of helping them learn to think about what information is most interesting and important. You may want to have your students work in partners to read and sticky-note the text, partnering struggling readers with stronger readers who will help them with difficult words.

When students complete the reading, gather them together and go through each part of the text, asking who has a sticky note on this page. Have them read what they wrote on the sticky note and explain why they think this is an important fact. You can use three sticky note think-writes in any subject area when students are reading informational text and you want them to think about what information is most important or interesting to them.

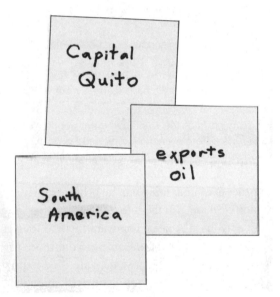

The thinking process of concluding or inferring requires the reader to take information in the text and "figure out" an idea that the text does not directly state. Our brains draw many different conclusions as we read but often these conclusions are drawn by comparing our world and experiences to the new world or experiences we are learning about. To use think-writes to help your students draw conclusions, pose a question that requires that kind of thinking. For Ecuador, you might have students write the words *climate, size,* and *geography* on a piece of scratch paper. Tell them that as they read, you want them to try to figure out how similar the climate of Ecuador is to the state in which they live. For size, they should try to figure out if Ecuador is larger or smaller than the state in which they live. And for geography, they should think about the different regions of Ecuador and how these are similar to or different from the regions of their state. Tell the students to jot down notes on these three topics as they read. After they read, have students share their comparisons and support their ideas with information from the Ecuador article and information they have previously learned about their state.

Everyone loves to give their opinions! Kids are no exception to this rule. If the kind of thinking you want your students to do falls into the evaluate/opinion category, ask them to decide something and justify that decision with facts from what they read. Here are some examples of opinion think-writes.

> "Your mom or dad has the chance to take a job in Ecuador. Your whole family would move to Quito and live there for two years. You would go to school there and learn to speak Spanish. Your family has decided that everyone gets a vote in this important decision. How will you vote and what reasons will you give to support your opinions?"
>
> "Imagine that you are grown up and have just been elected to the United States Senate. The deficit is large and the president has proposed eliminating the space program. How will you vote? Support your vote with facts you learn about what we have learned from space exploration."
>
> "As you are reading about sea turtles, you will discover that they are endangered in many parts of the world. Different people have ideas about how to save sea turtles from extinction. Which ideas do you think would work best and why do you think so?"

Even the thinking process of imagining can be prompted with a think-write. Give your students a large index card and ask them to "sketch" what they are reading about. Tell them to use pencils—not crayons—because you want them to focus on what they see in their "mind's eye," not on an artistic creation. Some of your more verbal students will experience some frustration with this task because they are used to processing information with words only. But your spatial and artistic students will enjoy this novel way to think about what they are reading. Maybe instead of a think-write, this activity should be called a think-draw!

Concluding is figuring it out. *Evaluating* is deciding "what *you* think." *Imagining* is putting yourself into the text and "being there." Your students will approach informational text with much higher levels of engagement if you include some higher-level think-writes—and think-draws—to your comprehension tool kit!

Summary

This chapter is all about "more." The more you read, the better you will read. The better you read, the more you will read. The more you write, the better you will write. The better you write, the more you will write. All our students—struggling and achieving alike—benefit from more! The obvious place to look when you are tallying up the minutes you can add is across your whole school day. Including some focused comprehension lessons, writing lessons, and vocabulary activities will allow you to provide all your students with more literacy encounters. "More" is also the essential idea when you think about how much they will learn during your math, science, and social studies instruction. Focus on the key vocabulary of the subject matter with engaging activities, and your students will learn more math, science, and social studies. Teach them how to read informational text by mining the graphics and using the index, table of contents, bold words, and pronunciation guide in math, science, and social studies texts, and they will understand and remember more important content. Use math, science, and social studies topics in focused writing lessons and think-writes, and force your students to think deeply about the concepts they are learning, and they will understand and remember still more content.

This common-sense notion that "more" results in better reading, writing, and content learning is supported by numerous research studies. Many studies have found that using effective instructional strategies in vocabulary or comprehension can improve student learning of subject matter (Hattie, 2009). Having students write during science, social studies, and other subjects increases their learning in all these subjects, and having students write regularly produces the greatest gains (Bangert-Drown, Hurley & Wilkinson, 2004; Graham & Perin, 2007).

chapter 10

Assessment

Assessment is part of everything we do in life. Most of us make an assessment of the weather each morning to decide what to wear. We assess the food, service, and atmosphere as we dine at a new restaurant. We assess our new neighbors as we watch them interact with each other and move their furniture in. This chapter provides some examples of how you can make assessment an extension of your teaching, rather than just one more chore that has to be done.

What Is Assessment?

Sometimes, it is easier to define something by beginning with what it is not. Assessment is *not* grading—although assessment can help you determine and support the grades you give. Assessment is *not* standardized test scores—although these scores can give you some general idea of what children have achieved so far. Assessment *is* collecting and analyzing data to make decisions about how children are performing and growing.

Caldwell (2002) describes four steps for assessment. First, identify what you want to assess. Second, collect evidence. Third, analyze that evidence. And fourth, make a decision and act on that decision. Caldwell suggests three main purposes for reading assessment: to determine student reading level, to identify good reading behaviors, and to document student progress.

Determining Student Reading Level

Reading level is affected by individual factors within each child, such as prior knowledge and interest, as well as by instructional factors, such as type of prereading instruction, amount of support provided by the reading format, and whether a first reading or a rereading of a selection is being considered.

Despite the fact that reading level is not static, you still need to determine an approximate reading level for each of your students. Knowing the level at which each student is reading early in the school year serves as a benchmark against which to judge how well your instruction is helping that child raise his or her reading level. First, you need to know how to determine whether the books your students are choosing for self-selected reading are too hard or too easy so you can help them make more appropriate choices. Next, you need to have a general idea of each child's reading level so you can decide how much support each child needs to experience success during comprehension lessons. Finally, you need to determine reading levels because many schools and parents expect you to know the reading level of and document progress for each student.

To determine reading levels, have individual students read passages at different reading levels. Many reading series include graded passages with their reading textbooks. Some school districts and states have created graded passages or selected benchmark books that you can use to assess reading levels. A number of published Informal Reading Inventories (IRIs) also include graded passages, such as the Basic Reading Inventory (Johns, 2008) and the Qualitative Reading Inventory (Leslie & Caldwell, 2005). These reading passages are graded in various ways. Traditionally, passages were specified as preprimer (early first grade), primer (middle first grade), first grade, early second grade, late second grade, third grade, fourth grade, and so on. Recently, books and passages have

A variety of systems have been developed for marking the oral reading of a child. Most systems work something like this:

> Once there was a farmer who lived with his wife and their ten children in a very small farmhouse. The farmer and his family were miserable. They were always bumping into each other and getting in each other's way. When the children stayed inside on rainy days, they fought all the time. The farmer's wife was always ~~shooing~~ _shooting_ children out of the kitchen so she could cook. The farmer had no place to sit ~~quietly~~ _quickly_ (SC) when he came in from _his_ work. The farmer ⟨finally⟩ could stand it no longer. He said to his wife, "Today I am going ~~into~~ _to_ the village to talk with a wise man about our crowded house. He will know what to do."

In reading this passage, the child read "shooting" for *shooing*; read "quickly" for *quietly* but then self-corrected (SC); inserted the extra word "his"; omitted the word *finally*; and read "to" for *into*.

been divided into more levels. In the Reading Recovery system, for example, books are divided into many levels; levels 16 through 18 are considered end of first grade.

Regardless of the source or leveling system of your graded passages, you can use these passages to determine the approximate reading level of each student. Generally, you have the child read aloud a passage, beginning with one you think he or she can handle. As the child reads, you mark the reading in some way that errors can be counted and analyzed. After the child reads the passage, you ask the student to retell the passage or you ask questions to determine how much was comprehended.

Once you have made a record of the child's oral reading and a determination about comprehension from the retelling or the answers to questions, you decide what level of oral reading accuracy and comprehension is adequate. Most experts recommend that a child have an oral reading accuracy level of about 95 percent and demonstrate comprehension of 75 percent of the important ideas in the passage. The passage about the farmer and his wife has approximately 100 words. If you do not count the self-correction (which we would not because self-correcting is a good reading behavior that indicates the child is self-monitoring), the reader made four errors, giving him an accuracy rate of 96 percent. If the child's retelling indicates comprehension of most of the important ideas in this short passage, we will know that this reader can read text at this level quite adequately. We will not, however, know that this is the just right, or instructional, level for the child.

Instructional level is generally considered to be the highest level of text that a reader can read with at least 95 percent word accuracy and 75 percent comprehension. To determine instructional level, you must continue to have the child read harder and harder passages until word identification falls below 95 percent or comprehension falls below 75 percent. Instructional level is generally considered to be the *highest* level of text for which the child can pass both the word and comprehension criteria.

When you know the approximate reading levels of all your students, you can use this information to choose materials for guided reading and decide how much support your different readers will need with the various materials. Remember that prior knowledge and interest have a large influence on reading level. Remember that during guided reading lessons, you build both interest and prior knowledge (including meaning vocabulary) before children read. You then choose your format to provide enough support so that they can be successful at meeting the purpose for the lesson. Children can read text that is a little beyond their level if they are given the appropriate support before, during, and after reading. Remember also that the size of the "leaps" children make has limits. If you determine that

Determining Reading Levels

1. Use passages or books that have been determined to get increasingly more difficult.
2. Have the child begin reading at the level you think he or she might be.
3. To get a measure of word reading accuracy, record oral reading errors as the child reads.
4. After the child reads, remove the text and ask the student to retell what was read or answer some comprehension questions.
5. If the child's word reading accuracy is at least 95 percent and comprehension is approximately 75 percent, have that child read the next harder passage. If the child's word reading accuracy is below 95 percent or comprehension is below 75 percent, have that child read the next easier passage.
6. Continue to have the child read until you determine the highest level at which the child can read and still meet the 95 percent word accuracy and 75 percent comprehension criteria. This is the best general indicator of that child's just right, or instructional, reading level.

a child's reading level is late first grade, that child can usually be given enough support to feel successful with some second-grade-level material. However, material written at the third-grade level is probably not going to be accessible for that child.

Once you understand how to listen to a child read and retell to determine instructional level, you can use this knowledge during your weekly independent reading conferences. You won't want to do formal oral reading records during these conferences. Rather, listen as the child reads a part he or she has selected, and then ask that child to tell about the most interesting part of the book or what has been learned so far. As the child reads and tells you about his or her reading, your informal 95 percent/75 percent meter is running, and if you realize that a child is choosing books that are way too easy or way too hard, you can steer that child toward some "just right" text.

Why Not Use Standardized Tests to Determine Reading Levels?

In many schools, children take a variety of tests that yield a grade equivalent. Teachers get a printout that tells them that Billy reads at 2.5 and Carla reads at 5.5. Being trusting, logical people, they assume that this means Billy's instructional reading level is middle second grade and Carla's instructional reading level is middle fifth grade. Unfortunately, life is not that simple. If Billy and Carla are both in the second grade, most of the passages they read on the test are second-grade passages. Billy's score of 2.5 means that he did as well on the test as average second-graders reading second-grade text. Carla read the same passages and she did as well as the average fifth-grader reading second-grade passages would have done. We can certainly say that Carla is a good reader—certainly a better reader than Billy. But we cannot say that her instructional reading level is fifth grade because she did not read any fifth-grade passages!

Another reason that we cannot use standardized tests to determine individual reading level is that all tests have something called *standard error of measurement (SEM)*. Look in the manual of any test and it will tell you what the SEM is. If the SEM is 5 months, then the score a child achieves is probably within 5 months of the true score. Billy's score of 2.5 has a 68 percent chance (1 standard deviation) of actually being somewhere between 2.0 and 3.0. If we want to be 95 percent sure, we have to go out 2 standard deviations. Then we will know that Billy's score is almost surely somewhere between 1.5 and 3.5.

Across groups of children, these SEMs balance out. One child's score is higher than his actual ability, but another child's score is lower. If your class average score is 2.5, you can be pretty sure that your class reads about as well as the average class of second-graders on which the test was normed. Standardized scores provide information about groups of children but give only limited information about the reading levels of individual children. To determine the reading level of a child, we must listen to that child read and retell and find the highest levels at which he or she can do both with approximately 95 percent word accuracy and 75 percent comprehension. Unfortunately, no shortcut will get us where we need to go.

Identifying Good Literacy Behaviors and Documenting Student Progress

Determining reading levels is generally done early in the year, then at specific points during the year, and again at the end of the year. Day in and day out, however, you need to be assessing and monitoring how well your students are reading and writing. To do this, you have to know what you are looking for. What are the good reading and writing behaviors? Throughout the chapters of this book, we have described instruction that develops good literacy behaviors. In this section, we suggest ways to assess these behaviors as your students engage in literacy activities.

Assessing Emergent Literacy

Chapter 3 described many activities for building the foundation for literacy and concluded that there are seven signs of emergent literacy. The seven signs shown on page 210 are the reading behaviors we look for as indicators that each child is moving successfully into reading and writing. These behaviors form the basis for our assessment of beginning readers. You can assess these behaviors as your students engage in their daily literacy activities.

If you teach young children, you may want to keep a checklist of emergent literacy behaviors. Each day, put the checklists of two or three children on your clipboard and observe and talk with these children as they engage in independent reading and writing to determine how well they are developing critical behaviors. Use a simple system, a minus (–) to indicate the child does not have that behavior, a question mark (?) when the behavior is erratic or it is unclear that the child has it, and a plus (+) to indicate the child does seem to have developed that behavior. Three pluses on three different dates is a reliable indicator that the child has indeed developed that behavior.

Assessing Word Strategies

As children move from the emergent literacy stage into the beginning reading and writing stages, you need to monitor and assess their development of fluency, sight words, decoding, and spelling strategies. Chapters 4 and 5 contained many activities for developing these strategies. Your assessment, however, must take place while the children are actually reading and writing. The goal of word instruction is to teach children words and strategies they can actually use when they are reading and writing. What you want to know is *not* how your students spell words during the daily word wall activity but how quickly they recognize these words when reading and how correctly they spell these words when they are writing.

There are many opportunities throughout the day to make these observations. During your weekly independent reading conferences with children, ask them to read aloud a short part of what they have chosen to share with you. Listen for how fluently they read;

• Emergent Literacy Behaviors •

	Dates Checked (− ? +)
Name _____	
"Pretend reads" favorite books, poems, songs, and chants	— — — — — — —
"Writes" and can "read back" what was written	— — — — — — —
Tracks print	— — — — — — —
Left page first	
Top to bottom	
Left to right	
Return sweep	
Points to each word	
Knows reading jargon	— — — — — — —
Identifies one letter, one word, and one sentence	
Identifies first word, first and last letter in a word	
Reads and writes some concrete words	— — — — — — —
Own name and names of friends, pets, family	
Favorite words from books, poems, and chants	
Demonstrates phonemic awareness	— — — — — — —
Counts words	
Claps syllables	
Stretches out words as attempts to spell	
Blends and segments words	
Identifies rhymes	
Demonstrates alphabet awareness	— — — — — — —
Names some letters	
Knows some words that begin with certain letters	
Knows some common letter sounds	

how automatically they identify the word wall words; and how they use patterns, context, and other cues to figure out unknown words. When your students are reading in partners or trios, circulate to the different groups and ask them to read a page to you. Notice how they are using what you are teaching them about words as they actually read text. Another opportunity to observe their sight word, word identification, and fluency behaviors is when you meet with small groups.

Sight Word, Decoding, and Spelling Behaviors

Name _____	**Dates Checked (– ? +)**

Identifies word wall words automatically when reading — — — — — — —

Spells word wall words correctly in first-draft writing — — — — — — —

Uses letter patterns, picture and sentence cues to decode — — — — — — —

Beginning letters of word (*br, sh, f*)

Rhyming pattern (*at, ight, ain*)

Endings (*s, ed, ing*)

Prefixes (*un, inter*), suffixes (*able, tion*) for big words

Combines letter cues, picture cues, and sentence cues

Uses letter patterns to spell words — — — — — — —

Beginning letters of word (*br, sh, f*)

Rhyming pattern (*at, ight, ain*)

Endings (*s, ed, ing, er, est*)

Prefixes (*un, inter*), suffixes (*able, tion*) for big words

Self-monitors — — — — — — —

Self-corrects when meaning is distorted

Self-corrects when nonsense word is produced

Rereads to correct phrasing

Rereads for fluency

Reads fluently — — — — — — —

With phrasing

Attending to punctuation

With expression

Writes fluently — — — — — — —

Words are written quickly

Handwriting is not slow and laborious

Focuses on meaning

You can observe their spelling behaviors by periodically looking at samples of their first-draft writing, by analyzing their spelling in writing samples you collect three times each year, and in your revising/editing/publishing conferences with individual children. As with emergent literacy behaviors, the – ? + system allows you to easily record what you observe on each child's word behavior checklist.

Assessing Comprehension Strategies

Chapter 7 described comprehension strategies and a variety of activities that teach comprehension and foster thoughtful literacy.

As with emergent literacy behaviors and word strategies, you can monitor and assess your students' development of these behaviors as you interact with them during comprehension lessons and in your independent reading conferences. Because comprehension is so dependent on prior knowledge and interest, it is not possible to feel secure in our judgments that a child can—or cannot—use a particular comprehension strategy. Often, children recall much information and respond to that information in a high-level way

● Comprehension Strategies–Story ●

Name _____	Dates Checked (– ? +)
Names and describes main characters	— — — — — — —
Names and describes settings	— — — — — — —
Describes the goal or problem in the story	— — — — — — —
Describes major events that lead to resolution	— — — — — — —
Describes the resolution to the story	— — — — — — —
Makes predictions	— — — — — — —
Makes connections	— — — — — — —
To self	
To world	
To other texts	
Makes inferences and draws conclusions	— — — — — — —
Imagines and visualizes characters and events	— — — — — — —
Expresses a personal reaction/opinion	— — — — — — —
Monitors comprehension and uses fix-up strategies	— — — — — — —

when the topic is familiar and of great interest but demonstrate little comprehension of less-familiar, uninteresting topics. You can use some checklists to indicate general use of comprehension strategies. Because we read informational text differently from the way we read stories, you probably need two comprehension checklists—one for stories and one for informational text.

Anecdotal records can also help determine how well your students are learning and applying comprehension strategies. Comprehension is complex, and often checklists just do not seem to capture children's thinking as clearly as you could by making comments, perhaps even including some of your children's "exact words."

Many teachers analyze the anecdotal records for one child each day. At this pace, every student's anecdotal records can be analyzed every 4 to 6 weeks. Alternatively, you can keep anecdotal records only for those students who appear to have difficulty comprehending and observe these students more frequently. No more reliable or valid means of diagnosing or evaluating students' ongoing learning is possible than anecdotal records collected regularly and systematically and consisting of objective and specific descriptions of children's reading behaviors.

● Comprehension Strategies—Information ●

Name _____   **Dates Checked (– ? +)**

Uses visuals to preview text and make connections   — — — — — — —

Makes predictions based on visuals   — — — — — — —

Summarizes important information   — — — — — — —

Accurately recalls important facts/details   — — — — — — —

Organizes ideas appropriately   — — — — — — —

    Sequence/chronology

    Topic/subtopic

    Comparisons

    Cause/effect

    Problem/solution

Makes inferences and draws conclusions   — — — — — — —

Imagines and visualizes information   — — — — — — —

Expresses a personal reaction/opinion   — — — — — — —

Monitors comprehension and uses fix-up strategies   — — — — — — —

Assessing Writing

As described in Chapter 8, writing is perhaps the most complex act people engage in. The best way to determine how well students write is to observe them each day as they are writing, to look at first-draft writing samples, and to interact with them during writing conferences.

You can observe many aspects of writing as you move around the classroom. Do students struggle to identify topics for writing? Do students do some planning first when asked to write? Is handwriting easy for them? Are they using resources in the room and spelling patterns they know to spell words? Are they automatically using some of the mechanical and grammatical conventions they have been learning? Do students move confidently through a first draft? Do students revise and edit some as they write, or do they wait until they are publishing a piece? To record these observations, you may want to make a checklist similar to the previous examples but specific to the age and starting point of your students.

In addition to the observations you record, you may want to take a focused writing sample during the first week of school. Give your students a prompt to which they all can relate, such as "What Third Grade Is Like" or "My Most Favorite and Least Favorite Things." Analyze these samples to determine where individual children are in their writing development and what the class as a whole needs to work on. Put this sample somewhere where you can find it in January. After the winter holidays, have your students write on the same prompt again. When your students have written the second time, return the first samples to them and let each child analyze the writing growth made. You can also analyze the second samples, comparing them to the first for each child and looking for indicators of things the class needs to work on. Repeat the same procedure once more at the end of the year and you and your students will be able to document the growth they have made.

Writing is a very complex process. No matter how good we get, there is always room for growth. Because writing is complex, it is easy to see only the problems children still exhibit in their writing and not the growth they are making. Having three writing samples on the same topic across the school year provides tangible evidence of growth to both teacher and student.

Assessing Attitudes and Interests

It is hard to overemphasize the importance of children's attitudes toward and interests in reading and writing. If developing avid readers and writers is one of your major goals, you need to collect and analyze some data so that you can identify needs and document progress.

Early in the year, it is important to determine what your students like to read and how they feel about reading. Many teachers start the school year with the following homework assignment: "Next Monday, bring to school the three best books you read all summer." They encourage students to go back to the library to check out a book previously read. If children can no longer find the book, the teachers ask them to tell why they thought it was such a good book. Young children are encouraged to bring favorite books they like to have read to them.

Children's Names	Books Shared	Magazines/ Newspapers	Current Interest (none, little, some, much)
Carol	Ramona the Pest Charlotte's Web	none	some
Sheryll	3 Bobbsey Twins mysteries	none	some
Sue Ann	Whales Dinosaurs Runaway Horse	U.S.A Today	much
Travis	none	Sports page	little
Ray	none	Fishing	little
David	3 Star Trek books	Sports Illustrated	some
Jason	Cannonball Death at High Noon Dirty Dozen	Time	some

Topics of interest to many children:

Sports, fantasy

Types of books read:

✓Realistic fiction   ✓Science fiction   Historical fiction
✓Mystery   Myths/legends   Folk/fairy tales
Fantasy   Biography   Autobiography
✓Informational   Other _____

When the children bring their books, encourage them to tell what they like about the books. As they share, note the titles of the books they bring and their reasons for liking them. This tells you a lot about their current reading interests and also suggests selections for read-aloud books to try to broaden interests.

Some children do not bring three books, or they bring books but have nothing to say about them and may not have liked or even read the books. This tells you a lot about the current interests, attitudes, and home environment of these children. It also lets you know that all the efforts you plan to make to encourage and support reading are truly important and needed.

You might want to follow up this "best-books" assignment with another homework assignment to bring in magazines and parts of the newspaper the children have read. Again, follow up this assignment with group sharing and make notes about what each child brings (or does not bring). Record your results on a "Beginning Interests and Attitudes Summary," such as that shown here. In addition to noting what each child shares, summarize the interests of the class by noting which topics and types of books are shared most. You have now assessed your students' entering interests and attitudes and can plan how much and what kinds of motivational activities to do.

Just as with any kind of assessment, your assessment of reading interests and attitudes should be ongoing. By linking your assessment directly to your instruction, you ensure

• Beginning Interests • and Attitude Summary

Name _____   **Dates Checked (– ? +)**

Seemed happy when engaged in reading   — — — — — — —

Seemed happy when engaged in writing   — — — — — — —

Talked about reading at home   — — — — — — —

Talked about writing at home   — — — — — — —

Showed enthusiasm when sharing a book with peers   — — — — — — —

Showed enthusiasm when sharing a piece of writing   — — — — — — —

Showed enthusiasm during self-selected reading conference   — — — — — — —

Showed enthusiasm during writing conference   — — — — — — —

Chose to read rather than engage in another activity   — — — — — — —

Chose to write rather than engage in another activity   — — — — — — —

that your assessment is valid. By assessing interests and attitudes on a regular schedule, you get a more reliable indicator than if you assess only once or twice a year. Also, as in any assessment, you can use a variety of methods to assess interests and attitudes. One of the best methods of assessing is to observe what your students actually do. Many teachers fill out checklists for everyone early in the year and then fill them out again for one-sixth of their class each week. If you do this all year, you should have six or seven indicators of reading attitude throughout the year and should be able to document which students have better attitudes at the end of the year than they did at the beginning.

Summary

Assessment is a part of everything we do. To make any kind of decision, we collect and analyze evidence and then act on that evidence. Literacy assessment includes determining reading levels for children, assessing and monitoring their reading and writing strategies and behaviors, and documenting their progress. The systematic use of checklists and anecdotal records gives you the most valid and reliable results. You can then use these records to document the progress of each child and report that progress to parents and other stakeholders. Assessment in real life is a natural and productive activity. We hope that the practical ideas presented in this chapter help make assessment a natural and productive part of your literacy instruction.

Differentiating Instruction for Diverse Learners

"The more different ways I teach, the more children I reach."

We don't know who the author of this quote is but we all recognize (and research supports) the common sense truth it communicates. The children in your elementary classroom are all individuals and they differ on any dimension you can name. We know from the research on multiple intelligences that children differ in the ways they learn. To meet the needs of your kinesthetic learners, you need to provide hands-on, concrete learning experiences. Your interpersonal learners thrive when you include small-group and partner activities as a regular feature of your literacy instruction. In today's multicultural classrooms, there are many cultural differences among our students. They have different cultural heritages and racial backgrounds, and they come to school speaking a variety of languages. In addition to cultural differences and differences in how your students learn, they also differ in how much they like to read and write and thus approach literacy activities with very different levels of engagement. The most obvious difference you probably notice among your students is their reading levels. Regardless of what grade you teach, your most achieving students probably read and write at levels several years beyond the levels of your struggling students. Although we have not used the word *differentiation*, the concept of teaching in a variety of ways to meet the needs of all your students has been an important agenda in all the preceding chapters of this book. Before we suggest some additional ways you can differentiate your instruction, think back to the possibilities already described.

This book began by inviting you into the classrooms of unusually effective teachers—teachers who year in and year out got better than expected results from their students. Common across all these classrooms was the variety factor. Teachers used a wide variety of materials, a wide variety of lesson formats, and a variety of student groupings. Another common factor was student engagement. Discipline problems were few and far between because the teacher viewed the classroom as a community and taught students to work together and to help and respect one another. Quantity of reading and writing was another common factor in successful classrooms. Students spent a lot of time reading and writing—not only when the schedule said "reading" and "writing" but also during science and social studies time. The research reviewed in Chapter 1 suggests that the most effective teachers know that "one size does not fit all" and that their instruction across the day incorporates the basic principles of differentiation.

The chapters that have followed Chapter 1 also incorporate the basic principles of differentiation. The essential question of Chapter 2 focused on how you can increase the quantity of reading done by *all* your students. Including some informational books and magazine articles in your teacher read-aloud and adding more informational pieces to your classroom library is a differentiation strategy because males often prefer nonfiction. Including multicultural books provides additional differentiation for your students of varying cultural and racial heritages. During your weekly independent reading conferences, you differentiate your instruction for both struggling and avid readers by spreading them out across the days and spending an extra minute or two with them, steering them toward materials at their optimal reading level. The most obvious way you differentiate your instruction during independent reading time, however, is by letting your students choose what they want to read. When they can choose, they will differentiate for themselves.

Glance through the activities for building the literacy foundation suggested in Chapter 3 and think about how they are differentiated. It is not by accident that many of the activities center on the names of your children. When you use your children and their names to build beginning literacy concepts, your children can view each lesson as "all about them!" When your fledgling readers choose what they want to read during independent reading time and write in the writing center, they are differentiating their own instruction by their choices.

The focus of Chapters 4 and 5 was on helping all children become fluent readers and writers who can automatically and quickly read and spell common words and who have strategies for quickly identifying and spelling unfamiliar words. In these chapters, differentiation is accomplished through quantity, variety, and choice. Everyone can find things that are easy for them to read because you have accumulated and created a wide variety of "everyone" books. Across the week, you engage your children in rereading through choral reading, echo reading, and reading along with recorded books they have selected. By having your word wall words always visible, you are supporting your visual learners. Auditory learners learn these important words as they chant them. The learning style of your kinesthetic learners is supported as they write the words.

The decoding and spelling activities in Chapter 5 were carefully designed to move all your students forward in their understanding of spelling patterns. During Guess the Covered Word activities, the words are always read in the context of a sentence or paragraph. Children learn how to use word length, all the beginning letters, and known words to figure out unknown words. In every Guess the Covered Word lesson, beginning sounds are reviewed for children who need more practice with beginning sounds. Advanced readers often learn to read all the words in the sentences used in Guess the Covered Word activities—greatly increasing the number of words they can read. Each Making Words lesson begins with short, easy words and progresses to longer, more complex words. Children who still need to develop phonemic awareness can do this as they "stretch out" words while making them and as they decide which words rhyme while sorting them. Using Words You Know Lessons begin with short, familiar words and proceed to longer, more complex words.

Differentiation in the vocabulary and comprehension activities described in Chapters 6 and 7 is supported by the great variety of activities and lesson formats you can use to help your students build their vocabularies and hone their thinking strategies. Beginning the year with Writer's Workshop, as described in Chapter 8, and letting your students choose their topics allows all your students to write about what they know about and care about. When you form revising and editing partnerships by pairing writers with similar abilities, you are using these partner groupings to differentiate your writing instruction. As you meet with individual students in writing conferences, you can tailor your conference to the individual needs of each writer. This writing conference provides the "teachable moment" in which both advanced and struggling writers can be nudged forward in their literacy development. Chapter 9 suggested a variety of ways you can incorporate comprehension, vocabulary, and writing opportunities into your science and social studies instruction. With these additional opportunities to engage your students in reading and writing, you can include more variety in your lessons and increase the quantity of reading and writing your students do. Assessment is essential to differentiation. Only when you know what your individual students can do and cannot yet do can you make good decisions about how to spend your instructional time and what kind of lessons and groupings will move all your students forward.

If you are incorporating many of the ideas from the previous chapters into your daily instruction, you already have a lot of differentiation going on in your classroom. The rest of this chapter will focus on some additional activities you can use to achieve an even more differentiated classroom.

Use a Variety of Collaborative Groupings

No matter how hard you try or how fast you move, if you are the only person in your classroom who is teaching, there is not enough of you to go around! The most obvious and available resource you have to provide more "just right" instruction to each of your students is your other students. In the most effective classrooms, teachers use a variety of collaborative groupings to help their students accomplish a variety of tasks. As you read about the various grouping possibilities, think about your class across the day and where each of these activities might help you lower the pupil-teacher ratio in your classroom.

Partners

Imagine that you and your best friend both have the same task to accomplish. Perhaps you need to learn PowerPoint to create a presentation for your graduate class. Would you be likely to get together to work on it? Would doing it together be more fun than doing it alone? Would you be able to do it better and perhaps faster together than alone (provided you did not get sidetracked by other mutual interests!)? In real life, when we have something to accomplish and someone we like has the same task, we often arrange to do it together, believing the old saying that "two heads are better than one." Partners are the easiest collaborative grouping to incorporate into your classroom routine. Here are some ways partners might fit into your classroom routines.

Talking Partners   Many teachers use a "Turn and Talk" routine to increase student talk and engagement. Before introducing Turn and Talk to your students, think carefully about who you will pair with whom. If you have children learning English, do you have other children who speak their language and whose English is more advanced so they could do some translating? Do you have a "budding teacher" who, although not able to speak the language of the child learning English, would enjoy teaching that child? If you have a child with attention or behavior problems, could you pair that child with someone he or she is friends with and thus more likely to want to talk with and listen to? Thinking about what kind of support you want the partners to provide for the various activities and assigning partners purposefully is the secret to the success of this collaborative grouping.

After you have decided on the talking partners, think about when you want to have the partners turn and talk, and seat your talking partners together for this activity. Many teachers use Turn and Talk regularly during their teacher read-aloud so they assign places on the carpet to the talking partners. Periodically, they stop during their reading and pose a question and give students 30 seconds to turn and talk.

> "Turn and talk to your partner about what you see in the pictures. How many things can you name?"
>
> "Turn and tell your partner what you think is going to happen next."
>
> "Turn and tell your partner if you think the boy has a plan that will work."
>
> "Would you like to take a trip to the moon? Tell your partner why or why not."
>
> "Do you think the things in this story could really happen? Explain to your partner what you think and why."

The possibilities for Turn and Talk during teacher-read aloud are endless. When you incorporate Turn and Talk into your read-aloud, you can raise the level of thinking your students do and their active engagement with the text. After students talk with one another, resist the temptation to let everyone share with the whole group. This will slow your read-aloud down considerably and you have accomplished what you wanted to accomplish by letting them share their thinking with each other. After the 30 seconds, return to your read-aloud and acknowledge their thinking with a general response.

> "You named a lot of the things in the picture. Listen and see if you called them what the author called them."
>
> "I heard lots of good predictions. Let's see what did happen."
>
> "Some of you think yes and some of you think no. Let's read on and see."
>
> "Thumbs up if you told your partner you would like to go to the moon."
>
> "Most of you thought the story was imaginary. Here are some of the good reasons I heard you use to explain your thinking."

Talking partners can also increase participation and engagement when you are introducing a new topic during reading, math, science, and social studies. Look back at the connection and prediction think-writes described in Chapter 9. On some days, instead of having your students write down their thoughts, seat them with their talking partners and give them a brief time to share ideas.

> "We are going to be learning about many of our nation's presidents this week. Turn and tell your partner everything you think you know about presidents. You have one minute."
>
> "Today we are starting a math unit on measurement. Have you ever measured anything? What can you use to measure things? Turn and share what you know about measurement."

"In science today, we are going to experiment with these objects and see if they sink or float. I am going to hold up the objects one at a time and give you and your partner 30 seconds to decide if you think they will sink or float. At the end of 30 seconds, I will ask you to give me a 'thumbs up' or 'thumbs down' to show me your predictions."

"Today we are going to learn more about Antarctica. Turn to page 67 in your social studies text. You have three minutes to mine the graphics with your partner. Talk about all the visuals on pages 67 to 70 and see what we can add to what we know about Antarctica."

Just as with think-writes, posing questions for talking partners to discuss gives your students the time and opportunity to gather and then share their connections and predictions. It forces you to do something most of us find very hard to do—wait! Wait-time has been shown to increase both the quantity and quality of student response. Incorporating think-writes and this talking partner routine, often called "Think-Pair-Share," into your lesson routines across the curriculum will result in much higher levels of talk, engagement, and thinking

Reading Partners   Another way you can use your students to teach each other is to assign them to reading partners. Just as with talking partners, you need to think carefully about who to partner with whom. Think about your struggling readers first and who would be the best partners for them. Ask yourself, "Who will be patient and not just tell them all the words?" "Who will be insightful and able to coach them and get them to talk about their thinking?" In most classrooms, there are a couple of very nurturing children who would love to help some of their struggling classmates. These are the children to try out as partners for your most struggling readers. In most classrooms, the best reader in the class is probably not the best partner for the most struggling reader.

When you have your partnerships formed, you need to make sure the partners have a clear purpose. If the Beach Ball activity is going to be done after reading, the partners should be reading and thinking about their answers to the questions on the beach ball. If they are going to add things to the KWL chart, they should be reading to find things to add. If they are going to participate in an Oprah Winfrey Interview, they should be thinking of questions to ask the "guest" and what they would say if they are picked to be the guest. When partners know exactly what they are going to do after reading, they not only help each other with the words but they also help each other with the thinking that allows them to comprehend.

Before the partners go off to read, tell them how long they have. Make it a reasonable amount of time, but don't give them more time than most of them will need. Most behavior problems during partner reading happen when children have time to fool around. Don't give them the same amount of time each day because selections vary in length and complexity. Always set a time limit. Write it on the board and/or set a timer. When the time is up, tell them you are sorry if they didn't finish but you need them to join the group, or tell them they may finish and then join the group. The course of action you choose doesn't matter, but be consistent and enforce your time limits. You will be amazed how much more they can read and how much better they behave when the "clock is ticking."

Inevitably when students are reading with partners, some will finish early and announce to all, "We're done!" Once this happens, your students may go into "race mode." Suddenly they are all trying to finish first! This race mentality does not promote thinking and comprehension! When your students are working in reading partners, give them a "filler"—something they should do if they finish early. Relate this filler as closely as you can to the purpose for reading. If they are reading to answer the questions on the beach ball and finish early, tell them they should take turns asking each other the beach ball questions and come up with "awesome" answers. If they are reading to find information to add to the KWL chart and finish early, tell them they should begin to write down the information. If the after-reading activity is "doing the book" and they have a few minutes, tell them to decide which character they would like to be and to practice what they will say and how they will act. Children are not in such a rush to finish first when they have to think and prepare for another task. (Do not turn the filler into a class requirement that must be turned in or completed in a specified amount of time, or you will be right back in the same old bind: "They don't all finish at the same time." Also, it is probably not a good idea to use the word *filler* with your students, but it is important for you to remember that is what it is!)

When introducing partner reading to your students, role-play and model for them what partners do, how partners help each other, how partners correct each other nicely, and how to ask good questions. Here are some of the different ways you can teach your partners to read, depending on their age and the purpose for reading that day:

- *Take Turns.* One partner reads the first page and the other partner reads the second page and so on. This is the most common way of partner reading—but not necessarily the most productive.

- *Read and Point.* One partner points to the words on one page while the other partner reads; then they switch reader/pointer roles on the next page. This is particularly helpful in the beginning, when print tracking is a big issue with some children. You will be surprised at how quickly some children pick up print tracking when a nurturing, helpful partner is pointing to their words and making sure the other partner points to the words correctly when it is his or her turn. We do not recommend this practice after the children become more fluent, however, because it slows down children's reading and can take their focus away from the meaning.

- *Ask Questions.* Both children read each page, silently or chorally. They then ask each other a "good question" about what they have read.

- *Say Something.* Say Something is also a good partner reading strategy. The simple notion is that after you read a page, you "say something." If you do not have anything to say, you may have been concentrating too much on the words and not enough on the meaning. You may need to reread the page, thinking about what you might say about it. Some teachers have partners take turns—one partner reads a page and the other partner says something; then they reverse roles. On other days, partners read the page together or silently and then each says something.

- *Echo Reading.* Once the children know how to echo read, they will enjoy echo reading some selections. Give the child who is the echo in each partnership something to designate his or her status, or have the children read the selection twice switching their reading and echo reading roles. For struggling readers, make sure they are the echo on the first reading.

- *Choral Whispering.* Choral whispering is a variation of choral reading. Children whisper with their partner. Children use a "whisper" voice so that their voices do not distract partners seated nearby.

Once you have your students reading in partners, you will find that partner reading is a wonderful opportunity for you to circulate around and both coach and monitor the reading of individual children. Tell your students that while they are reading, you will be coming around to most of the partnerships to listen to their reading and discussion.

> "When I join your partnership, I may interrupt and ask each of you to read a little aloud for me so that I can hear how well you are growing in your reading. I may ask you to retell or summarize what you have read so far. I will write some notes here on my clipboard so that I have a record of how well you are reading and how you are all becoming such good thinkers about your reading. If I don't get around to all the partners today, I will make a note of that too and make sure I get to listen to you read and tell about your reading next time we read in partners."

Writing Partners   Many teachers like to use writing partners who help and support each other during writing time. The partners can get ideas flowing by talking with each other for two minutes about what they are planning to write. As described in Chapter 8, they can help each other revise and edit their pieces before publishing. If you choose to form writing partnerships, you probably want to assign students of similar abilities to work together. Your talking partners or reading partners will very likely be different from your writing partners.

Literature Circles

Literature circles, sometimes called *literature discussion groups* or *book clubs*, are groups of four to six students who read the same book and gather to discuss and do activities related to that book. The groups have a clear purpose for reading and discussion. An alternative would be to have the group read different books that are somehow connected. For example, they might all be books related to the same topic, books by one author, or books in the same genre. Depending on the age, reading levels, and ability to work collaboratively together, you can organize your literature circles in a variety of ways and with varying amounts of teacher direction and group structure. Here are some possibilities to consider when thinking about using literature circles to differentiate instruction in your classroom.

Book Choice and Group Assignment   For each "lit circle" cycle, select four to six books that are related in some way. They might be books by the same author—Dr. Seuss, Patricia Palacco, Eve Bunting or Marc Brown; they might be related by genre—mysteries, biographies, fantasies, or plays; or they might be related by topic—animals, holidays, weather, or explorers. To achieve differentiation for the varied reading levels in your classroom, be sure to include at least one book that is easy enough for your most struggling readers and a book that will challenge your most able readers. Once you have chosen the books, your students need to make some choices among those you have chosen.

To enable your students to make good choices, devote the first day of each lit circle cycle to having students preview the books. If the books have lots of pictures, place the books around the room and have your students rotate to each book and spend three minutes previewing each book by mining the graphics. With chapter books that have few pictures, read aloud the first chapter of each book to your whole class of students. Based on this preview, have your students fill out a lit circle choice sheet on which they list their first, second, and third choice of the book they would most like to read. Explain to your students that you may not be able to give them their first choice but you will give them one of their choices.

To form groups, look first at the choices of your struggling readers. If they choose the easy book for any of their choices, assign them to that book. If any of your struggling readers do not choose the easy book for any of their choices, assign those students to their first-choice book, assuming the first choice is not the challenging book! Next, look at the choices of your most advanced readers and assign them to the challenging book if it is one of their choices. After the struggling and advanced readers are assigned to groups, assign your other students, giving as many first choices as possible and making good groups that can work well together.

When everyone is assigned, the group reading the easy book contains some struggling readers and some average readers who chose that book as their first choice. The group reading the challenging book likewise contains some advanced readers and some average readers who chose that book as their first choice. The groups reading the average-difficulty books contain mostly average readers with a few struggling and advanced readers who didn't choose the book closer to their level. If you take the time to have your students preview the books and to strategically assign them to groups, your groups will work together better because everyone is happy they got one of their choices. (Your students never need to know there is an easy or a challenging book. That is your secret for making lit circles differentiated collaborative groups!)

How Lit Circles Read the Books   After you decide on your groups, you can decide how they should read the book by considering how much support they need. You may want the students to meet together for the actual reading or you may want them to read the book on their own and come together for discussion or completing the assigned task. If you choose to have them not do the actual reading together as a group, you might want to assign partners within each group to make sure every student has enough support to successfully read the text. Perhaps you will decide that you want to have one of the groups read the book with you while the others read on their own or with partners.

When the group meets together, you need to decide how much structure they need to accomplish the task you want them to complete. For some groups, you might want to assign a teacher or coach in each group who leads the group to complete the task. If a written product is desired, you can appoint a recorder in each group and give that student a marker and some special paper on which to write the results. If the groups are going to report to each other their ideas or discoveries each day, you may want to appoint a reporter who will be the "voice" of the group. If illustrations will help the groups share their ideas, you can designate one student in each group to create these illustrations.

For some lit circles, you might want to appoint specific roles to each student in the group. To be sure your students understand their roles, create a role sheet for each role and model for your students how to use it. Tailor the roles to the maturity and talents of your students, the group size, and the task you want them to complete. Here are the roles used in one classroom:

- *Discussion Director:* Your job is to develop a list of questions that your group might want to discuss about today's reading. Try to determine what is important about today's text. Focus your questions on big ideas.
- *Passage Master:* Your job is to locate a few special sections of the reading that the group should look back on. You should help your group notice the most interesting, funny, puzzling, or important parts.
- *Vocabulary Enricher:* Your job is to be on the lookout for a few especially important words that your group needs to remember or understand. You should look for new, interesting, strange, important, or puzzling words.

- *Connector:* Your job is to find connections between the material you are reading and yourself and other students. Also look for connections to the world and to other books we have read.

- *Illustrator:* Your job is to draw some kind of picture related to the reading. It can be a sketch, diagram, flowchart, or stick figure scene.

Literature Circles Help You Differentiate in Numerous Ways   Literature circles provide many opportunities for you to differentiate instruction for all the different kinds of diversity you have in your classroom. Differentiation for the various reading levels is accomplished as you include at least one easy and one challenging book and assign students whose reading level matches that book if that book was one of their choices. You can further differentiate by deciding how much support you will give students to read the book. Your most struggling readers can be supported by partners or by being included in teacher-led groups. You can differentiate according to their learning strengths by assigning specific roles: Verbal students get to be reporters; artistic students are given the roles of illustrators.

Differentiation is also achieved as the students make choices. When they select the books they most want to read, their choices are based on their individual preferences and they are differentiating for themselves.

A Literature Circle Example

The teacher decides that all the children will read and do plays. He chooses four plays from the Rigby *Traditional Tales and Plays* collection, in which each book contains the tale told both in story format and in play format. The books chosen are *Goldilocks and the Three Bears* and *Town Mouse and Country Mouse* (average difficulty), *The Three Billy Goats Gruff* (easier), and *Robin Hood and the Silver Trophy* (challenging). The teacher decides to spend four days with these plays—previewing and choosing on the first day, reading the story and play in their groups for two days, and reading the plays in small groups and for the other groups on the final day.

Day 1   The teacher begins these book club groups by sharing the book covers and explaining that the books contain both a story and a play. The teacher explains that today they get to look at all the books and decide on their first, second, and third choices for which one they would most like to read. Eight books of each title have been placed in four gathering places in different corners of the room. The children circulate to the different corners and have three minutes to look at and talk about each book. When all the children have looked at all four books, they write down their first, second, and third choices and give these to the teacher. After school, the teacher looks at their choices and assigns children to groups, considering both their reading levels and their choices, and making sure to give everyone one of their choices.

Day 2 The teacher gathers the children together and tells them that today they will spend most of their time reading the tale told in story form. Each group has 22 minutes to read the tale, and then they will gather back together and do the Beach Ball activity. The teacher quickly reviews with the children the questions on each segment of the beach ball and the rules for Beach Ball activities. The teacher then distributes the appropriate books to members of the different groups and assigns each group a place to meet. The teacher tells the children that their group can decide how to read the story but that they must stop after every two pages and discuss their answers to the questions on the beach ball. As the children read, the teacher circulates and makes sure every group knows what to do. He spends more time with the group reading *The Three Billy Goats Gruff,* coaching them on word and comprehension strategies.

After reading the selection, they gather together again. Each group comes to a circle inside the big circle, and that group answers the questions on the beach ball as the others watch and listen. The children are very interested in all four stories and pay good attention as each group shares ideas from their particular story.

Day 3 The activity for the third day is reading the play. Today, the teacher tells the students to read the play in two-page segments. They first read each segment in an echo reading format and then read it again with different children reading different parts. The teacher appoints a child to be the "teacher" in each group. This child is the voice that all the other children will echo. For the second reading, the groups are instructed to take turns reading so different people read different parts. The teacher again circulates as the children read, coaching them to read with appropriate expression and settling a few disputes about who reads which part on which page.

After reading the plays in small groups, the teacher gathers the children together again, once more placing each group, in turn, in the inner circle. The teacher takes the role of narrator for each group and reads the narrator parts. Then the teacher lets all the children chorally read all the other parts. The children delight in listening to the choral reading of all the groups.

Day 4 Today, the children gather in their small groups once again and read the play with one person reading each part. The teacher has assigned each child a part. The child who is the narrator in each group is also given the role of "director." The children read their part and then do whatever acting is required. The teacher encourages all the groups and "rehearses" the billy goats and the troll so that they read and act with expression. After about 20 minutes of practice, the class reassembles. The members of each group read and act out their play for the other groups. Each group gets a round of applause, with the loudest applause given to the big billy goat.

Coaching Groups

If, in your assessment, you notice students having difficulty figuring out how to pronounce unfamiliar words in their reading, you can teach them to use their word identification strategies by meeting with small coaching groups. Coaching groups last only 10 to 15 minutes. As the children read and encounter problems, you can coach them to apply what they have learned when they actually need to use it.

When you begin a coaching group, tell your students that they are all going to learn to be word coaches. You may want to make an analogy to a sport your students play. Help your students understand that during soccer practice, you practice various moves, and then in game format the coach watches you play, stopping you from time to time to coach you to use the skills you have practiced. Tell them that in the coaching groups, you are going to show everyone how to be word coaches so they can coach each other on how to figure out a difficult word. Include all your students in coaching groups so they can all learn to be word coaches, but include those who struggle with word identification more often.

Demonstrate how to be a word coach, and as they understand how to coach, let different students play the role of "word coach." Choose reading material that is at the reading level of most of the students included in the group. Have students read a short section of the text to themselves first and then ask a student to read aloud so you can demonstrate what a word coach does. Before students begin reading, remind them of the strategies they can use to figure out an unfamiliar word. You might want to post a chart of steps such as this one.

How to Figure Out a Hard Word

- Put your finger on the word and say all the letters.
- Use the letters and the picture clues.
- Look for a rhyme you know.
- Keep your finger on the word and finish the sentence; then pretend it's the covered word.

Here is how to coach each strategy and why each strategy is important:

- *Put Your Finger on the Word and Say All the Letters* When readers come to a word they don't know, they should put their finger on the word and name all the letters. Naming the letters is not the same as pronouncing individual sounds to sound out the word. English is not a sound-it-out-letter-by-letter language, and the worst decoders are the ones who try this phonetic approach. You want them to name all the letters because having them do this is the only way to know for sure that they have indeed looked at all the letters and seen them all in the right order. Another reason for having them name the letters is that strong evidence suggests that retrieval from the brain's memory store is auditory. Just looking at an arrangement of letters and searching in the brain for the word, or a rhyming word that resembles the unknown word, is apt to be a more difficult way of identifying that word than saying the letters, which goes through the brain's auditory channel.

Sometimes when students name the letters of an unfamiliar word out loud, they can immediately pronounce that word, which may be proof positive that the auditory channel was needed for retrieval! After they name all the letters, if they successfully pronounce the word, cheer! They have scored a goal. ("See, it was in there. You just had to say it so your brain could find it!") If they still do not know the word after they name all the letters, give them *one* of the next three cues, depending on the word.

● *Use the Letters and the Picture Clues* Pictures often provide clues to words. The child who sees the word *raccoon* and names all the letters, then glances at the picture, may indeed see a picture of a raccoon. The picture, along with naming the letters, often allows readers to decode the word. Once the reader has named all the letters out loud and studied the picture, cue them to notice the picture clue if there is one:

> "I see an animal in the picture that looks to me like a *r-a-c-c-o-o-n.*"

● *Look for a Rhyme You Know* If the unknown word has a familiar rhyming pattern, cue the reader to some of the rhyming words that might be known:

> "We know that *w-i-l-l* is *will* and *s-t-i-l-l* is *still.* Can you make *t-h-r-i-l-l* rhyme with *will* and *still?*"

● *Keep Your Finger on the Word and Finish the Sentence; Then Pretend It's the Covered Word* Guess the Covered Word is an activity that helps children use beginning letters, word length, and context to figure out words. It is the "default" cue, the one to use when others do not work. If neither picture clues nor rhyming words help, cue the reader to try the Covered Word activity. Having your students read on and then go back is not the preferred method for decoding words because it interrupts their reading. Ideally, readers process unknown words as they encounter them. However, when they need the clues provided by the rest of the sentence to decode a word, coach them to use the sentence clues.

Coaching a Missed Word The procedure just described is what to do when a reader stops on a word. If instead of stopping, the student misreads a word, let the reader finish the sentence and then lead the child back to that misread word. Imagine, for example, that the child reads "There was not a cold in the sky" instead of *There was not a cloud in the sky.* At the moment the child misreads "cold" for *cloud, cold* does make sense. But by the end of the sentence, the child should realize that the sentence did not make sense and go back to try to fix the error. Let your students finish the sentence and they will develop their own self-monitoring systems. If, however, they do not notice any error and just continue to read, stop them and say something like, "That didn't make sense. Let's look at this word again. Say all the letters in this word." Then give them the appropriate cue to help them figure out the word.

Finding the Time to Do Coaching Groups Many teachers do coaching groups while those children not in the coaching group read with partners. In other classrooms, the teacher meets daily with an "after-lunch bunch" and does coaching at that time. All children are included in the after-lunch bunch at least once each week but readers who struggle with word identification are included almost every day. In some classrooms, teachers have a center time each day and do a coaching group that we call a "Fun Reading Club" during that time.

If you have help coming—a special teacher or trained assistant—and you have many students who need coaching, consider scheduling your independent reading at that time. The helping person can coach readers who struggle with decoding in their independent books while you hold your scheduled conferences.

Partner Older Struggling Readers to Tutor Younger Struggling Readers

This idea is based on a tutoring program set up at Webster Magnet School in Minnesota (Taylor, Hansen, Swanson, & Watts, 1998). Fourth-graders who were reading at beginning third-grade level tutored second-graders, most of whom were reading at primer level. The second-graders were all participating in an early-intervention program in their classroom in which they read books on their level. The fourth-graders spent 45 minutes on Monday and Tuesday with the reading coordinator or with their classroom teacher preparing for their 25-minute tutoring session on Wednesday and Thursday. On Monday, the fourth-graders selected a picture book to read to their second-grader and practiced reading the book. They also practiced word-recognition prompts that they would use when their second-grader read to them. On Tuesday, they practiced again and developed extension activities to develop comprehension strategies, including story maps and character sketches. They came up with several good discussion questions based on the picture book they were planning to read.

On Wednesday and Thursday, the fourth-graders met with their tutees. During this session, they listened to their second-grader read the book currently being read in their classroom's early-intervention program. While listening, they helped their second-graders identify words by giving them hints: "Look at the picture," "It starts with *pr*," "Sound it out in chunks—what would this part be (covering all but the first syllable)?" Next, they read from the picture book they had chosen, built meaning vocabulary from the book, led a discussion based on their discussion questions, and did the comprehension extension activity.

On Friday, the fourth-graders had debriefing sessions with their teacher in which they discussed how their tutees reacted to the book, how well their word-recognition prompts were working, the success of their discussion and comprehension activities, as well as problems encountered and progress noticed. They also wrote a letter to project coordinators detailing the successes and problems of that week. They received a response to their letter on Monday.

Data reported on this project show that both the second- and fourth-grade struggling readers made measurable progress. This is not surprising because this program combines all the elements essential for reading growth. Second-graders were getting daily guided reading instruction in materials at their level in their classrooms. In addition, during the tutoring session, they were reading material at their level to someone who knew how to help them with word recognition. They were also increasing their knowledge stores and comprehension strategies as they listened to their fourth-grade tutor read the picture book to them and as they engaged in the discussion and comprehension activities. Fourth-graders got a lot of practice using the material at their instructional level, reading the picture book, and learning word-recognition and comprehension strategies, as they prepared and carried out the tutoring with their second-graders.

Getting this system to work will take some organization, and if you have a reading specialist at your school, it would be good to get him or her involved. Given the results reported and the "just plain sensible" nature of the cross-age tutoring program, you are almost guaranteed to "get your money's worth" out of the time required to set up such a program.

Find and Train a Tutor
for Your Most Needy Child

Think now about the one child in your classroom who is most behind in reading and writing. Perhaps this child is just learning to speak English or has not attended school regularly. For whatever reason, this child is a beginning reader and needs a lot of reading practice in very easy materials. Most children who are far behind in reading and writing can make considerable progress if they have a strong classroom program and some one-on-one tutoring.

Training the Tutor

Before thinking about where you might find this tutor, you must decide what you would train the tutor to do. The most important component of any successful tutoring program is the repeated readings of materials at the child's instructional level. So your first task is to find some materials that are just right. Look back at the suggestions in Chapter 4 for finding and creating easy materials. You are looking for something your beginning reader would be interested in and can read at instructional level—no more than five errors per 100 words. If your student is a "nonreader" or such a beginning reader that you cannot find anything, you will have to create the materials. This is not as hard as it sounds. Simply sit down with your struggling reader and write an introductory paragraph of five or six sentences about him.

> Carlton is 9 years old. He goes to Washington School. He is in the fourth grade. Mrs. Cunningham is his teacher. He likes Washington School. He likes Mrs. Cunningham, too.

This paragraph will become the reading material Carlton reads with the tutor for the next several days until he can read it fluently and knows most of the words in it. When he demonstrates to you that he can do this, ask Carlton what else he would like the book to tell about him and have him watch while you write the second page:

> Carlton has six brothers and sisters. Their names are Robert, David, Manuel, Thomas, Patrice, and Jackie. They live on Willow Road. His father works at the Ford place. His mother works at Ken's Quik-Mart. His cousin, Travis, lives with them, too.

The procedure continues with the teacher creating the pages of Carlton's book and the tutor reading and rereading them with Carlton until he can fluently read each page and most of the words. Future pages tell about any pets Carlton has, places he has gone, friends and what they do together, foods he likes to eat, jobs he does at home, things he does not like, and so forth. Once Carlton can fluently read this beginning book, he will have a good bank of known high-frequency words and should begin being tutored in a very easy book.

When the material has been chosen or created for the child to read, tutoring procedures follow a predictable pattern.

Tutoring Procedures

- The tutor and child preview a new book or several new pages of a book, naming things, talking about what is happening in the pictures, and reading any headings or labels.
- The child reads one page without help from the tutor, figuring out words in whatever way he or she can.
- The tutor points out good strategies the reader used: sounding out an unfamiliar word, using picture clues, going back and correcting at the end of a sentence, and so on.
- The tutor then points out any words that the child did not read correctly and helps the child figure them out by showing how the picture, the letters in the word, and the sense of the sentence help with that word.
- The tutor writes the missed words on index cards along with the page number on which they were missed.
- The same procedure is repeated with each page. Pictures, headings, and labels are discussed. The page is read by the child unaided. The tutor points out good strategies the reader used and then gives help with missed words. The missed words are written on index cards with the page numbers.
- When several pages have been read and three to six missed words are written on cards, the tutor and child return to the first page read that day. The missed words are displayed in front of the child, but they are not pronounced by the tutor or the child.

When the child has finished the page, she or he puts a check next to any word correctly read in the text this time. The tutor and the child talk about words that were not correctly read and how they can be figured out. The child continues to reread pages with the index-card words for that page visible as she or he reads, checking those correctly read when the page is finished and getting help with those incorrectly read.

- The word cards are put in an envelope and clipped to the book and are ready for the next day's reading.

- Together, the tutor and the child write in a notebook a sentence or two summarizing what was read today. The child and the tutor first agree on what to write. Then the child writes, getting help from the tutor with spelling as needed. The tutor and child decide on one word each day to add to the child's portable word wall folder. This folder has the alphabet letters and spaces for words needed. By having the folder open while writing, the child can quickly find a word he or she remembers deciding that he or she needs to learn to spell.

- The child rereads pages for several days. After reading each page, the child puts checkmarks on index cards next to previously missed words that he or she was able to read correctly today. Words with three checks are "retired."

A	**B**	**C**	**D**	**E**	**F**
are also about	before	can't could	don't	enough	first favorite
G	**H**	**I**	**J**	**K**	**L**
getting	have	I'm into		know knew	let's
M	**N**	**O**	**P**	**Q**	**R**
myself	new	one our	people		really

S	**T**	**U**	**V**	**W**	**X**	**YZ**
said school	then there threw to	until	very	want was wear whether		your you're

For Carlton's book, this procedure should be varied somewhat. Because Carlton knows almost no words, each sentence should be written on a sentence strip, read, and then cut into words. Carlton should reassemble the words to match each sentence in the paragraph. Eventually, he should make the whole paragraph by matching and assembling the cut-apart words. Carlton should write a sentence at the end of each day, perhaps choosing his favorite sentence from the paragraph and then trying to write it without looking (but getting spelling help from the tutor). He and the tutor decide on a word each day to add to his word wall folder, and Carlton learns to find and use these words to help him write his sentence each day.

As you can tell, the trickiest part of this tutoring is finding the right book. If you find a book in which the child is missing a word every 20 words or so, the reading is fluent enough so that the child can figure out words and self-correct. The number of missed words you write on index cards should be small enough so that the child is able to learn these words and accumulate the three checks necessary to retire them. Once you have the tutoring set up, you need to monitor the progress of the child. When children are accumulating few index-card words, it is time to move them to slightly harder books.

Finding the Tutor

Are you convinced that your beginning reader could make more rapid progress if you could add this structured tutoring routine to the rich classroom instruction you are providing? Now all you need to do is to find a reliable tutor. Here are some places to look.

- Do you know a parent who drops off or picks up at school every day and could stay 30 minutes or come 30 minutes early? Many parents are on a tight schedule, but most schools have some parents with the flexibility to spend 30 minutes tutoring a child if they know they are needed and have a specific, workable tutoring system, such as that just described.

- Does a capable lunchroom worker or bus driver have 30 minutes a day to spare? Some part-time workers would love to have the opportunity to make a difference in the life of a child. Some schools even have money to pay this person a little extra each week for the extra hours worked.

- Does a high school nearby begin or end earlier or later than your school? Many high schools encourage (or even require!) volunteer service by their students. Perhaps a future teacher would love to have the experience of tutoring your child.

- Does your school have older students, one of whom might be a tutor? Ask a teacher friend who teaches older children if some student could afford the half-hour it would take each day to tutor your child. The schedule could be staggered so that the tutor did not miss the same thing each day, or the tutor could come when other students are going to band, chorus, and so forth.

- Do you have a student who could be the tutor? If you are an intermediate teacher and you have a sophisticated, nurturing, budding teacher in your classroom, you may already have the help you need. Most intermediate-aged children are not sophisticated or dedicated enough to do this, but there is often one in every class.

- If you cannot get one person to come for 30 minutes every day, could you get four people to come for 2 hours 1 day each week? One school found four retired people willing to give up one afternoon each week to tutor children. Two teachers worked together to find and train these tutors. On their day each week, each tutor worked individually with four children, two from each class. Each tutor knew the procedures and each wrote a note in the child's notebook for the next day's tutor, telling how far they had gotten and pointing out any "good things" the child had done that day. On Friday, the classroom teachers took turns meeting with each child being tutored while the other teacher read to both classes. During this Friday time, they monitored the progress of each child and decided when to move each child to higher-level books. They also wrote a note in the child's notebook letting the tutors know how much progress each child was making and how appreciative they were of the help.

Coordinate with Reading and Other Specialists

Many struggling readers participate in remedial or resource room instruction in addition to classroom reading instruction. Such programs can provide much needed support for the children, but they can also result in a confusing and unhelpful conglomeration of reading lessons and activities. Special programs are most effective when they provide supportive instruction that is designed to ease the difficulties that participating children are having in their classrooms.

To accomplish this, however, means that remedial and special education teachers must be familiar with the classroom reading program. Federal regulations for remedial and special education programs promote cooperative planning of instruction between classroom teachers and specialist teachers. In addition, the support instruction must be designed to improve classroom performance. The goal of these regulations is to accelerate children's reading development to move them back into the classroom with no further need for assistance.

Struggling readers who participate in remedial or resource room instructional support programs are the very children who need the kind of reading instruction that is coherently planned and richly integrated. We have seen a variety of ways in which classroom teachers work with support teachers to develop such programs.

In one school, the support teachers come into the classrooms to work with participating children. They support the children's progress through the books that are used in the core reading/language arts program. The special teachers may have the children reread a story and work on fluency and self-monitoring behaviors. At times, they reteach a strategy lesson from the basal or model summary writing for a *Weekly Reader* article. These teachers work with both small groups and individuals, depending on the classroom and the students. With support teachers in the room working at supporting progress through the core curriculum, less time is needed to meet and plan instructional roles.

In another school, the support teachers work in the classroom occasionally but more often work on extending classroom reading lessons in another room. In this case, the coordination is achieved through the use of a traveling notebook that the teachers have children carry back and forth each day. Both teachers jot down comments about what they are working on and the problems or successes the children had that day. The notebook allows the support program teacher to monitor core curriculum lessons and to develop lessons that extend or support this learning.

In another school, the support teachers work only with the books that children are reading in the classrooms. The support teachers focus on extending comprehension of the texts being read in the classroom by working with children to develop scripts from books and stories and to develop performances of these.

Another example of classroom/special teacher coordination is found in one school where the sixth-graders who attend the remedial program read books linked to their social studies curriculum. With the support of the specialist, these struggling readers read historical fiction and biographies; this adds greatly to their background knowledge and allows them to be active participants in social studies class discussions. A similar link could also be made between reading and science.

What is common among the very best remedial and special education programs is that children spend most of their time actually reading and writing in a way that supports classroom success. The support children receive from the specialist teacher provides immediate returns in improved reading and writing during classroom instruction.

Use the Latest Technology

When helping struggling readers, be careful about "plugging" them into the computer and hoping "the computer will do it." Many computer programs are just high-tech worksheets and do not teach children anything they can actually use as they read and write. Also, all children need the high-quality, responsive instruction that only a teacher can provide. There are, however, some computer programs that allow children with a variety of disabilities to read and write much better than they could "the old-fashioned way."

Mainstreamed into most classrooms today are children with a variety of physical limitations that make writing difficult or impossible. Children with limited vision often cannot write with paper and pencil. Children with speech difficulties often find writing and sharing their writing arduous. Children with cerebral palsy and various other physical problems may not be able to write with pencil and paper or even with a normal computer keyboard. Special computer devices and programs are absolutely necessary to allow these children to learn to write. It is even more critical that these children learn to write because many lack fluent speech, and being able to write gives them a way to express themselves and participate in classroom life.

There are word prediction programs that use what the child has written and the first few letters of the next word to predict what the whole word will be. There are also talking word processors that give immediate speech feedback as the student types words, sentences, and paragraphs. Many of these talking word processors include graphic organizers, clip art, talking dictionaries, and frames to help children organize their thoughts prior to writing.

No teacher can be expected to know the specifics of all the devices available. What you do need to know is that if you have a child with a physical disability that makes writing in the normal way impossible, devices are available that will allow this child to

RICH resources

Computer-Assistive Devices and Software

- *Co: Writer* (Don Johnston). This is a talking word prediction program. Based on what the child has written and the first few letters of the next word, it predicts what the whole word will be. When the child clicks on the word, it becomes part of the text. This software also contains Flexspell, which translates phonetic spelling.

- *Write: Outloud* (Don Johnston). This is a talking word processor that gives immediate speech feedback as the student types words, sentences, and paragraphs. Its spelling check includes a homonym checker, which recognizes homonyms and offers definitions so that the child can choose the correct word. Text also can be read back to the child. This program is particularly helpful for children with visual impairments.

- *Draft Builder* (Don Johnston). This program helps children organize ideas through a variety of visual maps. Speech feedback is included.

- *IntelliTalk II* (Intellitools). This talking word processor combines graphics, text, and speech. A variety of templates and overlays are included to produce different kinds of text.

- *Kidspiration* (Inspiration). This program is based on Inspiration but easier to use. It integrates pictures and writing to help children develop visual maps to connect and expand ideas. These maps, along with audio support, help children write organized text.

- *Special keyboards and other devices.* For children who cannot use a regular keyboard, there are special keyboards, switches, and eye gaze pointers that allow children with limited mobility to word process and create text.

write. Also, by federal law, the child is entitled to have access to these devices, regardless of the cost. If you need help to make writing a reality for a student who is physically disabled, contact your administrator or special education coordinator. If you need support to get what you need, contact the child's parents and let them know what is available and that their child is entitled to have it.

Increase the Support You Are Providing Your English Language Learners

Almost 25 percent of the children in U.S. elementary schools speak a language other than English as their home language. That means that one out of every four children in our classrooms must learn to *speak* English as they learn how to read and write English. Throughout this book, we have included suggestions for adapting instruction and providing additional support for our English language learners. Here's our Top 10 List of adaptations elementary teachers find to be most supportive of their children learning English.

1. Provide each ELL with a nurturing supportive partner. Ideally, this partner would speak the language of the ELL and also be fluent in English. Alternatively, choose a nurturing "budding teacher."

2. Include your English Language Learners in all coaching groups and other teacher-led groups.

3. Find a tutor who can provide an additional 30 minutes each day of structured tutoring in material at the child's instructional level or in a book you create about that child.

4. Explore the possibilities offered by computer technology. Some websites have picture dictionaries with the words in both languages. Other websites have books written in two languages. There are also websites that offer classroom-tested ideas and other teacher-to-teacher support.

5. Use your teacher read-aloud time as one vehicle for developing English vocabulary. Be sensitive to vocabulary that might not be understood and ask your students to explain what unfamiliar words mean. Be sure to include "everyone" books and informational books with lots of pictures as part of your teacher read-aloud. When reading an easy book, record that reading and let your ELLs listen to that book several times. If possible, include some books that reflect the culture of your English language learners.

6. Support your ELLs in choosing books they can read during independent reading time. Provide them with alphabet and simple picture dictionaries. If they can read in their home language, help them find books in that language. When they demonstrate that they can read some materials, encourage them to take those items home and share them with their families, who will be delighted with the progress their children are making in learning English.

7. Provide your ELLs with sticky notes to "flag" new words whenever they are reading. After reading, allow them to show their sticky-note words to their partner and let that partner play "teacher" and explain the new words.

8. Provide a partner to read and explain anything the class is reading that is beyond the current language capabilities of your students learning English.

9. Build a personal word wall in a file folder for each English language learner. Gradually add common words that each child needs to learn to spell, especially words such as *they*, *have*, and *come,* which don't follow the rhyming pattern.

10. Remember that writing in another language is the hardest language skill to acquire. Encourage your students learning English to write about their experiences, and accept and praise whatever writing they are able to accomplish. Provide one-on-one support so that your English language learners can publish something when the whole class is publishing.

If you have an older student who is just learning English, look back at the suggestions for building the literacy foundation included in Chapter 3. Regardless of age, all beginning readers need to build the emergent literacy understandings described in this chapter.

Summary

Differentiation is essential because children differ on so many dimensions. Faced with all the differences children in one classroom exhibit, teachers often feel overwhelmed and frustrated that they cannot give every child the amount of individual attention each child deserves. Differentiation cannot be achieved with any single strategy or program.

The most effective teachers use *variety* as one of their main tools for diversifying their instruction. They seek out and use a wide variety of materials. They use a variety of grouping structures including whole-class teaching, various collaborative grouping arrangements, and individual instruction during conferences. Knowing that students have individual learning styles, effective teachers use a wide variety of lesson formats so that across the day and week, all students experience success and enjoyment as they participate in different activities.

Choice is another principle you can use to differentiate your instruction. When students can make choices about what to read during independent reading time, what to write during Writers' Workshop, and which books they would most like to read during lit circles, they are differentiating that part of your instruction by their choices.

Increasing the *quantity* of reading and writing activities your students do by including literacy activities as you teach math, science, and social studies increases the amount of differentiation you provide. When you include reading, writing, and vocabulary activities in the different subject areas, you have additional opportunities to use a variety of lesson formats and collaborative groupings.

Some of your students will need additional instruction beyond what you are providing for others. When you include all students in coaching groups but your struggling students more often are part of these groups, you are providing those students with additional instruction and opportunities to read.

Many teachers have a "Little Red Hen" identity. They try to do everything all by themselves. In today's classroom, every teacher needs help to meet the needs of all the students. You can further differentiate your instruction if you incorporate various collaborative groupings in which children teach and help each other, coordinate tutoring for those who need it, and coordinate your instruction with any special teachers your children work with.

chapter 12

Inside Classrooms That Work

We began this book by sharing with you what we have learned from the research on the most effective classrooms. In Chapters 2 through 11, we took this complex puzzle of effective instruction apart and examined the critical pieces. In this chapter, we put those pieces back together and help you imagine what a kindergarten, primary, and intermediate classroom might look like when all the essential components of effective instruction are included. Your classroom will have a different time schedule and a different mix of students, but we hope these model classrooms will help you create for your students a classroom that works even better.

A Day in a Kindergarten Classroom

In kindergarten, you are building the foundation all children need to become fluent and avid readers and writers. Throughout the day, you engage your young learners in a variety of activities that help them develop these essential concepts:

- Why We Read and Write
- Background Knowledge and Vocabulary
- Print Concepts
- Phonemic Awareness
- Some Concrete Words
- Some Letter Names and Sounds
- Desire to Learn to Read and Write

Imagine that you are the kindergarten teacher carrying out the activities in this sample day. Think about how you are helping *all* your children develop these foundational concepts.

8:15–8:45 Choice Centers

Each morning, your children begin their day in a center of their choice. During center time, you circulate, greeting your children and helping them get their day off to a good start. You carry a clipboard with file folder labels and when you notice accomplishments, problems, or other things that you want to remember, you record these by putting the child's initials and date and the comment you want to make on one of the labels. At the end of the day, you peel these off and attach them to each child's anecdotal record folder. Today you jot down notes about Jerome "reading" a little book in the library corner to a stuffed animal, noting that his voice sounds like a reading voice and that he is doing a good job of inventing a story that matches the pictures. You also note that Elizabeth, at the writing table, has created strings of letters in rows and "reads" her "writing." You try to talk to each child during the morning center time and spend a few extra minutes with your children who are learning English and with others whose oral language skills are limited. You engage them in conversation about what they are doing at the center. Because these are one-on-one conversations and are related to something they are actually doing, your children are more willing to talk than when they are in a small group or whole-class setting. You also notice that your children talk with each other more during center time. In fact, knowing that listening and speaking are major goals of kindergarten, you encourage this child-to-child talk as you visit the various centers.

8:45–9:15 Opening, Calendar, Morning Message

When you go to the rocking chair and sit down, your children realize that center time is over and come join you. You begin the big group activities with the usual questions: What day is it today? What was yesterday? What day will tomorrow be? What is the date? What is the weather? How many days have we been in school? Your children answer each question then find the word cards (Thursday, Wednesday, Friday, October 24, windy) to finish the sentences on the sentence strips in the pocket chart. They count the three bundles of "tens" and the eight "ones" and conclude that they have been in kindergarten for 38 days. Next, you write a morning message as all your children watch. You call on different children to supply information and help you spell words.

Dear Class,

    Today is Thursday, October 24. It is a very windy day! We will need our jackets when we go outside. Did you wear your jacket to school today?

    Love,

    Miss Williams

When the message is written, your children read it chorally and you call on children to count words and sentences and share what they notice about today's message. Your students notice many things—the words they know, the capital letter at the beginning of each sentence, the periods, the exclamation and question marks at the end of the sentences, and so on. You end this big group session by leading the children in some of their favorite marching and moving songs and close with some finger-plays using familiar rhymes. All the children enjoy these songs and poems, and many of them still need this practice to build their phonemic awareness.

9:15–9:35 Shared Reading

Next, you lead the children in a rereading of *Brown Bear, Brown Bear* by Bill Martin. You and the children have read this book several times and this time, you pause before turning each page to see if the children can remember which animal is coming next. Your children all respond eagerly: "A red bird" . . . " "A blue horse." They are delighted when that animal appears when you turn the page. When you have completed reading the book, you remind them of the *Brown Bear* books they are making during their assigned center time.

9:35–10:00 Writing

You begin the writing time as you always do by modeling writing. You model using the print in the room to spell words and how you stretch out words and write letters for the sounds you hear when you can't find the correct spelling. Today you write two sentences.

> Mr. Hinkle will vizit us after lunch.
> He will bring his pet turtl.

Your children all watch carefully and try to read what you are writing. Before dismissing your students to their tables and their writing, you ask several children what they are going to write about today. As your children write, you circulate around the room encouraging and coaching them. When they ask for help in spelling a word, you help them use all the words around the room and stretch out words not displayed in the room.

10:00–10:30 Recess/Snack

As the children line up to go outside, you ask Jodi, your line leader today, what letter she wants the class to be as they go outside. Jodi chooses the letter *M* and your children march to the playground since *march* is the action they have learned for the letter *m*. When they return to the classroom, they find popcorn on each of their desks. They look up at the "food board" and notice that you have added a picture of popcorn as a key word for the letter *p*. As they munch on their popcorn and whatever else they might have brought for snack time, you review with them the other foods on the food board and the letter sounds they represent.

10:30–11:30 Assigned Centers

During this time, your children go to centers once more but, unlike the morning time when they chose the centers and activities, now they are assigned to centers and rotate through the activities. Today, you have four centers set up. In the math center, children will work in partners to count the number of letters in words from *Brown Bear* and sort these words into baskets labeled 1 through 8. In the reading center, children are making their own take-home books patterned on the *Brown Bear* book. In the listening center, they will listen to a recorded book about real zoo animals. You settle into your chair in the teacher center where you will work with small groups of children on particular skills you have noticed they need to work on.

11:30–12:00 Lunch

Just before they line up, you read the children the lunch menu. You make up a few riddles helping them review their beginning letter sounds.

> "Today, you are having another food that begins with a *p*. The one you are going to have just has cheese on it. I like it with cheese and with another *p* word—*pepperoni!*"

Your children make happy sounds as they realize their favorite—pizza—is on the menu.

> "With your pizza, you will have something that is very nutritious and contains lots of vitamins. It has lettuce and other vegetables and begins with an *s*."

The children quickly guess, "Salad."

> "For dessert, you will have something that comes in different flavors and colors. Sometimes it is yellow, sometimes brown, sometimes white. Today it is white with chocolate frosting and begins with the letter *c*."

The children guess "cake" and have no trouble knowing that their beverage will be the *m* food from their food board—milk.

12:00–12:30 Independent Reading
and Teacher Read-aloud

When your children arrive back from lunch, some children go to their tables. Others go to a corner of the room that contains all the predictable big books that they have read this year. Other children go to a table on which you have placed all the class books they have made this year. Some children go to the reading corner, which, in addition to books, has puppets and stuffed animals. Your students know exactly where to go because they have one day to read in the reading corner, another day when they can read the big books, and another day when they can read the class books. They read at their seats on the other two days. The children at their seats choose from trays of books that rotate each day to a different table. This procedure has been in place for two weeks now and is working quite well. Having all the children spread out in the room created problems because there just weren't enough good "spreading-out places." This new arrangement seems to have just the right balance of freedom and structure so that the children spend most of their time actually reading the books in whatever way they can. As your children read, you circulate and stop to read with them. You spend more time with your struggling students and with Juan and Carlos, who are making rapid progress with their English. When the children have read their own books for 10 minutes, you gather them at the rocking chair and read to them.

12:30–1:30 Math/Science/Social Studies

1:30–2:00 Specials

2:00–2:30

On three afternoons, your children have this half-hour to once again choose activities in the various centers. While they work in the centers of their choice, you pull individuals and small groups and provide coaching and instruction based on what you have observed their needs are. On Mondays, they go to the computer lab. On Thursdays, their "Big Buddies" from the fifth grade arrive to read and write with the children. Each fifth-grader is assigned one kindergarten buddy. They bring a book that they have practiced reading and read it "lap style" to their kindergartner. They then let the child choose a book to read to them. Next, they write whatever their kindergartner would like them to write in that child's "All about Me" book. The Big Buddy has learned to talk with the kindergartner about "the interesting things that have happened since I came last week" and then to record some of these things in simple sentences. These weekly journals are records of lost teeth, new jackets, birthdays, family moves, births, and deaths. The children love to have someone record what has happened in their lives and, once today's record is made, they pester their Big Buddies to "read all about me from the beginning of the year."

2:30 Dismissal/Homework

As your children prepare to go home, you help them choose a little book, an index card, and a pencil to put in a zippered bag. Each night, their "homework" is to read the book to someone or have someone read it to them and to write or have someone write something for them on the card. Today, given their interest in how foods are spelled, they are to try to copy some names of foods they like from the boxes and cans that they find at home.

After the children are gone, you peel the file folder labels off the backing and attach them to the appropriate children's folders. You think about how each child is developing and look again at the list of literacy goals you have set for them:

- They read or pretend read favorite books and poems/songs/chants.
- They write in whatever way they can and can read what they write even if no one else can.
- They "track print"; that is, show you what to read and point to the words using left-right/top-bottom conventions.
- They know critical jargon, can point to just one word, the first word in the sentence, just one letter, the first letter in the word, the longest word, and so on.
- They recognize and can write some concrete words—their names, names of other children, and favorite words from books, poems, and chants.
- They are developing phonemic awareness, including the ability to clap syllables, recognize when words rhyme, make up rhymes, and stretch out words.
- They can name many letters and tell you words that begin with the common initial sounds.
- They are learning more about the world they live in and are more able to talk about what they know.
- They can listen to stories and informational books and can retell the most important information.
- They see themselves as readers and writers and as new members of the "literacy club."

RICH
resources

Kindergarten

These books contain kindergarten-specific, classroom-tested activities:

The Teacher's Guide to Big Blocks, by Dorothy P. Hall and Elaine Williams, Carson-Dellosa, 2002.

Month-by-Month Reading, Writing and Phonics, by Dorothy P. Hall and Patricia M. Cunningham, Carson-Dellosa, 2008.

Writing Minilessons for Kindergarten, by Dorothy P. Hall and Elaine Williams, Carson-Dellosa, 2003.

A Day in a Primary Classroom

Now imagine that you are teaching first or second grade. You have a variety of literacy activities throughout the school day.

8:20–8:50 Opening

Your children arrive and prepare for the day. When they have their gear stowed, they gather around. They share things that have happened to them over the weekend, do some calendar activities, and talk about the events planned for the day. Next, you read them a few pages in *From Seeds to Plants* by Gail Gibbon and tell your students that they will learn much more about seeds and plants as they begin their new science unit. You put this book on the science table where you have placed several other books about seeds and plants. You pick up three or four of these books and show a few pages of each. You also show them a few pages from several seed catalogs you have brought from home and remind them that the science table is one of the spots they can choose to go to during their independent reading time.

8:50–9:20 Spelling and Phonics

Each morning at 8:50 you lead the children in two phonics and spelling activities. You spend 10 to 15 minutes with the word wall and 15 to 20 minutes in a second activity. Today is Monday, the day you add new words to the wall and your children are eager to see what the new words will be. As you begin to introduce the new words, you glance over at Roberto, who just arrived in your classroom last Wednesday and realize that he does not really know what the word wall is for. You decide to use this opportunity to remind all your children about how the word wall is useful to them.

> "Who can tell Roberto how the word wall helps us and how I decide which words to add?"

Carla raises her hand and gives a better explanation than you could.

> "You use the word wall words all the time. You can't read and write without them and a lot of them aren't spelled the way they ought to be so you will be wrong if you stretch them out and put down what you hear."

"Why are the words arranged according to their first letter?" you ask. Erin provides the answer to this question.

> "To make it easier to find them. When you need the word, you just think how it begins and then you can find it faster."

Satisfied with their understanding of how the word wall is useful, you proceed to show the children the five new words that you will add today.

> "Last week I was looking at your writing and I spotted three words that as Carla explained aren't spelled the way they sound. These three tricky words are *could*, *people,* and *some*. The other reason I choose words is if they have a rhyming pattern which will help you spell lots of words. That is the reason I chose *think* and *came*. Who can explain to Roberto why I highlighted the *i-n-k* in *think* and the *a-m-e* in *came*?"

Terry explains that words that have highlighting will help you spell lots of other words that rhyme with them. You add the words to the wall next to the letter they begin with and then get the children up out of their seats and lead them to cheer for each word three times.

> "Think t-h-i-n-k; t-h-i-n-k; t-h-i-n-k; think"
>
> "Could c-o-u-l-d; c-o-u-l-d; c-o-u-l-d; could"
>
> "People p-e-o-p-l-e; p-e-o-p-l-e; p-e-o-p-l-e; people"
>
> "Some s-o-m-e; s-o-m-e; s-o-m-e; some"
>
> "Came c-a-m-e; c-a-m-e; c-a-m-e; came"

Next, your children sit down and write the words on a half sheet of handwriting paper as you model the correct letter formation for each. They check their spelling and handwriting by "fencing in" each word as you "fence in" the words you wrote. When the words are all checked on the front, the children turn their papers over on the back, anticipating the "on the back" activity. You point to *think* and *came* and have them notice which letters are highlighted.

Next, you say some sentences that they might be writing and they decide how to spell some words that rhyme with *think* and *came*.

> Paula might be writing, *My favorite color is pink*. Which word will help her spell *pink*?
>
> Kevin might be writing, *I went to the skating rink*. Which word will help him spell *rink*?
>
> Roberto might be writing, *My brother's name is Hernando*. Which word will help him spell *name*?
>
> David might be writing, *The garbage truck stinks*. Which word will help him spell *stinks*?
>
> Liz might be writing, *My brother let the cat out and I got blamed*. Which word will help her spell *blamed*?

A Day in a Primary Classroom

1. pink
2. rink
3. name
4. stinks
5. blamed

For each sentence, the children decide which word has the helpful rhyming pattern and then use that word to spell the rhyming word.

With the daily word wall activity done, you begin your second phonics/spelling activity. This activity varies. At least one day each week, you do a Guess the Covered Word activity. On another day, you do a Using Words You Know lesson. On two or three days, you do a Making Words lesson. That is the lesson you are doing today. The children have picked up the letters they need and a letter holder when they came in and now they line up the letters in front of the holder. For this lesson, each child has five consonants, *c, r, r, s,* and *t,* and two vowels, *a* and *o.* You place large cards with these same letters in your pocket chart at the front of the room.

> "Let's get our brains and fingers warmed up with some short words you probably know. See how quickly you can put two letters in your holder to spell *at.*"

You notice that Roberto has *at* in his holder. You send him to the front of the room to make *at* with the big letters.

> "Add just one letter to *at* to make the three-letter word *sat.*"

You choose one of your struggling readers who has *sat* spelled correctly to go to the front of the room and make *sat* with the pocket chart letters. The lesson continues as you instruct your children what word to make and choose children with the word made correctly to go to the front of the room and make the word with the big letters. You don't wait for everyone to make the word before sending someone to the pocket chart, and some children are still making their word as the word is being made with the pocket chart letters. Before starting to make each word, you remind the children to fix their word to match the one made with the big letters.

> "Change one letter and change *sat* to *rat.* The cat chased the rat."
>
> "Change the vowel in *rat* and spell *rot.* The old tree stump will rot away."
>
> "Change one letter and turn *rot* into *cot.* Do you sleep on a cot at camp?"
>
> "Change the vowel again and *cot* becomes *cat.*"
>
> "Don't take any letters out and don't add any either. Just change the places of the letters and you can turn your *cat* into *act.* After we read stories, we like to *act* them out."
>
> "Clear your holders and start over and use 4 letters to spell Rosa. We read a story earlier this year about a girl named Rosa who was unhappy about always being too little. Make the name *Rosa.*"

"Clear your holders and start over and use 4 letters to spell *oats*. Horses eat oats."

"Add just 1 letter to *oats* and you will have *coats*.

"Move the letters in *coats* around and you can spell *coast*. In the summer, we go to the coast."

"Change just one letter and you can spell *roast*. Do you like to roast marshmallows?"

"I can tell some of you have figured out the secret word. Make it in your holder and raise your hand if you think you have it. I will come around and tap your head if you have figured out the secret word and you can all go together to the pocket chart and arrange all the letters to spell the secret word."

Four proud children who have figured out the secret word proceed to the pocket chart and spell *carrots*.

After making the words, it is time to sort for patterns and to use those patterns to read and spell a few new words. You put index cards with the word they made in your pocket chart and the children chorally read these words.

at	sat	rat	rot	cot
cat	act	Rosa	coat	oats
coats	coast	roast	carrots	

"Now we need to sort the words into rhyming patterns. I am putting *at* in the pocket chart. Who can come and hand me three words that rhyme with *at*?"

Drew hands you the words *sat, rat,* and *cat* and you line these up in the pocket chart under *at*. Three other helpers come up and find the words with the same pattern as *rot, oats*, and *coast*.

at	cot	oats	roast
sat	rot	coats	coast
rat			
cat			

"Now everyone take a piece of scratch paper and number it 1 to 4. I am going to say a sentence that has a word that rhymes with one of our sets of rhymes and you can use the rhyming pattern to figure out how to spell it:

"On the way to the mall, I got a flat tire. Stretch out *flat* and write the first letters you hear. Who can tell me which words *flat* rhymes with? Right, so use the pattern in *at, sat, rat,* and *cat* to spell *flat*.

"Soap floats in the water in the bathtub. Stretch out *floats* to get the first letter. Which words rhyme with *floats*? Right. Write *floats* next to number 2.

"I like peanut butter on my toast. Which words rhyme with *toast*?

"My baby brother cried when he got the shot. Which words rhyme with *shot*?"

A Day in a Primary Classroom

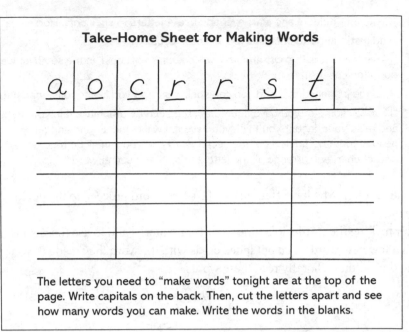

Take-Home Sheet for Making Words

a	o	c	r	r	s	t

The letters you need to "make words" tonight are at the top of the page. Write capitals on the back. Then, cut the letters apart and see how many words you can make. Write the words in the blanks.

When the four rhyming words have been written, you give the students their Making Words Homework Sheet. The letters *a, o, c, r, r, s,* and *t* are in boxes along the top, and beneath are larger boxes for your children to write words. "When you show this to someone at your house, do you think they will figure out the secret word or will you have to tell them?" you ask. Most children think that this will be a "toughie." They always enjoy their Making Words Homework Sheet. They cut the letters apart, write the capitals on the back, and fill the boxes with the words they can make—including some made in class and others they think of. Parents and older siblings often get involved, and because the letters formed the secret word made in class that day, the children are always smarter than anyone else and enjoy stumping their often competitive families!

9:20–10:00 Guided Reading

Guided reading is the time when you teach comprehension strategies and coach your students to use the decoding skills they are learning during the phonics and spelling time. Depending on what your students are reading, you use a variety of grouping strategies. On some days, you use big books and do shared reading activities with the whole class. Other days, your students meet in literature circles and read books together. This week, you will spend the week with your students in small groups reading from four of Arnold Lobel's beloved *Frog and Toad* books. Last week for your read-aloud, you read *Frog and Toad Are Friends,* so all your students are familiar with the characters and how to read chapter books. Today, your students are delighted to see that you have four more books featuring Frog and Toad. You remind your students that when they read in literature circles, they make a first, second, and third choice after previewing the books. Today, you will read them the first chapter of each book. Based on this preview of each book, they will make their choices and spend the next four days with their groups reading one chapter each day. You read them the first chapter of each book, *Days with Frog and Toad*, *Frog and Toad All Year*, *Frog and Toad Together,* and *Owl at Home.* After this preview, each child secretly fills out a sheet listing his or her first, second, and third choices. You promise them that they will all get one of their choices but you can't guarantee them their first choice.

While your students are at recess, you look at their choices and form your groups. Four of your struggling readers, Roberto, Paula, Todd, and Jacob, have chosen the easiest book, *Days with Frog and Toad,* as one of their choices. You assign them to this book, along with Liz and Kevin, who are average readers who chose *Days with Frog and Toad* as their first choice. Erin, David, Carla, and Ella, who are four of your best readers, have all chosen the hardest book, *Owl at Home,* so you assign them to this book, along with Jill, who is an average reader but who chose *Owl at Home* for her first choice. Drew, who is not a very good reader but didn't choose *Days with Frog and Toad,* is assigned to *Frog and Toad All Year,* along with five average readers. The other average readers, along with Gretchen, a very good reader who didn't choose *Owl at Home,* are assigned to *Frog and Toad Together*.

For the next four days, your students will read one chapter of their book each day in their literature circles. While they read, you will circulate and coach them on both decoding and comprehension. You will spend more time with the group reading *Days with Frog and Toad* because even though this is the easiest of the four books, the struggling readers in that group will need your support.

After reading each day, the groups will do activities to demonstrate their comprehension. Tomorrow, after reading the second chapters in their books, each group will do the Beach Ball activity in front of the whole class so that everyone can find out what happened in the second chapter. On Wednesday, the groups will work together to complete a story map summarizing the events in Chapter Three. On Thursday, they will share their thinking using the think-aloud procedure. Friday will be the most fun day. After reading the fifth and final chapter, the groups will work together and plan how to act out the book. Friday afternoon, each group will put on their improvised drama for all the other groups.

10:00–10:15 Break/Snack

10:15–11:00 Math

Today in math, you are starting a new unit on measurement. You have created a bulletin board on measurement that has some pictures of objects being measured and some of the key measurement vocabulary. Before you begin measuring objects in the room, you have your students do a prediction think-write. They write down the objects they are going to measure and predict their length and width. They then work with their talking partners to measure the objects and compare the measurements with their guesses.

11:00–11:40 Writer's Workshop

You begin the writing time each day with a mini-lesson in which you write something as the children watch. To demonstrate that writers write about many different things, you try to write on a variety of topics and use many different formats.

The children settle down on the floor in front of you, eager to see what you will write about today. They watch and listen as you think aloud about what to write.

> "I always have so many things I want to write about on Mondays. I could write about going shopping this weekend and seeing Drew and his dad at the mall. I could write about the exciting game my favorite team almost won. But I think I will write about what we just did in math."

As your students watch, you describe some of the activities just completed during the math lesson. As you write, you model for them how you use the print in the room, including the word wall and the words displayed on the measurement board you made for the new math unit. You also stretch out a few words to show your students how to spell words they are not sure of and can't find in the room. You circle these words to indicate they are probably not spelled correctly. You leave out one punctuation mark and don't capitalize the beginning word of the next sentence.

> This morning in math, we measured things. Before we measured each object, we wrote down our (gesses) about how big things would be then we worked together with our talking partners to measure them. We measured our desks, the teacher's desk, our thinking baskets, the Frog and Toad books and lots of other things. Some of our (gesses) were good and others were (terible) but measuring things is fun.

When you have finished writing, you ask the class to read it with you and be your editor. You direct their attention to the editing checklist and have them read it with you. You stop at the end of each sentence and students give you a thumbs up or thumbs down for each of the four items on the checklist. When they read the second sentence, they decide that you really have two sentences and direct you to put a period after *be* and start *then* with a capital letter.

Our Editor's Checklist

1. Every sentence makes sense.
2. Every sentence begins with a capital and ends with a punctuation mark.
3. People and place names have capital letters.
4. Words that might be misspelled are circled.

This writing mini-lesson takes 12 minutes, including the editing. When your mini-lesson is completed, your students go to their own writing. They are at various stages of the writing process. Two students are at the back table, happily illustrating their published books. Several children are working with their writing partners to revise and edit a piece they are planning to publish. Many children are writing drafts in their notebooks, busily producing the three good pieces they need before they can choose one to publish. After making sure everyone is doing what they need to do, you put your "editor-in-chief" hat on and hold individual conferences with several children, helping them get their piece ready to publish.

Your classroom is a busy working place for about 18 minutes. Then, at a signal from you, the children once again gather on the floor and the "Monday children" line up behind the Author's Chair. (All the children are designated by a day of the week; on their day, they get to share!) Each "Monday child" reads one piece he or she has been working on since last Monday and chooses two friends to tell something they liked and to ask a question.

11:40–12:20 Lunch/Recess

12:20–1:00 Science/Social Studies

You alternate science and social studies units and today you are starting a science unit on seeds and plants. You seat your students with their talking partners and tell them that today they are going to learn about different kinds of seeds. You ask them if they have ever eaten any seeds. You give them one minute to turn and talk to their partners about what they think they know about seeds. Next, you show them 10 different fruits and vegetables. You pause for 30 seconds after holding up each fruit or vegetable and give them time to talk to their partners about each and predict whether or not these have seeds inside them. Everyone is pretty sure that the apples and oranges have seeds inside them and that the bananas and onions don't. They are less sure about the tomatoes, walnuts, green beans, and carrots.

Most students don't know what the avocado and the guava are called and don't think they have seeds. After sharing their prior knowledge and predictions with their talking partners, your children eagerly watch as you dissect the fruits and vegetables and discover whether or not they have seeds. They are amazed to discover that they eat seeds when they eat nuts, tomatoes, and beans! You and the children begin a data chart to record your findings.

1:00–1:40 Specials

1:40–2:15 Teacher Read-Aloud/Independent Reading

Each day, when your students get back from specials, you read aloud to them for 10 to 15 minutes. You try to read from a variety of books and magazines and include both information and story text. Last week you read them *Frog and Toad Are Friends*, in preparation for the lit circles you are doing this week. Today you are reading them a book with a lot of true facts about real frogs and toads.

After reading to them, you dismiss them to their places for their own reading time. Each day, the boys and girls alternate who gets to "spread out" in the room and who goes to their seats. Today it is the boys' day to spread and they eagerly go to the science table, the *Zoobooks* rack, the library corner, and other places where you have placed books and

RICH resources

Primary Grades

These books contain grade-level specific, classroom-tested activities:

The First Grade Teacher's Guide to Four Blocks, by Patricia M. Cunningham and Dorothy P. Hall, Carson-Dellosa, 2008.

Month-by-Month Phonics for First Grade, by Patricia M. Cunningham and Dorothy P. Hall, Carson-Dellosa, 2008.

The Second Grade Teacher's Guide to Four Blocks, by Patricia M. Cunningham and Dorothy P. Hall, Carson-Dellosa, 2008.

Month-by-Month Phonics for Second Grade, by Patricia M. Cunningham and Dorothy P. Hall, Carson-Dellosa, 2008.

The Third Grade Teacher's Guide to Four Blocks, by Patricia M. Cunningham and Dorothy P. Hall, Carson-Dellosa, 2008.

Month-by-Month Phonics for Third Grade, by Patricia M. Cunningham and Dorothy P. Hall, Carson-Dellosa, 2008.

magazines. The girls return to their seats and read from their own books or from the crates you have placed at each grouping. Tomorrow will be their spreading day.

While the children read, you conference with the Monday children. Each Monday child brings you a book that he or she has selected and reads a few pages from that book. You make notes about what the Monday children are reading and about how well they are reading.

At 2:15 the bus riders pack up and line up at the door, waiting for their buses to be called. By scheduling your independent reading time at the end of the day, you make sure all of your students have at least 15 minutes of independent reading time. Car riders and walkers have a few more minutes to read since they are not dismissed until all the buses are gone.

A Day in an Intermediate Classroom

Now, transform yourself into an intermediate teacher. You know that much must be accomplished every day and that every subject wants more time than it can be allotted. Interruptions and schedule changes sometimes force activities to be "scrapped" or postponed until tomorrow. You have decided that the most crucial goal for your students is that they all become readers—people who choose to read even when they are not forced to. All your students can read some, although many do not read at grade level and a few read above grade level. You know that the major determinant of how well they will read by the end of the year is how much they read. You also know that many of your students do not read much at home and view reading as "something you have to do in school." Finally, you know that two activities have the greatest potential of getting your kids "hooked on reading"—reading to them and giving them consistent and ample time to read materials of their own choosing. To make sure that reading to the class and giving them time to read does not get crowded out as the day goes on, you schedule it first thing every morning.

8:30–9:10 Teacher Read-Aloud/Independent Reading

Each morning you read two pieces to the class. The first piece is a "quickread," and you try to make it as current and "in sync" with the interests of your students as you can. On Monday mornings, you bring in a newspaper and share some of the more interesting tidbits. You encourage your students to bring in interesting things from the weekend paper too. Pieces shared are added to the collage-style newspaper board. Other mornings, you read from informational books, magazines, joke and riddle books, brochures, and other "non-book" materials. The message you want to begin your day with is that reading is an essential part of the real world.

The second piece you read each day is a book—or a chapter of a book. You choose books of high interest to readers at this age but of varying genres so that all your students are exposed to a variety of literature. You include both fiction and nonfiction titles and are always on the lookout for good multicultural books. This week, you are reading *Get On Out of Here, Philip Hall* (B. Greene, 1981).

Next comes your students' time to read. Some students have a library book that they are in the middle of reading. Others choose a book from the trays of books that rotate to different tables each week. Each tray is filled with a wide variety of books, including some high-interest, easy vocabulary books and some informational books with lots of pictures. Children are grouped by days of the week, a fifth of the class for each day. On Day 1, the Day 1 people can read anywhere and anything in the room, including newspapers, magazines, joke books, the newspaper board, and so on. On the other days, they stay at their seats and read books. In this way, everyone gets a chance to "spread out" and read anything one day each week, but most of the class is seated quietly at their desks reading.

While your students read, you hold quick conferences with one-fifth of your students each day. The students have been taught how to prepare for the conference; they come to the conference with the pages they want to read and talk about marked with a bookmark. When making the schedule for the daily conferences, you spread out your most struggling students across the five days—beginning each day with a conference with one of your struggling readers and giving that reader a few additional minutes. You view these weekly conferences as "conversations" rather than "interrogations," and all your students look forward to their weekly one-on-one time with you.

9:10–9:40 Vocabulary/Spelling

At the beginning of the year, you were shocked at what terrible spellers many of your students were. They misspelled common words in their writing—frend, peeple, thay, becuz—spelling them the way they sound. Their academic vocabularies are also quite limited and they are not good at figuring out or spelling big words. So, for 30 minutes each day, you focus on the spelling and meaning for big words, which you choose from the key vocabulary for your science or social studies unit. You also spend a few minutes reviewing the word wall words—common words you see misspelled in their writing.

This week, your topic is *pollution* and you display these unit-related words on a board along with some pictures related to pollution.

pollution	environment	recycle
pollutants	environmental	conservation
resources	chemicals	fertilizers
pesticides	combustion	renewable

Because polysyllabic words are often related through their roots, you always include some words that have the same root— *pollution/pollutants, environment/environmental.* As you introduce the words to your students, you help them distinguish the different forms of the words from one another and see the relationships between words.

> "*Pollution* is the word we use to describe the whole problem. *Pollutants,* including *fertilizers, chemicals,* and *pesticides,* are some of the things that cause pollution. Does anyone know the root word in *pollution* and *pollutants*? Yes, the root word is *pollute.* How would you spell *pollute*?"

You remind your students that the *e* is often dropped when endings such as *tion* and *ant* are added and help them see that "*pollute* is what you do that causes the problem of *pollution.*" In a similar way, you help them understand that the *environment* is the surroundings in which we live, and *environmental* is the word we use as a describing word.

> "We can say that pollution is a problem for our environment or that pollution is an environmental problem."

As you introduce the other words, you also draw their attention to morphemes, meanings, and spelling changes.

> "*Recycle, renewable,* and *resources* all begin with the prefix *re* and have related meanings. When you *recycle* something, you use it again. *Renewable* resources, such as trees, will grow again. Does anyone know what we call resources that are not renewable? Yes, we call them *nonrenewable* resources."

Once all the words have been introduced and attention has been devoted to their meaning and to similar chunks, you lead them in a clapping/chanting activity similar to the cheering you would hear at a basketball game. Your students say each word, clap and chant its spelling, and then say the word again.

> "Pollution— p-o-l___l-u___t-i-o-n—pollution"
> "Pollutant—p-o-l___l-u___t-a-n-t—pollutant."

You end this part of the lesson by having your students write these words in their science notebooks. Tonight, for homework, they will write a sentence and/or draw a picture giving a personal example for each word.

Most of your spelling/vocabulary time each day is spent in activities focused on the polysyllabic words on your unit board. You do take a few minutes each day, however, to focus your students' attention on the commonly misspelled words you have placed on the word wall. Most weeks, you add three or four words to this wall—all common words you have seen misspelled in their writing. Today, you add the contractions *don't, wouldn't, can't,* and *didn't.* You help your students decide which two words make up the contractions and notice which letters have been replaced by the apostrophe. Then you have your students clap and cheer the contractions and write each word on a piece of scratch paper. You remind your students that the word wall is there to help them spell tricky words correctly when they are writing and that when a word is on the wall, there are no excuses for misspelling that word in their writing.

9:40–10:30 Math

In math, you have been doing a unit on decimals, fractions, and percents. Many students seem baffled by this concept so today you use a simple picture book to try to make the relationships concrete. You found *Piece = Part = Portion* by Frank Gifford and began today's math lesson with it. Watching the light bulb go on for some of your students as they looked at the enticing illustrations and listened to the clear explanations accompanying these visuals reminds you that there is probably a picture book out there to illustrate any difficult concept and the hunt is worth it. Students were much more able to do the conversions in their math book after enjoying this simple picture book. You put the book in one of the rotating trays and expect to find many students perusing it during their independent reading time.

10:30–10:50 Break/Recess

10:50–11:30 Guided Reading

Because your students read on many different levels, you use a variety of different formats and groupings during the guided reading time. Last week, your students worked in lit circles reading five different informational books about animals. You also have them read some of the selections in your reading textbook. When you have them read in the basal, you use the partner reading format making sure to partner up your struggling readers with someone who can and will support and coach them. Earlier in the year, you included all your students in coaching groups and they have gotten quite good at coaching each other.

Today your students are going to read a story that has a lot of interesting characters and will lend itself to an Oprah Winfrey interview. You tell your students to read the story and think about which character they would like to be if they are picked to be guests on Oprah's show and, of course, to come up with some good questions Oprah should ask or that they might ask when Oprah asks for questions from the audience.

While the partners read, you circulate and notice how well they are coaching each other. When you notice one partner just telling his partner the words he can't figure out, you intervene and model coaching with those students. When you notice some partners finishing, you remind them to decide which guest they would like to be, and if they have time, to write down two good questions Oprah or the audience might ask.

Most of your students are "hams" and pretending to be Oprah or one of Oprah's guests is one of their favorite reading activities. As you watch them perform after reading, you are reassured that in addition to having fun, your students are all engaging in higher-level thinking as they ask and answer the questions.

11:30–12:00 Specials

12:00–12:30 Lunch

12:30–1:15 Science/Social Studies

You begin your study of pollution with a connection think-write in which you ask your students to write down some things they think are pollutants and how these things hurt our environment. As they share their ideas, you add these to the *K* column of a KWL chart. Next, your students tell you some questions they have about pollution which you add to the *W* column. Then you watch a short video clip about pollution and add some information learned to the *L* column. There are still many unanswered questions and you tell your students to "stay tuned" because you and they will be finding much more information on this critical issue.

1:15–2:00 Writing

You alternate your writing time between Writer's Workshop, in which students choose their own topics and select pieces to publish, and focused writing, in which you have your students write on particular topics or in particular forms. Next week, when they have a lot more information about pollution, they are going to work in writing partners to write short articles describing different pollution problems and possible solutions. You will then publish these in the newsletter you send home to parents every two weeks. This week, you are in Writer's Workshop mode. You begin today as you do every day with a mini-lesson in which you write something and your students help you revise or edit.

> "Today, I am in a poetry mood and I am also worrying about pollution. I think I will write a cinquain with some of the information we learned about pollution. Remember last week, when we all wrote animal cinquains and published them in this class book? I will read a few of your animal cinquains to remind myself of the cinquain form."

After you read a few animal cinquains, you write a cinquain in the correct form and purposefully use some common, not very vivid words.

Pollution

Pollution.

Scary, bad.

Trash, litter, pesticides.

They hurt our environment.

Pollution.

When you finish writing, you ask students to read it with you and see if they can replace any of your boring words with more vivid words. The students decide that *scary, bad,* and *hurt* are not very vivid words and help you replace them. They also want to change the last word—which hadn't occurred to you but which does make your poem much stronger. Here is the revised cinquain that everyone agrees is even better than your first attempt.

Pollution

Pollution

Frightening, disgusting.

Trash, litter, pesticides.

They destroy our environment.

Recycle!

After this writing mini-lesson, you take some students who have a piece ready to publish to the back table with you while the other students pursue their own writing. Some students begin new pieces. You have clearly inspired two students who write their own pollution cinquains. Others continue writing an already begun piece. As they write, they glance at the word wall and other print in the room when they need spelling help. When they can't find a word they need, they stretch it out and then circle it to show this is probably not the correct spelling. They know that you will help them fix all spellings if this is the piece they choose to publish. Several students are working with their writing partners to revise and edit a piece that they will bring to you for the final edit before they publish it. Two students who you have already helped to edit their pieces are using the computers to type their final drafts. Three other students are adding illustrations to their final drafts.

It took a while to get the Writer's Workshop procedures established, but the students now seem quite comfortable with it. They know that they need to produce three good first drafts before picking one to publish. When they have chosen a piece to publish, they revise and edit it for the items on the editor's checklist with their writing partner and then they bring it to you for the final edit. Finally, they copy or type it and add their illustrations.

2:00–2:30

The last minutes of any school day are difficult to structure and, in many classrooms, are just "waiting-to-leave" time. You know, however, that if you are going to get everything accomplished that needs to happen in an intermediate classroom, you have no time to waste, so you have planned important activities for the last half hour that your students enjoy and thus will cooperate with during this restless end-of-the-day time.

On Tuesdays, your big kids read to their little buddies in the kindergarten. The kindergartners pick a book they want read to them and deliver them to your classroom on Monday. Monday afternoon, your students work with their reading partners to practice their books and prepare to read them. You have taught them specific steps they need to do with each book:

1. Read the book title and the author's name, and ask your little buddy what the book will be about.

2. Look through the book with your buddy, talking about the things you see in the pictures before reading.

3. Read the book and help your little buddy talk about it. Ask questions that get your little buddy involved with the book:

   What do you think will happen next?

   Would you like to do that?

4. When you finish reading, ask your little buddy to find his or her favorite page and tell why it was the favorite.

5. Go through the book again and let your little buddy tell you what is happening or help read it to you if some parts are very easy.

On Wednesdays, you divide your students into groups of four or five and let them share favorite parts from what they have been reading during their independent reading time. On Thursdays, they meet in groups and share something they have written since last week. On Fridays, you accompany them to the library and help them check out books and remind them that their only homework over the weekend is to read something. Although they are still not reading at home as much as you would like, parents report that the students are spending more time reading over the weekend when they have books they have chosen, and they see it as their "weekend job!"

Each day, when the children leave, you remove the labels on which you have written notes from the clipboard and put them on the outside of each student's folder. (Inside this folder are samples of writing, reading responses, and other work.) As you put on new labels with new comments, you look at the previous labels and consider how each student is growing. Sometimes, as you reflect on the different students whose reading and writing

RICH resources

Intermediate Grades

These books contain classroom-tested activities for intermediate grades:

The Teacher's Guide to Big Blocks, by Amanda B. Arens, Karen L. Loman, Patricia M. Cunningham, and Dorothy P. Hall, Carson-Dellosa, 2005.

Writing Mini-lessons for Intermediate Grades, by Dorothy P. Hall, Patricia M. Cunningham, and Amanda B. Arens, Carson-Dellosa, 2003.

Month-by-Month Phonics and Vocabulary for Fourth Grade, by Amanda B. Arens, Karen L. Loman, and Patricia M. Cunningham, Carson-Dellosa, 2007.

Month-by-Month Phonics and Vocabulary for Fifth Grade, by Karen L. Loman, Amanda B. Arens, and Patricia M. Cunningham, Carson-Dellosa, 2007.

Month-by-Month Phonics for Upper Grades, by Patricia M. Cunningham and Dorothy P. Hall, Carson-Dellosa, 1998.

you have focused on that day, you think of other questions you have about that child's literacy development. You then put this child's initials, tomorrow's date, and a few words to remind you of what to look for on the label and to spend some time focusing on the same student tomorrow. Although you focus on some students more often than others, you try to focus on each child at least once a week. The combination of weekly anecdotal records and samples of writing and reading responses kept in the folder gives you a basis for deciding how well individual children are progressing toward becoming more literate, as well as information that guides your whole-class, small-group, and individual instruction.

references

Allington, R. L. (2009). *What really matters in fluency: Research-based practices across the curriculum.* Boston: Allyn & Bacon.

Allington, R. L., & Johnston, P. H. (Eds.). (2002). *Reading to learn: Lessons from exemplary fourth-grade classrooms.* New York: Guilford.

Arens, A. B., Loman, K. L. & Cunningham, P. M. (2007). *Month-by-month phonics and vocabulary for fourth grade.* Greensboro, NC: Carson-Dellosa.

Arens, A. B., Loman, K. L., Cunningham, P. M., & Hall, D. P. (2005). *The teacher's guide to big blocks.* Greensboro, NC: Carson-Dellosa.

Artley, S. A. (1975). Good teachers of reading—Who are they? *The Reading Teacher, 29,* 26–31.

Bangert-Drown, R. L., Hurley, M. M., & Wilkinson, B. (2004). The effects of school-based writing to learn interventions on academic achievement. *Review of Educational Research, 74,* 29–58.

Baumann, J. F., Kame'enui, E. J., & Ash, G. E. (2003). Research on vocabulary instruction: Voltaire redux. In J. Flood, D. Lapp, J. R. Squire, & J. M. Jensen (Eds.), *Handbook of research on teaching the English language arts* (2nd ed., pp. 752–785). Mahwah, NJ: Erlbaum.

Beck, I. L., McKeown, M. G., & Gromoll, E. W. (1989). Learning from social studies texts. *Cognition and Instruction, 6,* 99–158.

Beck, I. L., McKeown, M. G., Hamilton, R. L., & Kucan, L. (1997). *Questioning the author: An approach for enhancing student engagement with text.* Newark, DE: International Reading Association.

Beck, I. L., McKeown, M. G., & Kucan, L. (2002). *Bringing words to life.* New York: Guilford.

Becker, W. C. (1977). Teaching reading and language to the disadvantaged—What we have learned from field research. *Harvard Educational Review, 47,* 518–543.

Biemiller, A. (2004). Teaching vocabulary in the primary grades. In J. F. Baumann & E. J. Kame'enui (Eds.), *Vocabulary instruction* (pp. 28–40). New York: Guilford.

Biemiller, A., & Slonim, M. (2001). Estimating root word vocabulary growth in normative and advantaged populations: Evidence for a common sequence of vocabulary acquisition. *Journal of Educational Psychology, 93,* 498–520.

Blachowicz, C. L. Z., & Fisher, P. (2000). Vocabulary instruction. In M. L. Kamil, P. B. Mosenthal, P. D. Pearson, & R. Barr (Eds.), *Handbook of reading research* (Vol. 3, pp. 503–523). Mahwah, NJ: Erlbaum.

Caldwell, J. (2002). *Reading assessment: A primer for teachers and tutors.* New York: Guilford.

Calkins, L. (1994). *The art of teaching writing.* Portsmouth, NH: Heinemann.

Carr, E., & Ogle, D. (1987). KWL plus: A strategy for comprehension and summarization. *Journal of Reading, 30,* 626–631.

Chomsky, C. (1971). Write first, read later. *Childhood Education, 46,* 296–299.

Cunningham, A. E., & Stanovich, K. E. (1998). What reading does for the mind. *American Educator, 22*(1&2), 8–27.

Cunningham, P. M. (2006). High-poverty schools that beat the odds. *The Reading Teacher, 60,* 382–385.

Cunningham, P. M. (2007). *Six successful high-poverty schools: How they beat the odds.* 56th Yearbook of the National Reading Conference, 191–207.

Cunningham, P. M. (2009a). *Phonics they use: Words for reading and writing* (5th ed.). Boston: Allyn & Bacon.

Cunningham, P. M. (2009b). *What really matters in vocabulary: Research-based practices across the curriculum.* Boston: Allyn & Bacon.

Cunningham, P. M., & Cunningham, J. W. (2010). *What really matters in writing: Research-based practices across the elementary curriculum.* Boston: Allyn & Bacon.

Cunningham, P. M., & Hall, D. P. (2001). *True stories from four blocks classrooms.* Greensboro, NC: Carson-Dellosa.

Cunningham, P. M., & Hall, D. P. (2008a). *The first grade teacher's guide to the four blocks.* Greensboro, NC: Carson-Dellosa.

Cunningham, P. M., & Hall, D. P. (2008b). *Making words 1st grade.* Boston: Allyn & Bacon.

Cunningham, P. M., & Hall, D. P. (2008c). *Month-by-month phonics for first grade.* Greensboro, NC: Carson-Dellosa.

Cunningham, P. M., & Hall, D. P. (2008d). *Month-by-month phonics for second grade.* Greensboro, NC: Carson-Dellosa.

Cunningham, P. M., & Hall, D. P. (2008e). *Month-by-month phonics for third grade.* Greensboro, NC: Carson-Dellosa.

Cunningham, P. M., & Hall, D. P. (2008f). *Month-by-month phonics for upper grades.* Greensboro, NC: Carson-Dellosa.

Cunningham, P. M., & Hall, D. P. (2008g). *The second grade teacher's guide to the four blocks.* Greensboro, NC: Carson-Dellosa.

Cunningham, P. M., & Hall, D. P. (2008h). *The third grade teacher's guide to the four blocks.* Greensboro, NC: Carson-Dellosa.

Cunningham, P. M., & Hall, D. P. (2009a). *Making words 2nd grade.* Boston: Allyn & Bacon.

Cunningham, P. M., & Hall, D. P. (2009b). *Making words 3rd grade.* Boston: Allyn & Bacon.

Cunningham, P. M., & Hall, D. P. (2009c). *Making words 4th grade.* Boston: Allyn & Bacon.

Cunningham, P. M., Hall, D. P., & Defee, M. (1991). Nonability grouped, multilevel instruction: A year in a first-grade classroom. *The Reading Teacher, 44,* 566–571.

Day, J. P., Spiegel, D. L., McLellan, J., & Brown, V. B. (2002). *Moving forward with literature circles.* New York: Scholastic.

Duke, N. K., & Pearson, P. D. (2002). Effective practices for developing reading comprehension. In A. E. Farstrup & S. J. Samuels (Eds.), *What research has to say about reading instruction* (3rd ed., pp. 205–242). Newark, DE: International Reading Association.

Durkin, D. (1979). What classroom observations reveal about reading comprehension instruction. *Reading Research Quarterly, 14,* 481–533.

Dyson, A. H., & Freedman, S. W. (2003). Writing. In J. Flood, D. Lapp, J. R. Squire, & J. M. Jensen (Eds.), *Handbook of research on teaching the English language arts* (2nd ed., pp. 967–992). Mahwah, NJ: Erlbaum.

Ehri, L. C., & Wilce, L. (1987). Does learning to spell help beginners learn to read words? *Reading Research Quarterly, 22,* 47–65.

Eldredge, J. L. (2005). *Teaching decoding: How and why.* Upper Saddle River, NJ: Prentice Hall.

Ellis, N., & Cataldo, S. (1990). The role of spelling in learning to read. *Language and Education, 4,* 47–76.

Fall, R., Webb, N. M., & Chudowsky, N. (2000). Group discussion and large-scale language arts assessment: Effects on students' comprehension. *American Educational Research Journal, 37*(4), 911–941.

Farnan, N., & Dahl, K. (2003). Children's writing: Research and practice. In J. Flood, D. Lapp, J. R. Squire, & J. M. Jensen (Eds.), *Handbook of research on teaching the English language arts* (2nd ed., pp. 993–1007). Mahwah, NJ: Erlbaum.

Graham, S., & Perin, D. (2007). A meta-analysis of writing instruction for adolescent students. *Journal of Educational Psychology, 99,* 445–476.

Graves, D. H. (1995). *A fresh look at writing.* Portsmouth, NH: Heinemann.

Graves, M. F. (2004). Teaching prefixes: As good as it gets? In J. F. Baumann & E. J. Kame'enui (Eds.), *Vocabulary instruction* (pp. 81–99). New York: Guilford.

Graves, M. F. (2006). *The vocabulary book.* Newark, DE: International Reading Association.

Graves, M. F., & Watts-Taffe, S. M. (2002). The place of word consciousness in a research-based vocabulary program. In A. E. Farstrup & S. J. Samuels (Eds.), *What research has to say about reading instruction* (3rd ed., pp. 140–165). Newark, DE: International Reading Association.

Guthrie, J. T., & Humenick, N. M. (2004). Motivating students to read: Evidence for classroom practices that increase motivation and achievement. In P. McCardle & V. Chhabra (Eds.), *The voice of evidence in reading research* (pp. 329–354). Baltimore: Paul H. Brookes.

Hall, D. P., & Cunningham, P. M. (2003). *Writing mini-lessons for intermediate grades.* Greensboro, NC: Carson-Dellosa.

Hall, D. P., & Cunningham, P. M. (2008). *Month-by-month reading, writing and phonics for kindergarten.* Greensboro, NC: Carson-Dellosa.

Hall, D. P., & Williams, E. (2002). *The teacher's guide to building blocks.* Greensboro, NC: Carson-Dellosa.

Hall, D. P., & Williams, E. (2003). *Writing mini-lessons for kindergarten.* Greensboro, NC: Carson-Dellosa.

Harris, A. J., & Sipay, E. R. (1990). *How to increase reading ability* (5th ed.). New York: Longman.

Harris, V. J. (Ed.). (1997). *Using multiethnic literature in the K–8 classroom.* Norwood, MA: Christopher Gordon.

Hart, B., & Risley, T. R. (1995). *Meaningful differences in the everyday experiences of young American children.* Baltimore: Paul H. Brookes.

Harvey, S., & Goudvis, A. (2000). *Strategies that work: Teaching comprehension to enhance understanding.* York, ME: Stenhouse.

Hattie, J. (2009). *Visible learning: A synthesis of over 800 meta-analyses relating to achievement.* New York: Routledge.

Hillocks, G., Jr. (1986). *Research on written composition: New directions for teaching.* Urbana, IL: National Conference on Research in English/ERIC Clearinghouse on Reading and Communication Skills.

Hodges, R. E. (2003). The conventions of writing. In J. Flood, D. Lapp, J. R. Squire, & J. M. Jensen (Eds.), *Handbook of research on teaching the English language arts* (2nd ed., pp. 1052–1063). Mahwah, NJ: Erlbaum.

Ivey, G., & Broaddus, K. (2001). "Just plain reading": A survey of what makes students want to read in middle school classrooms. *Reading Research Quarterly, 36,* 350–377.

Johns, J. J. (2008). *Basic reading inventory* (10th ed.). Dubuque, IA: Kendall/Hunt.

Juel, C., Biancarosa, G., Coker, D., & Deffes, R. (2003). Walking with Rosie: A cautionary tale of early reading instruction. *Educational Leadership, 60,* 12–18.

Juel, C., & Minden-Cupp, C. (2000). Learning to read words: Linguistic units and instructional strategies. *Reading Research Quarterly, 35,* 458–492.

Keene, E. L., & Zimmerman, S. (1997). *Mosaic of thought: Teaching comprehension in a reader's workshop.* Portsmouth, NH: Heinemann.

Knapp, M. S. (1995). *Teaching for meaning in high-poverty classrooms.* New York: Teachers College Press.

Langer, J., & Allington, R. L. (1992). Writing and reading curriculum. In P. Jackson (Ed.), *The handbook of curriculum research* (pp. 687–725). New York: Macmillan.

Leslie, L., & Caldwell, J. (2001). *Qualitative reading inventory—3.* New York: Longman.

Loman, K. L., Arens, A. B., & Cunningham, P. M. (2007). *Month-by-month phonics and vocabulary for fourth grade.* Greensboro, NC: Carson-Dellosa.

Macon, J. M., Bewell, D., & Vogt, M. (1991). *Responses to literature.* Newark, DE: International Reading Association.

Manning, G. L., & Manning, M. (1984). What models of recreational reading make a difference? *Reading World, 23,* 375–380.

Miller, D. (2009). *The book whisperer: Awakening the inner reader in every child.* San Francisco, CA: Wiley.

Nagy, W. E., & Anderson. R. C. (1984). How many words are there in printed school English? *Reading Research Quarterly, 19,* 304–330.

National Reading Panel. (2000). *Teaching children to read: An evidence-based assessment of the scientific research literature on reading and its implications for reading instruction: Reports of the subgroups* (National Institute of Health Pub. No. 00-4754). Washington, DC: National Institute of Child Health and Human Development.

Nye, B., Konstantopoulos, S., & Hedges, L. V. (2004). How large are teacher effects? *Educational Evaluation and Policy Analysis, 26*(3), 237–257.

Ogle, D. (1986). K-W-L: A teaching model that develops active reading of expository text. *The Reading Teacher, 39,* 564–570.

Palmer, B. M., Codling, R. M., & Gambrell, L. B. (1994). In their own words: What elementary children have to say about motivation to read. *The Reading Teacher, 48,* 176–179.

Pearson, P. D., & Gallagher, M. (1983). The instruction of reading comprehension. *Contemporary Educational Psychology, 8,* 317–344.

Pressley, M., Allington, R. L., Wharton-McDonald, R., Block, C. C., & Morrow, L. (2001). *Learning to read: Lessons from exemplary first-grade classrooms.* New York: Guilford.

Pressley, M., & Wharton-McDonald, R. (1998). The development of literacy, Part 4: The need for increased comprehension in upper-elementary grades. In M. Pressley (Ed.), *Reading instruction that works: The case for balanced teaching* (pp. 192–227). New York: Guilford.

Raphael, T. E., Kirschner, B. W., & Englert, C. S. (1988). Expository writing program: Making connections between reading and writing. *The Reading Teacher, 41,* 790–795.

Rasinski, T. V. (2003). *The fluent reader.* New York: Scholastic.

Rasinski, T. V. & Padak, N. D. (2008). *From phonics to fluency,* 2nd ed. Boston: Allyn & Bacon.

Read, C. (1975). *Children's categorization of speech sounds in English.* Urbana, IL: National Council of Teachers of English.

Shanahan, T. (1988). The reading-writing relationship. *The Reading Teacher, 41,* 636–647.

Share, D. L. (1999). Phonological recoding and orthographic learning: A direct test of the self-teaching hypothesis. *Journal of Experimental Child Psychology, 72,* 95–129.

Spivey, N. (1997). *The constructivist metaphor: Reading, writing and the making of meaning.* New York: Academic Press.

Stahl, S. A., Duffy-Hester, A. M., & Stahl, K. A. D. (1998). Everything you wanted to know about phonics (but were afraid to ask). *Reading Research Quarterly, 33,* 338–355.

Stahl, S. A., & Nagy, W. (2006). *Toward word meanings.* Mahwah, NJ: Erlbaum.

Stanovich, K. E. (1986). Matthew effects in reading: Some consequences of individual differences in the acquisition of literacy. *Reading Research Quarterly, 21,* 360–401.

Stanovich, K. E. (1991). Word recognition: Changing perspectives. In R. Barr, M. Kamil, P. Mosenthal, & P. D. Pearson (Eds.), *Handbook of reading research* (Vol. 2, pp. 418–452). New York: Longman.

Stanovich, K. E., & West, R. F. (1989). Exposure to print and orthographic processing. *Reading Research Quarterly, 24,* 402–433.

Sudduth, P. (1989). Introducing response logs to poor readers. *The Reading Teacher, 42,* 452–454.

Sulzby, E., & Teale, W. (1991). Emergent literacy. In R. Barr, M. Kamil, P. Mosenthal, & P. D. Pearson (Eds.), *Handbook of reading research* (Vol. 2, pp. 727–757). White Plains, NY: Longman.

Taylor, B. M., Hanson, B., Swanson, K., & Watts, S. (1998). Helping struggling readers in grades two and four: Linking small-group intervention with cross-age tutoring. *The Reading Teacher, 51,* 196–209.

Taylor, B. M., Pearson, P. D., Clark, K., & Walpole, S. (2000). Effective schools and accomplished teachers: Lessons about primary grade reading instruction in low-income schools. *Elementary School Journal, 101*(2), 121–166.

Topping, K., & Paul, T. (1999). Computer-assisted assessment of practice at reading: A large scale survey using Accelerated Reader data. *Reading and Writing Quarterly, 15,* 213–231.

Visser, C. (1991). Football and reading do mix. *The Reading Teacher, 44,* 710–711.

Wharton-McDonald, R., Pressley, M., & Hampston, J. M. (1998). Literacy instruction in nine first-grade classrooms: Teacher characteristics and student achievement. *The Elementary School Journal, 99,* 101–128.

Wylie, R. E., & Durrell, D. D. (1970). Teaching vowels through phonograms. *Elementary English, 47,* 787–791.

Yopp, R. H., & Yopp, H. K. (2004). Preview-Predict-Confirm: Thinking about the language and content of informational text. *The Reading Teacher, 58,* 79–83.

Yopp, R. H., & Yopp, H. K. (2007). Ten important words plus: A strategy for building word knowledge. *The Reading Teacher, 61,* 157–160.

Young, S. (1994). *The Scholastic rhyming dictionary.* New York: Scholastic.

index

Acting out stories to help students think actively,
    141, 143
    steps for, 142
Activities for classroom (*see* Books of activities)
Adding revising strategy, 161–162, 167
"After Lunch Brunch" reading club, 53
Alphabet books and songs, 45
    for building vocabulary, 107, 186
Anchored vocabulary, 34
Anchored word instruction, definition of, 6
Anecdotal records for assessing reading
    comprehension, 213
Anticipation guides, 186–189
Assessment, 204–217, 220
    of attitudes and interests of students, 214–215
    of comprehension strategies, 212–213
    definition of, 205
    of emergent literacy, 209, 210
    of good literacy behaviors, 209–217
    of reading level of student, determining,
        205–208
    steps for, 205
    of student progress, 209–217
    of student reading, 13–14
    of word strategies, 209–212
    of writing, 214
Attitudes and interests of students, assessing,
    214–217
Author's Chair, 147–151, 156–157
    mini-lessons, 153, 161, 162, 163, 164, 165

Background knowledge (*see* Experiences of students;
    Prior knowledge)
Balanced instruction, 8
    positive effects of, 7
Balanced reading program, 52–53
Basic Reading Inventory, 205
Beach Ball activity for reading comprehension,
    139–140, 185, 224
    steps for, 142
Behavior expectations, 3

Big Blocks, 7
Big Buddy readers, 20, 52
Blending and segmenting games, 42
Blends, teaching, 70
Book crates, rotating, 21
Book reports, 26
Books:
    about words, 115
    alphabet, 45, 107, 186
    availability of, 4
    sharing, 24–26
    students' selection of for independent reading,
        19, 23, 50, 226–227
Books of activities:
    intermediate grades, 266
    kindergarten, 249
    primary grades, 258
Buddy reading program, 20, 52
Building Blocks, 7

Chanting words, 61, 220, 261
Choral reading, 55–56, 220
Choral whispering, 225
Chunking words, 66–67, 85
Chunks, transferable, 90
Cinquains, 171–174
CIPCOMS, 193
Clapping/chanting activity, 261
Classroom bookboard, creating, 24
Classroom centers, scheduling for, 244, 247
Classroom conversations about what has been read,
    121–126
Classroom environment, research on, 2–9
Classroom management, 10–11
Classroom schedules:
    intermediate grades, 259–266
    kindergarten, 244–249
    primary grades, 250–259
Classroom/special teacher coordination, 237–238
Classrooms, effective, 2–8
Coaching by teacher, 3, 5, 229–232

Collaboration by students, 5

Collaborative groupings, 221–232

    coaching groups, 229–232

    literature circles,226–229

    partners, 221–225

Collaborative learning, 10

Comprehension (*see also* Reading comprehension)

    fluency and, 49 (*see also* Fluency in reading)

    low levels of, 9

    questions, 5

    strategies, 120–121, 212–213

    vocabulary and, 186–192 (*see also* Vocabulary)

Computer-assistive devices and software for students

    with limitations, 238–240

Concrete words, 40

    and literacy, 32–33

    teaching, 36–40

Conferences:

    about independent reading, 22–24

    to monitor struggling reader, 53

Connecting reading with photos, illustrations, visuals,

    182–183

Connection think-writes, 194–197

Connections:

    for conversations about reading, 122

    cross-curricular, 3

    of reading and photos, illustrations, visuals,

    182–183

Constructivist strategy for reading comprehension,

    123

Content-area instruction (*see* Integration of

    content-area instruction)

Context:

    pictures and building vocabulary, 107, 186

    use of to learn new words, 110–111

    visual aids and, 182–183, 186

Conversations (*see also* Conferences)

    about what has been read, 121–126

    in the classroom, 121–126

    student-to-student, 4

    student-to-teacher, 4

Cross-curricular connections, 3

Curriculum integration (*see* Integration of

    content-area instruction)

Daily independent reading time, 18–20

Data charts for helping students organize information,

    135, 184, 185

Decoding:

    assessing skills in, 211

    big words, 84–87

    spelling activities and, 220

    unfamiliar-in-print words, 66–67

    vocabulary, 6

    words, 66–67, 118 (*see also* Spelling)

Desire to learn to read and write, 33

Dialogue, adding to writing, 163

Dictionaries:

    creating, 186

    use of to refine new vocabulary, 111–112

"Dictionary Disciple," 112

Differentiating instruction (*see* Diverse learners,

    differentiating instruction for)

Digraphs, 69

Diverse learners, differentiating instruction for, 218–242

    collaborative groupings, 221–232

    coordinating reading with other specialists, 237–238

    partnering old with young students, 232–233

    support for ELLs, increasing, 240–241

    technology use and, 238–240

    tutors, 233–237

"Doing" the book, 140–141, 143, 224

    steps for, 142

Dramatization for building vocabulary, 102–103

Dysfluent reading, definition of, 50

Early-intervention program for struggling readers,

    232–233

Easy reading, mandated, 50–53

Echo reading, 54–55, 220, 225

Editing:

    in focused writing, 169–171

    in Writer's Workshop, 151–155

Editor's Checklist, 153

Effective classrooms, 2–8

Effective teachers, 219

Emergent literacy, assessing, 209, 210

Engagement of students, 4, 5, 8, 10,

    221–222

English language learners (ELLs):
  Author's Chair, 157
  Beach Ball activity, 139
  book selection for independent reading, 24
  book sharing, 25
  building meaning vocabulary, 103
  coaching groups, 240
  computer knowledge, 240
  concrete words, 40
  easy books, 241
  focused writing, 174
  graphic organizers, 136, 177
  learning letter names and sounds, 46
  literate conversations, 130
  modeling fluent reading for, 56
  peer editing, 155
  plays, 141
  providing supportive partners for, 240, 241
  reading comprehension, 130
  publishing works of, 159
  root words, 110
  sounds of letters, 71
  Spanish-English cognates, 110
  support for, 240–241
  supportive peers, 189
  teacher read-aloud time, 240
  think-alouds, 130
  tutoring for, 240
  vocabulary building, 103
  word walls, personal, 241
  writing, 147, 241
Evaluate/opinion writing, 202
Events as opportunities for vocabulary development, 100
"Everyone books," 220
  definition of, 51–52
Experiences of students, 120 (*see also* Prior knowledge)
  and making word connections, 105
  and reading, 118
  relating vocabulary to, 99–103
  simulated with dramatization, 102–103

Feature matrix, 134–136, 177, 185
Finger-plays, 56
First letter-sound relationships, 44

Fluency Development Lesson (FDL), 58–59
Fluency in reading, 13, 48–64, 220
  comprehension and, 49
  definition of, 49
  easy reading, mandated, 50–53
  high-frequency words, 59–63
  modeling by teacher, 53–57
  reading rate and, 53
  rereading and, 57–59
  word wall, 59–63
Focused writing, 168–178
  cinquains, 171–174
  connected to reading, 174–178
  editing, 169–171
  graphic organizers, 175–177
  modeling and demonstrating, 168–169
  publishing, 170, 171
  response logs, 177–178
  revising and editing, 169–170
"Follow the Letter Leader" activity, 46
Four Blocks framework for literacy instruction, 7

"Goldilocks" words, 104–106
Graded passages for determining reading level, 205–206
Graphic organizers, 184, 193–194
  for comprehension of informational text, 133–136, 137
  in focused writing, 175–177
  steps for, 137
Grouping structures, 4
"Guess the Covered Word" activity, 68–71, 220, 252
"Guess Yes or No" activity, 186–189
Guided Discovery, 75–76 (*see also* Making Words lessons and activities)
Guiding reading:
  in intermediate grades, 262–263
  in primary grades, 254–255
Guided Reading Block, 7

High-achievement classrooms, 2–3
High-frequency spelling patterns, 75
High-frequency words on word wall, 59–63
Home-school connection via new vocabulary, 101

Incentive programs for reading, 26
Independent reading, 5, 12–27, 52–53
  assessing and documenting, 13–14
  conferences, 22–24, 219
  daily scheduling, 18–20
  in intermediate grades, 259–260
  in kindergarten, 247–248
  in primary grades, 258–259
  read-alouds, 14–18
  sharing and responding, 24–26
  variety of materials, 20–22
Independent reading time, 34, 219
Informal Reading Inventories (IRIs), 205
Informational books, easy, 51
Informational text for shared reading, 181–184
Informational text lessons for reading comprehension,
  132–137
  graphic organizers, 133–136, 137
  KWL, 132–133, 137
Instruction (*see also* Diverse learners, differentiating
  instruction for)
  events and formats, 3, 5, 10
Integrated curriculum, 9, 220
Integration of content-area instruction, 180–203, 220
  to learn, 193–194
  reading and writing, 3, 5, 9
  shared reading, 181–184
  think-writes, 194–202
  transfer strategies to other subject matter, 184–185
  vocabulary and comprehension lessons, 186–192
  vocabulary in other subject matter, 185–186
Intermediate classroom, daily schedule, 259–266

Jargon, definition of, 31

Kindergarten classroom, daily schedule, 244–249
King or Queen for a Day, 37
KWL strategy for guiding students' thinking, 132–133,
  137
  steps for, 137

Letter actions, 46
Letter names and sounds and literacy, 33, 43–46
Limitations of students, physical, 238–240

Listening/meaning vocabularies, 66
Literacy, 28–47:
  activities for development of, 34–46
  attitudes, assessing, 216
  concrete words and, 32–33, 36–40
  foundations of, 30–34
  letter names and sounds, 33
  phonemic awareness and, 32
  print concepts and, 31–32
  reading and, 13
  vocabulary and, 96–98
Literate conversations, 121–126
  about what has been read, 121–126
  Oprah Winfrey Interview, 125–126
  Questioning the Author (QTA), 123–125
  steps to promote, 126
Literature circles, 122, 226–229
  example of, 228–229

Magazines for children, 20–22, 50, 52
Making Words lessons and activities, 75–87, 252
  big words, 83–87
  easy words, 76, 78–79
  one-vowel lessons, 82–83
  sorting into patterns, 76, 80
  steps in lesson, 78
  steps in planning, 77
  steps in teaching, 85
  transfer, 76, 81–82
Managed choice, 10
Meaning vocabularies, 6, 9
  development of, 96–98
  increasing via reading, 104–108
Misreading a word, 231
Modeling and demonstrating by teacher, 9
  choral reading, 55–56
  comprehension lessons, 120–121, 185
  echo reading, 54–55
  fluent and expressive reading, 53–57
  focused writing, 168–169
  how to decode big words, 84–87
  thinking strategies, 4
  transference of comprehension strategies, 185
  writing, 35, 246

Morning message in kindergarten, 245
Morphemes, 92, 186
   use of to learn new words, 108–110
Multicultural literature, 18

Names of students:
   to build phonemic awareness, 40–41
   to develop understanding of words and letters, 37–40
   to learn letter names and sounds, 43–46
News magazines for children, 21–22
Nifty-Thrifty-Fifty words, 87–90
No Child Left Behind (NCLB), 1
Nursery rhymes, 42–43, 56

"One Wonderful Word" activity, 115
One-vowel lessons in Making Words activity, 82–83
Onsets, 92
Open-ended questions after reading, 121–122
Oprah Winfrey Interview strategy, 125 126, 185, 262–263
Oral vocabulary, 6

Pantomimes for building vocabulary, 102–103
Parents, communication with, 5
Partner reading, 223–225
Partner talking, 221–223
Partner writing, 225
Partnering older and younger struggling readers, 232–233
Partners as collaborators, 221–225
Peer editing, 153–155
   example of, 154
Phonemic awareness, 32, 220
   development of, 40–43
   using names to build, 40–41
Phonics, decoding words, 66–67 (*see also* Spelling)
Phonics spelling, 41
Photos/illustration connecting to reading, 182
Physical limitations of students, 238–239
"Picture walks" to build vocabulary, 107, 186
Plays, 185
   echo reading and, 54
   as a way to increase story comprehension, 140

   with multileveled scripts, 54
   repeated patterns in, 55–56
Pocket charts for Making Words lesson, 76, 78–80, 252–253
Poems:
   integrating with other curricula, 193
   to model fluent reading, 58
   for read-alouds, 18
   repeated patterns in, 55–56
Prediction and vocabulary, 186–192
Prediction think-writes, 198–200
Prefixes, 87, 88, 90, 92, 108, 109
Pretend reading, 29–30, 34
Pretend writing, 34–35
Preview-Predict-Confirm (PPC) lesson, 189–190
Primary classroom, daily schedule, 250–259
Print concepts and literacy, 31–32
Print-rich classrooms, 36
Prior knowledge, 120, 190
   as an influence on reading level, 207
   in a new topic, 194–196
   and reading, 118
   relating vocabulary to, 99–103
   and think-writes, 194–202
   and vocabulary, 30–31
Pronouncing unknown words, 66–67
Prosody, 57
Publishing students' writing, 157, 159, 160

Qualitative Reading Inventory, 205
Quantity of reading/writing time, 219
Querying students on reading comprehension, 123–124
Question-and-answer sessions after reading, 121
Questioning the Author (QTA) strategy, 123–125

Read-Aloud Words Poster, example of, 106
Read-alouds, 14–18, 34
   and building vocabulary, 104
   for older students, 15 16
   rhyming books, 43
Reader's Chair activity to share books, 25
Readers' Theatre, 55

Reading (*see also* Reading comprehension)
  across the curriculum (*see* Integration of content-area instruction)
  club, 53
  connected to focused writing, 174–178
  connected to photos/illustrations, 182
  expressive, 57
  fluency and, 13
  incentive programs, 26
  informational text, steps for, 184
  integrating with other curricula (*see* Integration of content-area instruction)
  literacy and, 13
  level of, 205–208
  materials for, 20–22, 119
  partners, 223–225
  providing opportunities for, 3, 8–9
  rate, 53
  sharing parties, 25
  vocabulary development and, 98, 104
Reading comprehension, 117–144
  informational text lessons, 131–137
  literate conversations, 121–126
  modeling by teacher, 120–121
  Oprah Winfrey Interview strategy, 125–126
  Questioning the Author strategy, 123–125
  story text lessons, 138–143
  strategies, 120–121
  think-alouds, 126–131
  transfer to other subject matter, 184–185
Reading conferences, 22–24
"Reading and Me" form, 14
Reading/writing skills, 3, 4
  desire to learn, 33
  increasing volume of, 181
  and word walls, 63
Recorded reading, 58, 220
Remedial and special education teachers, 237–238
Removing revising strategies, 166–167
Reordering writing, 166, 167
Replacing revising strategy, 163–166, 167
Rereading, 105, 225
  providing opportunities for, 57–59

Resource room instructional support for struggling readers, 237–238
Responding to others' book selections, 24–26
Response logs in focused writing, 177–178
Revising and editing writing:
  focused writing, 169–171
  partnerships, 220
"Revising pens," 162
Revising writing, 160–167
  adding to writing, 161–163
  to publish focused writing, 170, 171
  removing writing, 166–167
  reordering writing, 166
  replacing writing, 163–166
Rhyming books, 42–43
Rhyming words, 72–75, 76
Rimes, 92
Root words, 76, 109
Roots, 92
Rotating book crates, 21

Say Something partner reading strategy, 225
Scaffolding by teachers, 3
Schedules in classroom (*see* Classroom schedules)
School environment related to vocabulary, 100
Segmenting and blending words, 41, 42
Self-evaluation by students, 5
Self-regulation/self-monitoring by students, 3
  reading habits, 13
  vocabulary knowledge, 3, 112–113
Self-Selected Reading Block, 7
Shared reading:
  and informational text, 181–184
  in kindergarten, 245
Sharing books, 24–26
"Showing" words, 164–165
Sight words, assessing, 211
"Skeleton books" for children to publish in, 159
Skits and vocabulary development, 102–103
Small-group conversations, 122
Small-group instruction, 5
Sound-letter combination, 76
Spanish-English cognates, 110

Spanish-speaking students, 71 (*see also* English language learners)
Special education and remedial teachers, 237–238
Spelling:
  assessing, 211
  automaticity of, 89
  patterns, 71–75, 76, 80
  and phonics in primary grades, 250–254
  responses to students' questions, 149
  rhyming words, 72–74, 76
  writing and, 91–92
Standardized tests as a determination of reading levels, 208
"Sticky-Note New Word Day," 107–108
Story maps for guiding students' thinking, 138–139
  steps for, 142
Story text lessons for understanding story structure, 138–143
  Beach Ball activity, 139–140, 142
  "doing" the book, 140–141, 142, 143
  story maps, 138–139, 142
Strips of letters for Making Words activity, 83–84
Struggling readers:
  boys, 15–16
  and comprehension, 50–51
  partnering older with younger, 232–233
Students, expectations, of, 3
Students choosing books for independent reading, 23, 50, 219, 226–227
Students with limitations, 238–240
Students' attitudes toward reading/writing, 214–217
Suffixes, 87, 88, 90, 92, 108
Support teachers, 237–238
Supporting and encouraging writing, 34–36
Syllables, clapping the number of, 42

Take-Home Sheet for Making Words, example of, 254
Talking partners, 221–223
Teacher monitoring fluent and expressive reading, 53–57
Teacher read-alouds, 14–18, 219
  in intermediate grades, 259–260
  in kindergarten, 247–248
  in primary grades, 258–259
  and "Turn and Talk" routine, 222

Teacher Record Sheet (for various genres), 17
Technological-assisted instruction, 238–240
Technology and media, 186
"Telling" words, 164–165
Ten Important Words, 191–192
Text structures, 119
Think-alouds for reading comprehension, 126–131, 184
  example of, 128–130
  steps for, 131
Thinking skills, 9
"Think-Pair-Share," 223
Think-writes, 194–202, 222–223
  connection, 194–197
  prediction, 198–200
  summarizing, concluding, evaluating, and imagining, 200–202
Three Read-Aloud Words activity, 104–106, 107
Time lines, 185
Tongue twisters, 43
Transference of comprehension strategies, 185
"Turn and Talk" routine to increase student engagement, 221–223
Tutoring needy children, 232–237
  finding the tutor, 236–237
  training the tutor, 233–236
20 Questions, 99

Using Words You Know lessons, 71–75, 220, 252

Vocabulary (*see also* Vocabulary building; Vocabulary development and comprehension lessons):
  background knowledge and, 30–31
  building (*see* Vocabulary building)
  home environment and, 101
  in integrated curricula, 185–186
  notebooks, 114
  prediction and, 186–192
  reading comprehension and, 6, 95–96, 97
  school environment and, 99, 100
  skits, 102–103
  and spelling in intermediate grades, 260–262

Vocabulary building, 94–116, 220
  alphabet books, 107
  context, 110–111
  dictionary, 111–112
  dramatization for, 102–103
  events as opportunities for, 100
  how to learn words, 96–98
  meaning vocabularies, 104–108
  morphemes, 108–110
  "picture walks," 107
  questions to build vocabulary, 187–188
  read-alouds and, 104
  "real" experience, providing, 99–103
  self-assessment of, 112–113
  size of vocabulary, 97
  "word wonder," 114–115
Vocabulary development and comprehension lessons,
    186–192
  Guess Yes or No, 186–189
  Preview-Predict-Confirm (PPC), 189–190
  Ten Important Words, 191–192
Volunteer readers, 16

Wait-time, 196
Wall words, 220
Webs, 134, 169, 175, 176, 184, 185
Wheel, The (game of letters), 91–92
Word introduction, example of, 88–89
Word play, 114
Word strategies, assessing, 209–210
Word study, 5
Word wall, 250
  to teach high-frequency words, 59–63
"Word Wonder," promoting, 114–115
Words:
  connecting to students' environment, 100
  counting, 41–42
  decoding, 66–67, 84–87, 118
  "Goldilocks," 104–106
  how to figure them out (steps), 230–231

how to learn vocabulary, 96–98 (*see also*
    Vocabulary building)
  introduction, example of, 88–89
  ways to display, 114
"Words Are Wonderful Day," 115
Words Block, 7
Words and letters, using names to development
    understanding, 37–40
Writer's Workshop, 147–167
  Author's Chair, 147, 156–157, 160
  in intermediate grades, 263–264
  mini-lesson, 147–148, 150–151
  peer editing, 153–155
  in primary grades, 256–257
  publishing writing, 157, 159, 160
  removing words, 167
  reordering words, 166–167
  replacing revising strategy, 163–166
  revising, 160–167
  starting the year with, 147–151
  writing conference, 158, 160
Writing:
  across the curriculum (*see* Integration of
    content-area instruction)
  assessing, 214
  conference, 158, 220
  focused writing, 168–178
  integration with other curricula, 9
  to learn, 193–194
  materials, 35–36
  providing opportunities for, 3, 8–9
  purposes, 35–36
  reordering, 166–167
  support for struggling writers, 158–159
  supporting and encouraging, 34–36
  thinking and, 146
Writing Block, 7
Writing conferences, 158, 200
Writing partners, 225
Writing/reading and word walls, 63